SECRETS OF THE CHINESE HERBALISTS, REVISED EDITION

Richard Lucas

Plant Drawings by Steven Talbott

Parker Publishing Company, Inc.
West Nyack, New York

Fourth Printing . . . . . January 1988

This book is a reference work based on research by
the author. The opinions expressed herein are not
necessarily those of or endorsed by the publisher.
The directions stated in this book are in no way
to be considered as a substitute for consultation
with a duly licensed doctor.

Library of Congress Cataloging-in-Publication Data

Lucas, Richard Melvin
  Secrets of the Chinese herbalists.

  Includes bibliographical reference and index.
  1. Herbs—Therapeutic use. 2. Materia medica,
Vegetable—China. 3. Botany, Medical—China.
I. Title.
RM666.H33L8 1987   615'.321'0951   86-25241
ISBN 0-13-797879-0
ISBN 0-13-798174-0 PBK

INTRODUCTION

In recent years the medical academies of China have been studying the centuries-old art of herbal remedies, and developing this art along scientific lines. This involves a comprehensive study of ancient records, and the screening of folklore remedies. Secret plant formulas, described in traditional terminology, are translated into modern terms and immediately submitted to the Chinese Medical Research Institute for re-evaluation, utilizing laboratory techniques.

As a result, the medical journals of China continually report many new discoveries in the ancient art of herb medicine, and these reports have attracted international interest. For example, Dr. Anna Cummings, a member of a British medical team sent to China to observe Oriental Healing methods, stated: "They [the Chinese] have frightfully modern pharmacies with white-coated, efficient technicians who go through these old remedies with fine-tooth combs, finding out what's in them and then working out modern recipes that duplicate and surpass the old remedies. Their achievements in this area are absolutely remarkable."

Dr. Dean, another member of the British medical team, had this to say: "Chinese medicine is, in my opinion, the best in the world. In my report I am urging that the British government send teams of specialists over there as soon as possible to learn anything they can about Chinese methods."

Approximately one-half of the population in China uses more than 1,500 different herbs, plus over 1,000 patent herbal remedies, and many of these herbs and formulas are exported to other countries. In Japan alone, consumers spend more than $2 billion annually on Chinese medicinal herbs and herbal products.

Here in the United States, people are becoming more health conscious and are searching for alternative healing methods to synthetic chemical drugs. Traditional Chinese herb medicine has developed into one of the most successful medical systems in the world;

therefore, anything that leads us in a more natural direction is to be welcomed.

With the publication of my book *Secrets of the Chinese Herbalists* I began receiving scores of letters from my readers, telling of the benefits they received from the use of Chinese herb remedies, and requesting more information on this fascinating subject. Because of these requests, and the new updated material on Chinese herbs, I decided to revise the original text.

Now, here, in this revised edition, you will find recent information on Oriental herb remedies that are safe, effective, and affordable. Consider the following:

- In Chapter 5 you'll read where extensive medical studies in China and other lands have determined that a natural herbal product helps relieve arthritis, peptic ulcers, liver ailments, menopausal problems, and many other disorders.
- In the same chapter you'll learn of a plant remedy which is one of the National Award Winners in China where it is considered effective for various ailments, and also valued as a general health tonic which assists memory and concentration, and helps prevent premature aging.
- Another chapter informs you of the remedial use of a scientifically developed Oriental herb product for treating a variety of conditions, including *Candida albicans,* high blood pressure, constipation, and so on. This remarkable remedy also detoxifies the body ravaged by environmental pollution.
- Turning to Chapter 6, you'll read of a Chinese herbal liniment used for relieving the pains of rheumatism, sprains, sore muscles, and similar aches and pains. The effectiveness, quality, and strict manufacturing process of this product has earned it a Gold Award and Silver Award by the Regional People's Government of China, and the State Council.

Are you concerned about the side effects of pharmaceutical tranquilizers prescribed for stress, tension, nervousness, anxiety, and insomnia? In Chapter 11 you'll read of an updated preparation of an ancient Chinese herb formula considered *par excellence* for stress and stress-related ailments. This formula produces no side effects, and is medically approved by the Japanese government.

Along with ample coverage of modern, updated Chinese herb remedies, this book also presents impressive case histories. For example:

- You'll read the case of Mr. L.,Sr., who suffered so many heart attacks for a period of 15 years that his physician said he might hold the Guinness world record for the most heart attacks and still survive. Although Mr. L,.Sr., was under continued medical supervision, his condition began to deteriorate to the point where he was bedridden. His son then urged him to try an Oriental herb product. Within six weeks of taking the herb remedy daily, Mr. L.,Sr.'s condition improved to such a degree that he was able to engage in various activities including driving a car for the first time in many years. After six months of continued use of the herb remedy, he was able to play golf and lead a virtually normal life.

That's just one of the remarkable case histories you are going to read about, but there are many, many more. For instance:

- Mrs. M. V. suffered from the menopausal symptoms of "hot flashes" which she found miserable to endure. She refused her doctor's recommendation to use estrogen as she heard it can cause side effcts. Seeking more natural methods of handling her problem, she began taking a specific Chinese herb remedy daily, and reports that the "hot flashes" have become a thing of the past.
- Then there is the case of a Chinese-American gentleman who suffered a stroke and fell to the floor. Although barely able to speak, he managed to tell a friend who was visiting, to get the Chinese remedy he kept on hand in the other room. He was immediately given the herbal compound, and shortly after was able to get on his feet, and was rushed to the hospital. His doctor confirmed that he did suffer a stroke, and was amazed that he was able to walk into the hospital, and had recovered so quickly.
- You'll also read the report by a medical doctor on a case of prostate infection he had been unable to completely cure in five years of orthodox treatment. His patient finally decided on his own initiative to use an herbal remedy. He took six of the herb

tablets daily, and his physician said the improvement was "like a miracle."

But these herb tablets did not help just one man alone.

- In a medical study by a urologist, ten patients suffering from prostatitis (with no infection) were treated with the herb tablets. At the end of the treatment, all ten patients had improved, and no longer complained of their symptoms.
- In another study at a urological clinic, nine prostate patients were also treated with the herbal tablets, and all responded with definite improvement.

Granted, not everything will work for everyone (there are too many individual differences, too many variables), so you will notice the majority of chapters in this book include listings of several different herb remedies for each particular ailment cited. In this way, a person may select one of the remedies or herbal products most appropriate for his or her own individual need, and if after giving it a sufficient trial it does not help, a switch can be made to another. (Herbs are natural food substances which tend to have a gradual effect, so patience is necessary.) This procedure does not, of course, guarantee success, but it does increase an individual's chances of finding a remedy that might prove helpful.

In case you are wondering whether it will be difficult to locate the herbs and herbal products mentioned in the pages of this book, the answer is no. Health food stores carry many of these items, and if your local store cannot provide some of them, a list of herb firms is given for your convenience at the back of this book.

There is so much more in this revised edition that I can't go into here without making the Introduction as lengthy as the text. You are about to discover many of the herbal secrets tested and perfected by some of the greatest healers of all time—the Chinese herbalists.

Richard Lucas

OTHER BOOKS BY THE AUTHOR:

Nature's Medicines: The Folklore, Romance, and Value of Herbal Remedies

Common and Uncommon Uses of Herbs for Healthful Living

The Magic of Herbs in Daily Living

Magic Herbs for Arthritis, Rheumatism, and Related Ailments

Ginseng—The Chinese Wonder Root

Siberian Ginseng

Herbal Health Secrets

TABLE OF CONTENTS

8. CHINESE HERB REMEDIES FOR MEN'S AILMENTS 117

9. BUILDING FEMALE HEALTH WITH CHINESE HERBS 133

1

THE WISDOM
OF CHINESE HERBALISTS

THE WISDOM OF THE ANCIENTS

The practice of herbal medicine dates back to the very earliest periods of Chinese history, and over a great span of time many pharmacopoeias were written and revised. Of these works, the oldest is the *Pen Ts'ao Ching,* in which the Red Emperor, Shen-ung, described various medicaments and included instructions for their use. Shen-ung died in the year 2697 B.C. and was succeeded by Huang Ti, the Yellow Emperor, who reigned from about 2697 to 2595 B.C. He composed the celebrated *Nei Ching (The Yellow Emperor's Book of Internal Medicine).* This was later divided into two main sections referred to as *Su Wen* and *Ling Shu.*

A striking similarity with modern thought on preventive medicine can be found in the remarkable *Nei Ching* manual. It states that the human body can be protected against disease by adaption to environmental changes. Ailments must be cured before they arise, says the *Nei Ching,* by proper diet, rest, and work, and by keeping the mind and heart calm. To cure an illness after it arises is like forging weapons after the battle has started or digging a well after you have become thirsty.

And in the *Su Wen,* the first part of the *Nei Ching,* we find the following question asked by Emperor Huang Ti: "I have heard that in ancient times human beings lived to the age of 100. In our time we are exhausted at the age of 50. Is this because of changes in circumstances, or is it the fault of man?" His physician, Ch'i Po, answered: "In ancient times, men lived in accordance with the Tao, the 'Principle.' They observed the law of Yang and Yin, were sober, and led regular, simple lives. For that reason, being healthy in body and mind, they could live to the age of 100. In our time, men drink alcohol as if it were water, seek all pleasures, and abandon themselves to intemperance. The sages teach that one must lead a simple and peaceful life. Thus keeping all its energy in reserve, the body cannot be attacked by illness... By living in such simplicity, men can still reach the age of 100 in our time."

Modern Medical Discoveries Known to Ancients

The *Nei Ching* described the circulation of the blood through the body, which was not discovered by the Western world (by Harvey) until the sixteenth century A.D.

Anesthetics were administered by Chinese surgeons as far back as the third century B.C., and the catheter, which the West invented in 1885, was described in *The Thousand Golden Remedies* in the seventh century B.C.

Another remarkable fact is that the concept of psychosomatic ailments (stress-induced illnesses), generally believed to be a modern medical discovery, was known to Chinese healers thousands of years ago. This can be seen very clearly in the following passage from the *Su Wen:* "We must know how to determine whether a disorder is caused by perverse energy coming from the outside [e.g., wind, cold, dampness, heat, dryness], or by emotional stress. Psychic disturbances, like perverse energies, can give rise to muscular disorders and all sorts of illness."

Diagnosis by Pulse

The taking of the pulse was discovered by Pien Ch'ueh, a famous physician of the second century A.D. According to ancient Chinese chronicles, Pien Ch'ueh saved the life of a prince who was unconscious and given up for dead by his court physician. Pien Ch'ueh felt the pulse, found that the prince was still alive, and administered treatment which brought about his recovery.

In the centuries that followed, the method of taking the pulse was highly developed into an intricate system of diagnosis. This system is still practiced today by Chinese healers. With his right hand the

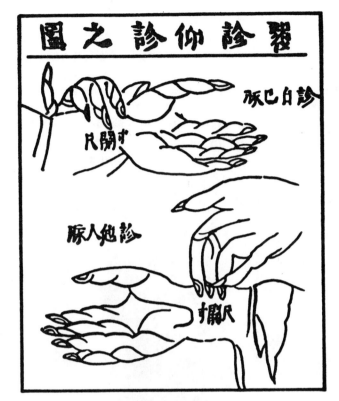

Taking the Pulse

herbalist feels the patient's left pulse, and with his left hand he feels the right pulse. He places three fingers—the index, middle, and ring finger—over the pulse and applies weak, moderate, and strong pressure with each finger. The position of the finger and the amount of pressure applied reveal the condition of various parts of the body, such as the stomach, spleen, gall bladder, liver, large intestine, small intestine, heart, and so on.

The Pen Ts'ao Kang Mu

As time passed, Chinese healers, each in their own generation, collected the medicinal knowledge of earlier periods and supplemented it with their own findings. In this way, the number of Chinese pharmacopoeias continued to increase and expand. Although each was important, the most outstanding of all is the immense work titled the

Pen Ts'ao Kang Mu or *General Compendium of Remedies,* published in China in the sixteenth century A.D. It is composed of 56 chapters containing 1,100 illustrations and nearly 12,000 formulas, the result of more than 25 years of labor by Li Shih Chen, a physician and pharmacologist who catalogued the remedies of previous eras together with his own discoveries. When treating patients, Li Shih Chen often preferred to be paid for his services by obtaining information of any remedies the patient might have heard of. He then carefully wrote down the recipe and later tested and evaluated it.

Enlarged Reproduction of Postage Stamp Honoring Li Shih Chen

Today the pharmacopoeia of Li Shih Chen is still considered highly important to the Chinese materia medica. Modern Western science has established that many of the herbs listed in the *Pen Ts'ao Kang Mu* contain valuable medicinal properties. In 1956, the People's Republic of China honored Li Shih Chen by issuing a postage stamp bearing his image.

The Chinese Concept of Yang-Yin

Five thousand years experience of compounding and processing roots and herbs has taught the Chinese many things about the rhythm and balance of nature. According to Oriental philosophy, there are two basic and opposing principles that regulate the Universe, and all phenomena are created by their continuous interplay. These two principles, called Yang and Yin, are natural opposites and may be briefly defined as follows (a complete list of Yang-Yin contraries would be endless).

YANG—Male, light, hot, strong, positive, active, sun, spring, summer.

YIN—Female, dark, cold, weak, negative, passive, earth, autumn, winter.

The Chinese texts explain, "If Yin and Yang are not in harmony, it is as though there were no autumn opposite the spring, no winter opposite the summer." Although Yang and Yin may be opposites, they are not hostile to one another. Each needs the other; without one, the other could not exist. Yang is not superior to Yin, nor is Yin superior to Yang.

Man is a miniature Universe, a microcosm or "small world" in relation to the "greater world" or macrocosm. Being an integral part of the whole, he is subject to the same Cosmic laws. As the whole order of the Universe results from the perfect balance between the two forces of Yin-Yang, so the health of man depends on the equilibrium of Yin-Yang in his body.

Incorrect Balance between Yin and Yang
Results in Illness

The Chinese believe that the action of these dual forces on the human level manifests through the various organs of the body, such as the heart, lungs, spleen, kidneys, stomach, and so on. For example, the contraction (systole) and dilation (diastole) of the heart, which follow each other rhythmically to circulate the blood; the rhythm of inhalation and exhalation of the lungs; the functions of the sympathetic and parasympathetic nervous systems; the act of waking and sleeping.

According to the Chinese, all diseases are the result of a disturbed harmony between Yin and Yang in the body. For example, if the Yin principle in the body predominates, there is weakness, exhaustion, debility; if the Yang predominates, there is irritability and excitation. The ancient medical book, the *Nei Ching,* states: "If Yang is predominant, then the body will grow hot, the pores close, and the patient begins to breathe heavily and gasp for breath. Fever will arise, the palate will become dry; the person becomes tense and irritable."

Comparison with Modern Scientific Concepts

This Chinese concept that disease will result if the Yin-Yang balance in the body is disturbed is remarkable when you consider that modern 20th century science is saying practically the same thing. When science discovered the important functions of the sympathetic and parasympathetic nervous systems, the relation to the Chinese theory of Yin-Yang become quite striking. Many physicians are convinced that if the sympathetic and parasympathetic nervous systems are not in harmony with each other, illness will surely follow Stress diseases which are so rampant today—high blood pressure, heart trouble, stomach ulcers, headaches, insomnia, and so forth—are believed to be partly due to an impaired nervous system caused by the stress and tension of modern living. Science tells us that a harmonious functioning of the nervous system and a well-balanced disposition are essential to good health.

Yang-Yin Symbol

The Yang-Yin symbol is generally depicted by a circle divided into two parts, one black and the other white, each of which resembles a comma or a fish. The circle represents the Universe (without beginning or end), and the dark and light divisions within it represent the Yang-Yin.

Basic Yang-Yin Symbol

Another Yang-Yin symbol is called the pentagram. It was devised by a Chinese emperor around the year 2900 B.C. It consists of combinations of broken lines (Yin) and straight lines (Yang) surrounding a circle and its two divisions, making a perfect emblem of the balancing of the forces of the Universe.

Pentagram—Another Type of Yang-Yin Symbol

In China, the dressing used for the treatment of a fracture or wound often bears a Yang-Yin symbol.

Yang-Yin Guidelines

The concept of Yang-Yin has guided everything Chinese, from government to family relations, from music to art, farming, health, and healing. This is the philosophy which Chinese housewives use to balance their families' diets for health. Many of the roots and herbs they use in supplementing and flavoring the daily meals are the very same as those used by herbalists when preparing herb teas or herbal blends, and the same careful attention to balance is followed by both.

As a result of their age-old Yang-Yin theory, Chinese herbalists do not claim to cure anything. They simply work to support and assist Nature in her endeavor to heal the ailing organism. Since natural foods—e.g., vegetables, fruits, legumes, and herbs—are live substances which have been formulated by countless ages of evolution, the herbalists of China believe that nonpoisonous plant medicines supply to the body the appropriate constituents it lacks, in a way similar to that of natural foods. Thus, by providing the body with what it needs or what it cannot produce in sufficient quantities, the Yang-Yin vital force is harmonized, strengthened, and sustained in an indirect way. This method embraces prevention as well as healing. The great modern Chinese scholar, Lin Yutang, wrote: "The Chinese do not draw any distinction between food and medicine. What is good for the body is medicine and at the same time food."

Basic Rules for Preparing Chinese Herb Teas

Generally, Chinese remedies consist of one principal herb or root and at least three or more assistant herbs, roots, or other natural substances. However, there are instances where less are used, and in some cases a domestic remedy may consist of one single botanical (ginseng root and garlic are among a number of such examples).

In preparing the herb teas, aluminum utensils are never used. The most satisfactory, according to the Chinese, are earthenware, crockery, enamel, or pyrex.

Unless the recipes state otherwise, hard substances, such as roots and barks, are prepared as decoctions (boiled continuously for a certain length of time), whereas soft substances, such as flowers, leaves, or blossoms, are prepared as ordinary teas (the herb or herb mixture placed in a cup or pan, boiling water poured on, and the tea allowed to steep). In each case, the container is covered with a lid until the boiling or steeping period is ended. If only one cup rather than a pint or more of the herb substance is steeped as tea, the cup is simply covered with a saucer.

2

CHINESE HERB REMEDIES
FOR STOMACH DISORDERS

The word dyspepsia means to digest with some difficulty or pain. Indigestion may be a more old-fashioned term, but it means the same thing.

An estimated 30 million people in the United States suffer from chronic digestive disturbances. The usual causes of indigestion are wrong food combinations, eating too fast, drinking too much fluid with meals, not chewing the food properly, overeating, anxiety and nervousness, swallowing air while eating, and intolerance toward sugars, fats, and starches. The common symptoms are heartburn, sour belching, a heavy uneasy feeling in the stomach after a meal, headache, coated tongue, nausea, vomiting, flatulence, a bad taste in the mouth, foul breath, and sometimes difficult breathing and palpitation.

The Dangers of Nonabsorbable Antacids

Throughout the United States, sufferers from indigestion gobble up antacid tablets by the ton every day. An occasional antacid tablet to relieve stomach upset is harmless enough, but to take the tablets constantly, week in and week out, as some people do, is asking for trouble.

According to a medical report, a team of doctors found that phosphorus depletion results from the frequent use of antacids that are not of a dietary nature and cannot be absorbed. (Your bones are the "storehouse" for phosphorus, and when this mineral is inadequately supplied, your bones are in danger of becoming soft or brittle.) Many of the drug store patent antacid preparations available in tablet or liquid form contain either or both, magnesium hydroxide and aluminum hydroxide. Right here we'd like to point out that there is a great difference between magnesium hydroxide, which cannot be digested by human stomachs, and the fully absorbable magnesium mineral which occurs naturally in various foods and plants and is so valuable in human nutrition.

To quote the medical doctors who submitted the report: "It has long been known that nonabsorbable antacids containing magnesium-aluminum hydroxides can bind gastrointestinal absorption of phosphorus." In their studies, phosphorus depletion was achieved in subjects by prolonged administration of antacids containing magnesium hydroxide and aluminum hydroxide. The doctors stated that in all subjects a number of striking events occurred, which included "a state of debility characterized by weakness, anorexia [loss of appetite], and malaise [a feeling of being ill]. In the patient A.S., severe bone pain and stiffness developed and persisted throughout the study. M.I., in addition, manifested an intention tremor of the hand..."

You Have a Choice

No doubt if you suffer from stomach distress you want to take something to relieve it. But why use indigestible forms of antacids that threaten to demineralize your bones and make you a very ill person indeed, when wholesome and digestible antacids are so easily available from natural herb remedies? Mother Nature is the true alchemist, and the precious treasures of her plant kingdom can neutralize the acidity gently, safely, and effectively.

A Word About Ulcers

It is estimated that one out of ten people will develop a duodenal ulcer at some time in their lives. This type of ulcer occurs in the short tube directly following the stomach. Some duodenal ulcers are very large—as much as 4 inches in diameter, while others are microscopically tiny.

Sufferers from duodenal ulcers may secrete as much as four times the amount of gastric juice in the empty stomach as normal persons. The pain of duodenal ulcer is often called "hunger pain" since it can be relieved by eating food.

The gastric type of ulcer occurs in the inside of the stomach area. Pain is felt in the stomach, and it also radiates upwards and to the back. It almost always starts shortly after a meal and produces a sort of burning sensation which is intensified by indigestible food, but relieved by a milk-diet.

A peptic ulcer simply means an ulcer occurring in the esophagus, stomach, or duodenum.

Many people carry an ulcer through life with nothing more serious than chronic annoyance, while some ulcers cause intense suffering and even death.

Chinese Herb Remedies for Stomach Disorders

Certainly medical doctors who employ surgery get good results in treating ulcers. Sometimes there is just no other way to save the patient's life. But when there is no real emergency, the ulcer victim may find relief through the use of natural Chinese herb remedies. The remedies are soothing and gentle, and many people have found them very effective. The same is true, of course, of specific Chinese remedies for coping with acid indigestion and other forms of stomach distress.

The natural ingredients called for in the recipes that follow are easy to use, easy to prepare, and easy on your pocketbook.

PROPOLIS

Propolis is a sticky, resinous substance collected by bees from the leaf buds or bark of trees, especially poplars (known in Chinese as *Pai-yang*),—the most important source. Its remedial value has been known to the Chinese since ancient times. Reference to its use was also cited in the Persian, Arabic, and Korean manuscripts of the sixth and eighth centuries.

Today, interest in this natural healing substance has been revived, and its effectiveness in treating various ailments is being scientifically proven in many parts of the world.

In Yugoslavia, a case was reported of a man age 50, who suffered from stomach ulcers. He experienced such severe pain after each meal that he began eating less and less, and this practice resulted in considerable weight loss and weakness. He was advised to take one propolis capsule three times daily, one-half hour before meals. From the first day he was free of pain, and by continuing to take the capsules faithfully, he soon found he could eat anything he wanted.

Doctors at the Klosterneuberg Hospital in Austria employed propolis for treating 250 patients suffering from ailments ranging from stomach ulcers to colitis and severe gastric conditions. Two hundred and forty-four were reportedly healed within two weeks. In one study, Dr. Franz K. Feiks reported that a group of patients suffering from stomach ulcers were given three drops of propolis before meals, three times daily. In seven out of ten cases, pain had disappeared within three days. After ten days, no wounds could be detected in six out of ten patients.

Dr. Feiks also reported the results of 15 out-patients with confirmed stomach ulcers who were treated exclusively with propolis. Fourteen of the patients remained in their own homes and the ulcers were completely healed. Only one case subsequently required hospital treatment.

DIRECTIONS FOR USING PROPOLIS

Propolis is available in many forms; e.g. capsules, tinctures, and lozenges. For stomach and intestinal ulcers, most practitioners advise that propolis be used in capsule form—one capsule three times a day, one-half hour before meals.

Note: Although propolis is a natural substance, and harmless for most people, in some rare cases a person may be allergic to it. Therefore, its treatment should be discontinued if a rash develops after using it.

CHIANG

English Name: Ginger
Botanical Name: *Zingiber officinale*

Ginger is among the top-ranking botanicals in the Chinese materia medica. It is given for dyspepsia, loss of appetite, nausea, vomiting, and alcoholic gastritis. Chewing the root and swallowing the juice causes copious saliva to flow and stimulates the digestive juices. It is also chewed to relieve nausea and vomiting. Some professional

Chinese cooks keep a small piece of ginger root in their mouth to prevent nausea from prolonged exposure to strong cooking odors.

The root prepared in the form of a tea improves sluggish digestion, relieves gas bloat, and stimulates the appetite. One-half ounce of the powdered root is stirred in one pint of boiling water, and two to three tablespoons of the tea are taken three times a day.

For upset stomach due to that morning-after "hangover," prompt relief may be obtained by sipping one or two cups of hot ginger tea for breakfast.

Chinese Ginger Remedy for Building a Healthy Digestion

The following remedy is reputed to be excellent for restoring strength and tone to the stomach and building a healthy digestion. The Chinese claim it is especially good during the cold weather as it has a warming and comforting effect on the stomach and is felt throughout the entire system.

Step 1. Put one-half cup of white rice in a flat bowl. Pour in enough water to barely cover the rice. Let stand overnight so that the rice can completely absorb the water. In the morning if there is any water still standing in the bowl drain it off. Put the rice in a dry frying pan, and gradually heat it until the pan is quite hot. Use a spatula, and keep turning the rice slowly so it doesn't burn. When the rice is parched dry and golden brown, put it in a glass jar and cap tightly against moisture.

Step 2. Bring one cup of water to a boil; add one teaspoon of the parched rice and a small piece of ginger root. Boil for one minute, and then turn off the burner and let stand for five minutes. Strain. Take one teacupful once or twice a day.

Motion Sickness

According to a report titled, *Motion Sickness, Ginger, and Psychophysics,* which appeared in a British medical journal [1], doctors in the U.S. have found that the natural root of ginger in powdered form

---

[1] *The Lancet,* 20/3/82.

was more effective than conventional drugs in preventing sickness from motion, such as travel by ship, plane, or car.

Thirty-six student volunteers, all highly susceptible to travel sickness, were divided into three groups. One group was given an antihistamine, another group took capsules of powdered ginger, and the other group a placebo. They were all blindfolded and seated in a tilted revolving chair.

None of those given the antihistamine or placebo was able to last the full six minutes of the test. But half the students who had taken ginger completed the ride. The doctors suggest that the natural remedy has the advantage of acting directly on the stomach, where it speeds up the absorption of acids and toxic substances; whereas, antihistamines block nerve impulses to the part of the brain that triggers vomiting.

PO CHAI

Po Chai is a Chinese product made with several select herbs formed into tiny pills about the size of buckshot. The pills come in small phials, which are packed ten to a carton.

To thousands of Chinese-Americans, Po Chai is a well-known and proven remedy for the relief of acid indigestion, heartburn, and gas bloat.

> Dosage: Adults—the contents of one phial. If necessary repeat in two hours. The pills may be swallowed with hot water or mild tea.

Woman Praises Po Chai

"I was raised near San Francisco's Chinatown," writes Mrs.T.L., "and had many wonderful Chinese-American friends. I learned to eat Chinese food with chopsticks, play the fascinating game of mah-jong, and even to speak a little of the language.

"One Thanksgiving Day, right after eating a sumptuous meal, mother and I dropped in for a visit with some of our Chinese friends. We hadn't been there 15 minutes before my mother began feeling ill. She complained of heartburn, a heavy feeling in her stomach, said that she was nauseated and couldn't seem to take a deep breath.

"I was alarmed, but one of our Chinese friends said, 'Too much turkey, pumpkin pie, and other rich Thanksgiving food,' while the others nodded in agreement. He took a small bottle of tiny herb pills out of the kitchen cabinet, gave the pills to my mother, and told her to take them with a glass of water. Ten minutes after she took the pills, she was feeling fit as a fiddle again.

"That evening before we left for home, mother wrote down the name of the herb pills. They were called Po Chai. From that time on we have followed the custom of our Chinese friends and have always kept a supply on hand as a stand-by home remedy for indigestion."

HUANG-LIEN

English Name: Gold Thread
Botanical Name: *Coptis teeta*

Among its many virtues, gold thread is considered an excellent bitter tonic for dyspepsia. It improves digestion, restores appetite, and relieves inflammation of the stomach lining. Gold thread is also employed to assist the treatment of alcoholism.

How to Use Gold Thread

The root may be used either in the form of a tincture or a decoction.

To prepare the decoction, place 2 ounces of the cut root in one quart of water, bring to a boil and simmer slowly for 20 minutes, and then strain. Dose: One tablespoonful four to six times a day.

To make the tincture, place one ounce of the cut root in a pint of good brandy. Cap tightly and allow to stand for one week, shaking the bottle once or twice a day. Strain. Dose: One teaspoonful in half a glassful of water three times a day.

HU-LU-PA

English Name: Fenugreek
Botanical Name: *Trigonella foenum-graecum*

The demulcent and carminative properties of fenugreek are considered valuable in relieving stomach gas and inflammation of the stomach and intestines. For any of these conditions, the powder is sprinkled over foods or a tea is prepared by adding one teaspoonful of the seeds to one cup of boiling water. The cup is covered with a saucer, and the tea is allowed to stand for 15 minutes, then strained. One cupful is taken three times daily.

Fenugreek is also employed for mild forms of peptic ulcers. The following account is but one of many examples of its effectiveness:

"I had a stomach ulcer for a great many years. It never bothered me so long as I stayed away from raw fruits, fruit juices, coffee, and meat. But I love these things, and every once in a while I couldn't resist the temptation to have some of them, and of course my ulcer let me know about it.

"Then I remembered that someone once told me of a Chinese herbalist who recommended fenugreek for stomach ulcers. I made a tea out of the powdered seeds, just like you make instant coffee, and drank one cup before each meal. Well, after three weeks of drinking the tea, I had a meal of my 'forbidden fruits' with absolutely no stomach distress whatsoever. I continued to drink the tea for several weeks more. At the end, I found that I could eat anything I wanted."— Mr. T.P.

JENSHEN

English Name: Ginseng
Botanical Name: *Panax schinseng*

Ginseng tea is considered an excellent stomach tonic. One cup taken daily before meals stimulates the appetite, prevents sour eructations, and restores normal digestion.

Directions: Place the contents of one small envelope of powdered ginseng in a cup and add boiling water. These little envelopes are called "Instant Ginseng Tea" and are available from herb companies and health food stores.

HSUN-TS'AO

English Name: Melilot
Botanical Name: *Melilotus arvensis*

The name melilot is derived from the words *mel* (honey) and lotus, meaning honey lotus. The plant grows abundantly in the Yangtse region of China and contains aromatic and carminative properties.

CHIANG
(Ginger)

HU-LU-PA
(Fenugreek)

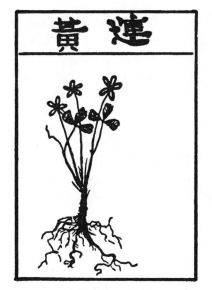

HUANG-LIEN
(Gold Thread)

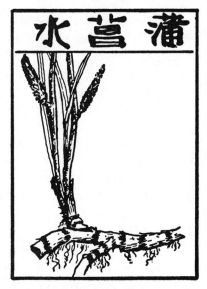

SHUI-CH'ANG-PU
(Sweet Flag)

A tea of melilot helps induce belching for the relief of gas bloat. The Chinese claim that it will also impart a lovely fragrance to the whole body.

Prepare as ordinary tea, and take one cupful three times a day.

SHUI-CH'ANG-PU

English Name: Sweet Flag
Botanical Name: *Acorus calamus*

Sweet flag has long been credited with medicinal virtues both by ancient and modern Chinese herbalists. In olden times the herb was also regarded as a magical plant. On the Chinese New Year, Cantonese cleaned out their homes and posted the sword-shaped leaves of sweet flag near the door. Beneath them they placed a pair of red scrolls bearing an inscription such as "The sweet flag like a sword destroys a thousand evil influences."

Medicinal Use

Sweet flag is a specific for the type of heartburn that is accompanied by sour eructations. This is a distressing condition in which belching brings up from the stomach a hot, searing, watery fluid, sometimes in considerable amounts. For prompt relief a few small pieces of the cut root of sweet flag are chewed and the juice (not the roots) swallowed. This should be continued for five or ten minutes. In chronic conditions, the roots may be chewed several times a day until the stomach is back in good healthy working order.

If you prefer to drink the tea rather than chew the roots, mix 1 ounce of the powdered root in 10 ounces of boiling water. The tea is taken warm, in doses of 2 ounces, twice or three times a day.

Case History

Mrs. J.G., a postal clerk, relates the following:

"For almost five years I suffered periodically from sour belchings, with all that terrible scalding water and sometimes even small pieces of food coming up in my mouth and throat. I tried all sorts of things that are supposed to help this particular condition, but they didn't help.

"One day a friend of mine told me that she was going to a Chinese herbalist for her rheumatism and about how much he was helping her. I made an appointment with him, and while there I began to have that miserable sour belching. I was frantic and asked the herbalist to please get me a glass of water.

"He left the room and quickly returned, but instead of bringing the water he handed me some small pieces of what he called sweet flag root and told me to chew them immediately and swallow the juice.

"I did as he asked. Almost at once, the terrible burning in my throat subsided, and in a matter of minutes my stomach quieted down.

"I took home a good supply of the roots and chewed the little darlings every day for a few weeks. That was over six months ago, and I have never had an attack of that horrible sour belching since. Isn't that remarkable?"

MI-TIEH-HSIANG

English Name: Rosemary
Botanical Name: *Rosmarinus officinalis*

According to tradition, rosemary was brought to China from the Roman Empire during the reign of Wenti of the Wei Dynasty.

Medicinally, the herb is used for nervous, sick stomach, to clear the stomach of mucus, and to restore appetite and normal digestion.

Prepare as ordinary tea, add a pinch of ground ginger, and drink three or four cups daily.

CH'IAO-MAI

English Name: Buckwheat
Botanical Name: *Fagopyrum esculentum*

Buckwheat is very nourishing and digestible and has always been an important food crop in the central provinces of China.

Honey made from buckwheat has proven effective in some cases of peptic ulcers. Consider the following examples:

• Mr. R., a business executive, suffered from a duodenal ulcer for several years. medical treatments helped for a while, but sooner or later the ulcer trouble always returned.

A Chinese herbalist told him to eat buckwheat honey and to use it in place of sugar as a sweetening agent. Mr R. announced, "It's hard to believe that something so simple would prove so effective. Not only did it heal my ulcer, but taking the buckwheat honey daily, as I continue to do, has prevented any further recurrence of the trouble in over two years."

• Mrs. C.V., a housewife, writes: "With five children, an invalid father-in-law to care for, and a husband who is a chronic complainer, I wasn't too surprised when an X-ray showed that a small ulcer was forming in my stomach. I'm deathly afraid of any kind of surgery, and since food is one of the few pleasures in my life, I just couldn't face the thought of a milk diet.

"On the other hand, I knew that I had to do something or the ulcer might get progressively worse and I'd probably land in the hospital. So I got the idea to try a Chinese herbalist. He told me to take a teaspoon of buckwheat honey four or five times a day and to stay away from fried foods, bread, coffee, smoking, and alcohol.

"I don't know if this treatment would help everyone, but for me it was excellent. In less than a month the ulcer was healed. I still use the buckwheat honey daily as a preventative measure, and I can eat anything I want."

• A woman, age 30, took several spoonfuls of buckwheat honey every day during the hay fever season to prevent hay fever. When the season ended, she was astonished to find that a long-standing ulcer condition had cleared up.

• A salesman in his early forties suffered periodic bouts of ulcer pains. Buckwheat honey cleared up the ulcer, and he reports that he takes the honey daily as a preventative against any further trouble.

Buckwheat's Anti-Ulcer Power

Every effort is made by medical doctors to neutralize stomach acid, because the acid is highly irritating to ulcers. Honey is an alkaline food, and darker honeys such as buckwheat have a higher alkaline level than the lighter ones. Honey also provides many valuable minerals, and, interestingly enough, the mineral content is higher in those darker honeys.

Among its many constituents, honey contains magnesium, the spark plug which starts the chain reaction which metabolizes food. It is one of the richest sources of rutin, the nutrient so useful in strengthening the capillaries (tiny blood vessels). It also contains an anti-hemorrhage factor believed to be vitamin K.

Honey is assimilated rapidly and easily, and it is very soothing to the delicate membranes of the digestive tract.

WU-PA-HO

English Name: Peppermint
Botanical Name: *Mentha piperita*

Peppermint grows almost everywhere in China, but since the supply coming from Suchou is reputed to be of the best quality, the plant is called Wu-pa-ho, Wu being the former name for Suchou.

Peppermint tea has a delightful, comforting effect on the stomach and imparts a nice fragrance to the breath. Since it is carminative in action, one cup of the beverage after meals induces belching and therefore relieves the heavy, distressed feeling of gas distention in the stomach.

For gas cramps, nervous upset stomach, nausea, or vomiting, one cup of the hot peppermint tea is sipped slowly every hour for three hours.

The tea is prepared by placing one teaspoonful of the leaves in a cup and adding boiling water. It is covered with a saucer to retain the aromatic properties, allowed to stand for five minutes, and then strained.

MU-SU

English Name: Alfalfa
Botanical Name: *Medicago sativa*

The reputation of alfalfa as an important healing agent for various ailments, including those of the stomach, can be traced back to the writings of the ancient Chinese. In an early Oriental herbarium, 896 plants are cited, and alfalfa tops the list. This herb originated in Persia and was allegedly brought to China by General Chang Chien of the Han dynasty.

Remarkable Plant

Alfalfa possesses deep feeder roots which burrow far into the earth, seeking out valuable minerals in the deep subsoil which are unavailable to other plants. Many instances are on record in which roots were found to have penetrated to depths of 38 feet, while even greater depths of 50 to 68 feet and over have been recorded.

This plant contains protein, calcium, phosphorus, iron, potassium, choline, sodium, silicon, magnesium, and eight essential enzymes. It also provides vitamins A, D, B_6, K, U, and P(rutin).

Alfalfa Used in Chinese Ulcer Treatment

Alfalfa tea is used to strengthen digestion and to stimulate a lagging appetite. It is prepared in the same manner as ordinary tea and taken freely as a daily beverage. Alfalfa also forms an important part of a Chinese remedy for stomach ulcers:

Directions:

- One tablespoonful of powdered alfalfa in a glass of water once a day.
- One teaspoonful of olive oil before meals.
- Diet: No fried foods, no bread, no alcohol, and no smoking.

Interesting Case Histories

Here are some examples of sufferers who improved by using the Chinese ulcer treatment. These accounts were submitted by Mrs. V.C., who writes:

"I began having stomach pains, which proved to be caused by an ulcer. My doctor told me to start drinking milk, first half-and-half, and that later I would be drinking three quarts of milk every day. I told him I was allergic to milk and cream, that they cause my asthma to flare up. He then suggested surgery, but the thought of an operation terrified me, so I politely left his office as quickly as I could.

"I decided to try a Chinese-American herbalist, but didn't realize how difficult it would be to find one. Finally I succeeded in doing so, but only by making a trip to one of the large cities in another state.

"The herbalist put me on alfalfa, one tablespoon of the ground powder dissolved in a glass of water once a day, and olive oil, one teaspoonful before meals. I was sure he would mention diet, and I was

WU-PA-HO
(Peppermint)

MU-SU
(Alfalfa)

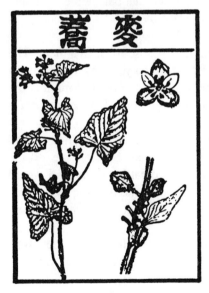

CH'IAO-MAI
(Buckwheat)

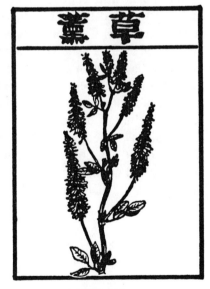

HSUN-TS'AO
(Melilot)

scared stiff it would be milk or cream and my whole trip would have been for nothing. So you cannot imagine how relieved I was to see that the diet did not stress dairy products. And it was such an easy diet, just no fried foods, no bread, and no smoking or drinking (I never drank or smoked anyway).

"The relief from the stomach pains was astonishingly prompt, and after I followed the treatment for a few weeks, my stomach ulcer had completely healed. This was not my imagination because I had my family physician check out the healing, and it was confirmed by X-rays.

"I have told many others who suffered from ulcers about this remarkable Chinese treatment, and they, too, have been helped. My brother was one. His doctor had him on a milk diet and bland foods, but the milk made him very constipated. He was terribly nervous and cross as a bear from the constipation, so after I told him about the wonderful results I got with the Chinese remedy, he stopped taking the milk and used my treatment. There was no more constipation or nervousness, and several weeks later his ulcer had disappeared.

"And then there was my neighbor. He tried the remedy, but didn't like the taste of olive oil, so he dropped that part of the treatment and just followed the rest of it. And even though it took longer, his ulcer cleared up. Can you imagine that!

"I also told a lady friend about the Chinese ulcer treatment. The poor dear had been on a starvation diet for over a year and a half, and in all that time her ulcer had only partially healed. She told me that the thought of continuing the prescribed diet for much longer gave her a terrible feeling of despondency.

"She switched to the Chinese remedy and was delighted to find that she could eat more liberally with no distress. She told me, 'If the treatment did nothing more than allow me to eat better meals I would always be more than grateful.' So you can imagine how happy she was when, some weeks later, X-rays showed that her stomach ulcer was healed.

"I could go on and on about others who have also been very successful in using the Chinese treatment for their stomach ulcers."

Possible Clues to the Effectiveness of Alfalfa

Some of the elements contained in the Chinese ulcer treatment may offer important clues as to why many people have found the remedy effective. Let us examine these elements in the light of modern science.

Alfalfa. As we have seen, among its constituents alfalfa contains vitamins A, B, K, U, P (rutin), and eight important enzymes. Their therapeutic value is scientifically defined as follows:

- Vitamin A: Important for keeping the mucous linings of the stomach healthy.
- Vitamin K: Helps the blood clot properly and protects against hemorrhages.
- Vitamin U: This vitamin is known as the anti-peptic ulcer dietary factor. It is also present in cabbage juice and was discovered in 1949 by Dr. Garnett Cheney, a physician from Stanford Medical School. Dr. Cheney treated his ulcer patients with cabbage juice and found that 62 out of 65 of his patients responded in half the time necessary for the usual type ulcer therapy.

  Following Cheney, other reports on vitamin U studies began to appear. In 1954, George Kohler discovered that alfalfa was a good source of this important vitamin. In 1960, two German scientists studied the inhibitory effects of vitamin U on ulcer formation in dogs.

  In 1971, after years of encouraging results from testing vitamin U on lab animals, Soviet scientists began clinical testing of vitamin U on human patients suffering from gastric and duo-denal ulcers. To date, more than 1,000 patients have been treated. The therapy included five to six vitamin U pills daily for 30 to 40 days. Results showed that whereas only 40% of ulcer patients are cured with the standard method of treatment, 80% were cured with vitamin U therapy and the remaining 20% were notably improved.
- Vitamin P (rutin): The appearance of an ulcer is generally preceded by inflammation of the stomach lining, and this in turn is the result of capillary weak-ness. Rutin is one of the bioflavinoids, and these

natural substances reduce lining inflammation and build capillary strength.

Three medical doctors reported marked success with bioflavinoids in treating 36 cases of bleeding duodenal ulcers. In all 36 cases treated, the mucous membranes and duodenal contour returned to normal, usually in about three weeks.

• Enzymes: According to Dr. Jacobson, food scientist of Reno, Nevada, there is a sufficient quantity of enzymes in alfalfa to be of considerable aid in the digestion of all four classes of food—starches, proteins, fats, and sugars.

Olive Oil. It is well known that olive oil has a soothing effect on the lining of the stomach. Devett Fox, M.D., treats his ulcer patients with olive oil and reports that it does the same or an even better job than the cream given in traditional ulcer diets. Some medical doctors have speculated that olive oil contains vitamin U, the ulcer healing substance.

The Chinese Ulcer Diet

You will notice that the Chinese diet is not the traditional ulcer diet prescribed by orthodox medics. This is very impressive, since a number of modern medical experts conceded years ago that there is very little advantage in the standard milk-heavy, bland ulcer diet, and recently the editors of *Drug and Therapeutics Bulletin* have reaffirmed these opinions.

The *Bulletin* says that a diet of steamed fish, milk, and purées over a long period of time is apt to cause a patient to suffer from iron and vitamin C deficiency, plus complications of diarrhea, gas, and constipation. If the patient has surgery, he is especially cautioned to avoid the traditional ulcer diet afterwards.

The *Bulletin* adds that the patient who eliminates fried foods, stops smoking, and stops heavy drinking is taking sensible anti-ulcer action.

Summary

1. Symptoms of indigestion may appear as heartburn, sour belching, gas bloat, foul breath, flatulence, nausea, vomiting, headache,

coated tongue, bad taste in the mouth, and sometimes palpitation and difficult breathing.

2. There is a distinct possibility that frequent use of antacid preparations containing magnesium or aluminum hydroxides can render the bones more fragile than they ought to be.

3. Natural Chinese herb remedies can do the job of neutralizing stomach acids safely and effectively.

4. Many other forms of stomach distress can also be relieved by wholesome, select Oriental plant remedies.

5. Specific Chinese herb formulas have coped effectively with some cases of peptic ulcers.

3

CHINESE HERB REMEDIES FOR RESPIRATORY AILMENTS

According to Chinese herbalists, there are a large number of specific plant remedies that can deal effectively with various ailments of the respiratory tract. These natural healing agents help fight infection, reduce fever, loosen stubborn phlegm, soothe inflamed air passages and linings, make breathing easier, and bring an end to dragged out respiratory miseries that cause considerable suffering.

If you are badgered by colds, sore throats, or other infections or ailments of the respiratory tract, you may find Chinese herb remedies of great benefit. However, please remember that nature demands cooperation, which means proper diet, rest, and clean living habits.

YIN-HSING

English Name: Ginko Tree
Botanical Name: *Ginko biloba*

The name "Ginko" comes from the chinese and means "silver fruit" or "white nuts." This tree grows abundantly south of the Yangtse and in other regions of the Far East, but has also been cultivated in Europe and the United States. The fruits are highly prized in the Orient, and the roasted pits are considered a delicacy. In our own country, however, the fruits are rarely seen on the Ginko because the staminate and pistillate flowers occur on different trees and usually only the staminate types are planted.

AN-HSI-HSIANG
(Gum Benzoin)

YIN-HSING
(Ginko)

LIN-MU
(Wild Plum)

Centuries ago, the Ginko was found growing in a courtyard of a Chinese temple, and it has since been classified as one of the oldest living species of trees. Today the Ginko is familiar to tree lovers everywhere, not only because of its great beauty, but also because it has a peculiar and mystifying immunity to insects and diseases which attack other trees. Even though its remarkable resistance to such pests has made the Ginko a horticultural curiosity, scientists have yet to discover what substance in the tree imparts the immunity. The Ginko is also very tolerant of dust and city smoke and is not usually damaged by storms.

A Specific for the Common Cold

The Chinese have long claimed that the leaves of the Ginko contain medicinal properties that can cure the common cold very quickly and that these properties are also effective in relieving sinus congestion, stubborn coughs, and asthma. For any of these purposes, the leaves are infused in boiling water and the vapors from the steam inhaled.

Those who may be skeptical of the Chinese claim for the Ginko as a curative remedy for the common cold may want to hesitate in their criticism and ponder the following report.

According to a German newspaper, Dr. Joachim H. Volkner, a nose, ear and throat specialist in Berlin, announced the discovery of a "lightning" cure for the common cold. Dr. Volkner found that if a person inhales an essence prepared from the leaves of the Ginko tree, his cold will get better. Two hundred and twenty-four people tried the Ginko treatment, and the results were "staggering." The German report stated that, "The inflamed areas healed immediately."

Dr. Volkner confesses that he hasn't as yet identified the exact substance in the Ginko leaves that produces the therapeutic effects, but he does explain how the treatment works. When a person catches a cold, the cells of the mucous membranes are damaged and are unable to store moisture. The efficiency of the cell walls becomes impaired because substances in the cell press against these walls. Apparently, the Ginko essence forces these components of the cell back into its interior. Dr. Volkner explains that "The microbes which have collected inside die off, and very shortly after inhalation [of the Ginko essence] they completely disappear."[1]

---

[1]*Hamburger Abendblatt,* October 8, 1966.

Ginko Combination

Ginko *seeds*, called *Pai-kuo*, are contained in a traditional Chinese herbal formula known as *Mahuang and Ginko Combination*.

The plant, Mahuang, has been highly esteemed among the Chinese since ancient times as a remedy for respiratory disorders. These claims were vindicated when modern scientists examined the plant and found that it contained a substance called *ephedrine* which proved helpful for certain pulmonary complaints.

In addition to the two principal herbs of Mahuang and Ginko seeds, the formula is augmented with eight assistant herbs. It is used as a tea by the Chinese for treating asthmatic attacks, bronchial spasms, colds, and coughs. The loss of appetite which sometimes accompanies these conditions is said to also be remedied by use of this herbal tea.

PIEN-HSU

English Name: Knotgrass
Botanical Name: *Polygonum aviculare*

Pien-hsu (knotgrass) is a low-growing herb which has been used in China as a remedy for lung ailments since the second millenium B.C. The Chinese often call the plant Fen-chieh-ts'ao because of the white powder that covers the stem.

Along with tannin, mucilage, and small amounts of volatile oils, knotgrass contains salicylic acid, a powerful pharmaceutical agent which no doubt accounts for the herb's long-standing reputation as a remedy for lung diseases. In modern Chinese medicine the plant is employed for treating bronchitis and whooping cough. It is prepared as a tea, one teaspoonful of the cut herb to one cup of boiling water. Three to four cups of the strained infusion are taken daily.

K'UAN-TUNG

English Name: Coltsfoot
Botanical Name: *Tussilago farfara*

K'uan-tung is commonly known in Western countries as coltsfoot or coughwort. The botanical name, *tussilago*, signifies "cough dispeller." Some of the Chinese names refer to the herb's early flowering and its resistance to cold and frost.

Nature's Cough Remedy

Coughing helps you to eject excessive mucus or food particles and other foreign material that interferes with your breathing. However, when the mucus deposits are stubborn and very deep-seated the cough persists. And it may also persist when the lungs are irritated due to smoke, dust, or infection, even though there is no material to eject. This is the type of cough that gives you that aggravating "tickle."

It is important to take every possible step to reduce the severity and persistence of coughing so that you can get your sleep and proper rest. The experience of Chinese herbalists has shown that a tea made of coltsfoot leaves and other select herbs is very helpful for relieving stubborn coughs and irritations of the lungs and air passages. The formula consists of the following:

K'uan-tung (coltsfoot leaves) .... 1 oz.
Hu-lu-pa (fenugreek seeds) .... 1 oz.
Chiang (crushed fresh ginger root) .... 1/4 oz.

Put the fenugreek seeds and ginger root in one quart of cold water and bring to a boil. Simmer for 10 minutes. Strain. Pour the boiling decoction into a container in which 1 ounce of coltsfoot leaves has been placed. Mix well, cover, and allow to stand until cold. Strain, reheat, and add one tablespoonful of honey and a small amount of powdered Kan-ts'ao (Chinese licorice root). Three to four cups of the tea are taken daily for irritable cough, wheezing, or throat irritation.

PEI PA KOA

English Name: Loquat Syrup

Loquat syrup, a translation of the Chinese language pronunciation of the name Pei Pa Koa, was originated by Kingto Nin Jiom in the Ching dynasty. This herb formula has a fascinating history. According to the story, which is reportedly true, Governor Yeung of Peiping (the city where the King lived) was extremely filial to his mother and terribly grieved because she suffered frequent attacks of painful sore throat and severe coughing spells. Many famous doctors were consulted, but none were able to help.

Then one day Governor Yeung heard of a learned Chinese physician named Yip Tin Sie and immediately engaged him to cure his

TSE-LAN
(Boneset)

K'UAN-TUNG
(Coltsfoot)

HSUAN-FU-HUA
(Elecampane)

SHU-WEI-TS'AO
(Sage)

mother's illnesses. This wise doctor bethought himself of the formula originated by Kingto Nin Jiom and decided to treat her with the herb syrup. After Governor Yeung's mother fully recovered, the doctor gave Governor Yeung the secret formula for the syrup and told him how to prepare it. The Governor was further instructed to give his mother some of the syrup twice a day, once in the morning and once in the evening, to maintain her health and to prevent any further recurrence of her ailment.

Governor Yeung was so grateful for his mother's recovery that he prepared bottles of the syrup and gave them away free to anyone who suffered from the same illness.

After the Governor's death, the demand for bottles of the syrup became so great that his descendants were forced to charge a little money for them, but to every bottle they attached the complete formula and the mark and words "Filial to Mother Device" in honor of their ancestors.

The gesture of revealing the exact contents of the precious formula is quite amazing since the Chinese, especially long ago, went to great lengths to keep the ingredients of their remedies a carefully guarded secret. For example, they would hire blind people to roll the herb ingredients into pill form or other forms, so that no one aside from the herbalist himself could possibly know what the formula contained. Thus, by revealing the ingredients of the Loquat Syrup, Governor Yeung's descendants certainly performed a humanitarian act.

Pei Pa Koa Comes to the United States

Pei Pa Koa (Loquat Syrup) contains absolutely no chemicals of any kind. It is a purely natural formula containing 11 herbal ingredients, and it is still prepared by the traditional method.

This syrup, which has been used for centuries in China, is now imported into the United States, and many people are claiming excellent results with its use. One young man who suffered from weak lungs and coughing spells for over a year reported that the syrup worked for him where orthodox medicine had not. He said, "I really didn't think the Chinese herb syrup would do much more than bring me a little relief, but after taking it every day for several weeks I was entirely free of my chronic lung trouble." An elderly woman reported that the use of the syrup cleared up a stubborn condition of nasal

Front Label of Loquat Syrup

Section of the Loquat Syrup label showing Governor Yeung giving the herb remedy to his beloved mother. Note the yin-yang motif of the circle—half white and half black.

congestion. In another case, a man wrote: "Constant tickle of 'smoker's cough' yielded entirely with the use of Loquat syrup, and I found the same to be true of an aggravating cough due to a bad cold."

HSUAN-FU-HUA

English Name: Elecampane
Botanical Name: *Inula chinensis*

This plant is native to North China, Manchuria, Mongolia, and Korea and appears to be the same as *Inula britanica*, the English elecampane. Other Chinese names for the plant are Chin-ch'ien-hua and Chin-ch'ien-chu, applied generally to the cultivated variety which resembles the herb *calendula*.

Sometimes the whole dried plant—including the leaves, roots, flowers, and stalks—is found on sale in Chinese herb shops. However, the root is the part chiefly used in Chinese medicine.

The medicinal action of elecampane is cited as diaphoretic. It is used in combination with other specific herbs for the relief of bronchitis, hay fever, and asthma.

For example:

Hsuan-fu-hua (elecampane) .... 1/2 oz.
Han-t'ao (cherry bark) .... 1/2 oz.
Sung (white pine) .... 1/2 oz.
Ch'ien-hu (angelica root) .... 1/2 oz.
Kan-ts'ao (Chinese licorice root) .... 1/4 oz.

Place the herbs in one quart of boiling water; boil slowly down to one pint, strain, and add honey to make a syrup. One tablespoonful is taken four times a day or more often if the cough is very troublesome.

The Chinese claim for elecampane as an important remedial ingredient for various respiratory ailments has received some scientific support. It was established that inulin, the chief constituent in the plant, is a powerful antiseptic and bactericide especially destructive to the tubercule bacillus.

LIN-MU

English Name: Wild Plum
Botanical Name: *Prunus spinulosa*

The flowers of the wild plum are single or in pairs and are very small compared to those of the domestic or garden plum. The wild species grows in Central China and Europe and appears in our own country in the double flowered variety.

The antispasmodic action attributed to wild plum bark is said to be of considerable value for treating asthma. Place one teaspoon of the cut, dried bark in one cup of boiling water, cover, and allow the tea to stand until cold. Strain, reheat, and add a little honey. Dose: One cupful one hour before meals three times a day.

Following are some interesting reports on the use of wild plum bark tea:

• "I am using wild plum bark tea before bedtime and upon arising for asthma and bronchitis. It certainly has been helping me. I have given this a long trial and can testify to the wonderful help received. Of course, right living and eating has also aided materially."—Mrs. S.B.

• "I have spent a small fortune on medicine for asthma in the last three years, and with no results. I heard about wild plum bark and purchased a supply, and I have been able to sleep from the first night on."—Mr. B.Y.

• "I want to tell you what the good wild plum bark has done for me. I have suffered for 15 years with asthma, and this spring I was down for 12 weeks. Three doctors could not help. One of my neighbors, a Mrs. J.G., ordered some wild plum bark, and it put me on my feet in a week. I certainly can never say enough for it."—Mrs. R.V.

TIGER BALM

Tiger Balm is a popular Oriental herb ointment developed more than a half a century ago by two Chinese brothers, Aw Boon Par and Aw Boon Haw. Aw is the surname, Boon means "gentle," and Haw means "tiger," so the brothers decided to call their formula Tiger Balm.

This Chinese herb product comes packed in three sizes—large jars, medium jars, and small tins. It also comes in two colors, red and white, and in two strengths, mild and strong. The jars and tins containing the stronger formula, called Red Tiger Balm, are wrapped in a reddish-pink paper, whereas those of the milder product, White Tiger Balm, are wrapped in white paper.

Remedial Benefits of Tiger Balm

Tiger Balm relieves tightness of the chest and produces a soothing effect on the pains due to colds, fatigue, exposure, strain, or rheumatism. For such conditions the parts are well rubbed with the Chinese ointment two or three times a day and covered with a warm flannel.

Tiger Balm is also used as an inhalant for stuffed up noses, nasal drip, and head colds. A few whiffs of the vapor soothes the upper air passages and gives your head a clear feeling.

Some Interesting Reports on the Use of Tiger Balm

• "For years I have suffered from sinus congestion with very little relief. Then I heard about Chinese Tiger Balm. Dabbing a little of the ointment under each nostril and inhaling the vapors brought such relief that I will never be without it."—Mrs. R.B.

• "Inhaling the fumes from the open jar of Tiger Balm is the only thing that has given me relief from the discomfort of hay fever."—Miss P.M.

• "Whenever I get neuralgia pains I use Tiger Balm. It relieves the pain considerably."—Mrs. V.S.

• "I had the flu, and my muscles and bones ached so badly I couldn't sleep. My wife bought a jar of Chinese Tiger Balm, which worked like magic. And we found that Tiger Balm is good for other things too. My sister was troubled with nasal drip and had to carry a packet of Kleenex in her purse at all times. At our suggestion, she agreed to try Tiger Balm. Two days later we got a phone call from her. 'I could kiss you both,' she said. 'That Chinese product is absolutely marvelous.'"—Mr. T.P.

BALASHIN SAI
(Pat Kwa Tan)

Balashin Sai is another famous herb formula developed by the two Aw brothers. The active ingredients of this Oriental product are Gambier, peppermint oil, and Chinese licorice powder. These ingre-

TIGER BALM
Medical Ointment

dients are compressed into tiny square lozenges which are used for the relief of coughs, colds, catarrh, sore throat, and nausea. Balashin Sai also sweetens the breath, counteracts perspiration odor, and serves as a refreshing stimulant for exhaustion.

• Mrs. J.R., a department store clerk, writes: "All my life I have suffered miserable spells of catarrh. Sometimes the aftermath of a cold or poor diet is the triggering cause. Other times I cannot detect the cause. Getting to sleep at night was a dreadful chore because I'd be constantly trying to clear my throat to keep from choking on the phlegm. During the day, frequent clearing of my throat while serving store customers was terribly embarrassing.

"I got very little relief from drug store patent medicines. Then I discovered the little Chinese herb lozenges called Balashin Sai. They are so effective and so easy to use. I simply put a few of the tiny pellets on my tongue and let them dissolve slowly. The catarrh soon clears up."

• The following comes from Jim R., a hard-working auto mechanic: "At least once or twice a year I catch a cold that isn't serious enough to keep me home in bed, but the scratchy sore throat and dragged out feeling really get me down. These bouts have never been any picnic for my wife and kids either because my disposition goes sour.

"One of our neighbors told my wife about a Chinese herb product call Balashin Sai and explained what the lozenges were. At my wife's insistence, I used them. The soothing effect on my throat was out-of-this-world, and I also experienced quite a refreshing pickup, no longer had that lousy dragged out feeling. Hope you'll pass the news of this Chinese remedy along to others."

HSIEH-TZU-TS'AO

English Name: Chinese Nettle
Botanical Name: *Urtica dioica*

Following is one of the specific remedies used by Chinese healers for treating the condition of pleurisy.

Boil 2 ounces of dried Chinese nettles (or the seeds) slowly in one quart of water for 20 minutes. Strain when cool, reheat, and take one teacupful every two hours. In addition, apply hot fomentations to the painful side. For this purpose prepare a second quart of the nettle decoction. Dip a flannel in the hot tea, wring out and place on the affected part, cover with a dry towel, and retain until cool. Then renew the flannel, and continue the hot fomentations until relief is obtained. Chinese herbalists have reportedly cured many a severe case of pleurisy with the above treatment.

PROPOLIS

Very good results have been reported with the use of propolis for treating various respiratory problems and related ailments.

- Dr. R. Chauvin of Paris, France, stated that he found the use of propolis helpful in preventing viral infections such as colds, flu, and tonsillitis.
- Dr. M.M. Frenkel of Russia reported that propolis is effective for treating diseases of the sinuses and upper part of the respiratory tract.
- Professor Osmanagic of Yugoslavia tested 270 volunteers who were exposed to influenza. Eighty-eight took propolis, and 182 did not. Of the group who used propolis, only 7% caught the flu, while 63% of the group who had not taken the substance contracted the flu.
- Professor Kern, also of Yugoslavia, reported impressive results with the use of propolis on patients with inflammation of the mucous membranes of the throat and mouth. The patients dissolved a propolis lozenge in the mouth every two hours. Within six to ten hours after starting the treatment, almost all patients were free of fever, and swallowing was painless.

In cases of patients suffering from chronic inflammation of the mouth and gums, symptoms were scarcely noticeable by the next day. In some instances, especially of children, improvement had taken place within a few hours.

How Propolis May Be Used

- For colds and coughs a propolis lozenge is sucked as often as needed.
- For tonsillitis, the lozenge is used three or four times daily.

- In conditions of sore throat, a propolis lozenge is taken every hour until relief is obtained.
- For sinusitis, a propolis lozenge is chewed as often as required.

TSE-LAN

English Name: Boneset
Botanical Name: *Eupatorium perfoliatum*

Tse-lan (boneset) is an important ingredient of a Chinese formula for colds, catarrh, and especially for influenza symptomized by fever, headache, aching muscles, and pains in the bones and joints. Generally after four or five doses have been taken profuse sweating occurs and relief is obtained:

Tse-lan (boneset) .... 1/2 oz.
Wu-pa-ho (peppermint leaves) .... 1/2 oz.
Chieh-ku-mu (dried elder blossoms) .... 1 oz.

Simmer the elder blossoms in one pint of water for 20 minutes, then strain. Place the boneset and peppermint leaves in a separate container and add one pint of boiling water (do not allow the infusion to continue boiling). Cover, allow to stand for one-half hour, and then strain. Add this brew to the elder tea, and then reheat the mixture and drink one-half pint hot every 15 minutes until relief is obtained.

Note: There are different species of elder. The one cited in this formula is known botanically as *Sambucus canadensis*.

AN-HSI-HSIANG

English Name: Gum Benzoin
Botanical Name: *Styrax benzoin*

A medicinal aromatic gum resin is obtained from an Asiatic tree called *Styrax benzoin* and is imported into Southern China from Sumatra and Borneo. The "An-hsi" in the Chinese name, An-hsi-hsiang, probably refers to the Persians, whose country, along with Sumatra and Central Asia, is a source of supply for this foreign balsamic resin. The aromatic resin is obtained by making triangular cuts in the bark of the tree. From these incisions exudes the sap which coagulates, and after it has sufficiently hardened it is collected and packed for export.

At one time in China, the fumes resulting from burning this lovely smelling substance were believed to drive away devils and attract good spirits.

Benzoin for Croup

The active ingredient of the gum resin is extracted and made into a tincture called "benzoin." This valuable tincture is universally used, both in Chinese and orthodox medicine, as an inhalant for dry, hacking coughs, those which doctors call "unproductive." This is a condition in which it is extremely difficult to cough up apparently immovable sputum from the bronchial tubes. It is commonly known as "croup."

Any mother whose infant has had the miserable ailment of croup knows how terrifying it is to watch the feverish child desperately trying to cough up the obstructive phlegm. For such emergencies, benzoin tincture is added to one pint of boiling water. Under a sheet arranged like a tent, the vapors from the mixture can be inhaled by the youngster. This loosens up the unproductive sputum, much to the great relief of the croupy child and the alarmed mother.

Laryngitis

Laryngitis is an inflammation of the larynx (voice box). Symptoms include hoarseness, irritation, difficulty in breathing (you wheeze), and frequently a dry, rasping cough. Your voice may be reduced to a mere whisper, break into a high falsetto pitch, or descend to a deep bass. Talking is very uncomfortable, and if you overuse your voice the laryngitis condition may become serious.

The benzoin inhalation method outlined for treating croup may also be used by adults suffering from laryngitis. Steam from one-half hour to one hour four times a day.

Along with recommending the steam inhalation, Chinese herbalists suggest that you take it easy, drink plenty of liquids, and spare your voice as much as possible. They also point out that laryngitis is aggravated by temperature changes, so you will recover more quickly if you stay at home when you have this ailment.

KAN-TS'AO

English Name: Chinese Licorice
Botanical Name: *Glycyrrhiza glabra*

Kan-ts'ao (Chinese licorice) grows abundantly in Northern China, and quantities are also brought from Mongolia, especially from the region of Kokonor. Other names for the plant are Mi-kan, Mi-ts'ao, Mei-ts'ao, Lu-ts'ao, Ling-t'ung, and Kuo-lao. The last name cited is applied because of the herb's great virtues as a remedy.

Licorice root is considered to be of great importance in Chinese pharmacy, being the corrective and harmonizing ingredient in a large number of prescriptions. In Chinese herb shops the root is commonly sold in long, dry, wrinkled pieces.

Demulcent, pectoral, alterative, emollient, expectorant, and slightly laxative properties are attributed to Chinese licorice root. It is used to relieve thirst, feverishness, coughs, hoarseness, sore throat, and distress in breathing. The extract enters into the composition of cough lozenges, syrups, and pastilles.

- For irritable cough, scratchy sore throat, or laryngitis, boil 2 ounces of licorice root in 1 quart of water until reduced to one and a half pints. Add 1 ounce of K'uan-tung (coltsfoot leaves) and two tablespoons of lemon juice to the simmering decoction, and immediately remove the container from the burner. Keep the brew covered and allow to stand until cold. Strain, reheat, and drink one cup of the hot tea three or four times a day.
- The following formula lubricates the throat, loosens stubborn phlegm, and affords relief in hoarseness, coughs, and bronchial irritations:

Kan-ts'ao (licorice root) .... 1/2 oz.
Chih-ma (flaxseed) .... 1 oz.
Boil in 1-1/2 pints of water for 10 minutes, then strain.
Dose: One cup of the hot tea, three or four times a day.
Sip the tea slowly.

YÜEH-KUEI

English Name: Cinnamon
Botanical Name: *Cinnamomum cassia*

In the Far East, the cinnamon tree is native to Kuangsi, but is now grown in other parts of southern China. Since ancient times, cinnamon has been used as a medicine, and regarded as the most desired of all the flavoring seasoning spices.

Remedial Use

Chinese herbalists explain that older people in their 70s and 80s often develop a cough accompanied by frequent spitting of whitish-colored phlegm. They consider the problem to be a Yin (weak) condition. As a helpful remedy, they suggest chewing and swallowing a very small pinch of powdered cinnamon. The cinnamon should be of the highest quality, which can be determined by a bitter-sweet taste. If the taste is too bitter, and not oily, the quality is poor.

CHINESE GUM WALL HERB TEA

This Chinese herb combination comes packed in tiny square boxes, ten to a carton. Each individual box contains many of the herbs most commonly used in Oriental medicine, such as atractylis, alisma, almond, lotus, scutellaria, licorice, platycodon, agastache, and others.

Gum Wall herb tea is used as a remedy for the first signs of a cold. It does not help if the cold has already been in progress for several days.

The tea is prepared by placing the contents of one or two of the tiny square boxes in a tea pot and adding two cups of boiling water. The tea is allowed to steep (stand) for five minutes. It is then strained and drunk hot, before bedtime.

Reported Use

• "Never in my life have I known anyone to catch a cold as easily as my husband does. It seemed as though all anyone had to do was sneeze and he was sure to catch their cold.

"A Chinese friend of ours suggested he try an Oriental herb remedy called Gum Wall tea whenever he felt he was coming down with a cold. My husband agreed to try the remedy, and were we ever surprised to find it worked! Please pass the good word along to others."—Mrs. L.P.

HUA-HSIAN

English Name: Anise
Botanical Name: *Pimpinella anisum*

Anise is of Eastern origin but is now cultivated in many parts of the world. The seeds are well-known flavoring agents for cakes, relishes, soups, sauces, and wines. In the old days it was a popular custom to chew anise seeds to sweeten the breath.

Remedial Uses

The therapeutic action of anise is classified by herbalists as pectoral, expectorant, and carminative. It is especially valued as a remedy for hard, dry cough where expectoration is difficult. For this purpose it is generally used in the form of lozenges.

The volatile oil of anise forms part of the preparation for the liqueur anisette[2], which reputedly is helpful for bronchitis and spasmodic asthma. If anisette is taken in hot water it is said to be an immediate palliative.

Five to ten drops of anise oil placed on top of a small amount of honey in a teaspoon, taken one-half hour before meals, has reputedly proved helpful in some cases of emphysema.

Fifteen drops of *essence* of anise added to one quart of hot water and used as an *inhalant* has relieved some stubborn cases of laryngitis.

CHINESE HERB GARGLES AND MOUTH WASHES

Germs that trigger colds, tonsillitis, influenza, and similar ailments generally gain access by the mucous membranes of the mouth and throat. As an accessory treatment to the various plant remedies previously covered, Chinese herb gargles and mouth washes are of great value since they remove germs from your mouth and throat, and help speed your recovery.

These natural herb solutions are also helpful for treating canker sores, mouth ulcers, ulcerated gums, bleeding gums, and similar conditions.

---

[2]Anisette is sold in most liquor stores.

Beneficial for Oral Hygiene

When you are exposed to chilly winter months or a barrage of sneezing and coughing, infection may hover all around you, but the full force of the attack may be repelled if you indulge in a melodious herbal gargle or mouth wash every morning before going to work and before going to bed at night. Along with their protective powers, these herbal preparations build mouth and gum health and also modify unpleasant odors that linger in the mouth after certain meals or beverages.

Directions for Use

Some of the Chinese recipes cited in the following list are used solely for treating a specific condition of the mouth and throat, while others may be used either as a treatment or for daily oral hygiene.

For treatment purposes, an herb gargle or mouth wash is used four times a day, or more often if necessary. In conditions of sore throat, tonsillitis, and similar ailments, herb gargles are more effective if used as hot as possible, but not so hot that they burn. Mouth washes are used warm or cool. For bleeding gums, the herb preparations are used cold.

For daily oral hygiene, a mouth wash or gargle may be employed once in the morning and once again at night, or you may clean and rinse your mouth with the herbal solution whenever possible after eating. When you use an herb gargle for daily oral health, it should be used warm, not hot.

MU-YAO

English Name: Myrrh
Botanical Name: *Balsamodendron myrrh*

From remote antiquity, the fragrant gum-resin of the myrrh tree has been a constituent of Oriental medicines, perfumes, incense, precious ointments, and sacred oils. Originally imported from Persia, the gum-resin of myrrh is now produced to some extent in the southern regions of China.

As a mouth wash, one-half teaspoon of myrrh tincture in a glass of warm water soothes delicate mucous membranes of the mouth and throat. It is also very soothing and healing for troublesome canker sores, denture irritated gums, or when gums are sore from rough brushing or sensitive dental work. The lovely aroma and flavor of myrrh tincture imparts a lasting, refreshing taste and fragrance to your mouth and breath after strong-flavored foods. Try it also every morning to refresh your mouth after that stale overnight taste and mouth odor.

Tincture of myrrh may be applied full strength to cold sores.

HUANG-LIEN

English Name: Gold Thread
Botanical Name: *Coptis teeta*

Huang-lien (gold thread) is used as a gargle or mouth wash for minor sore throat, canker sores, and irritation of the mouth due to smoking. It is also used warm for aphthous sore mouth in children (a condition symptomized by many white blisters in the area of the mouth and throat).

Boil 2 ounces of the cut roots of gold thread in one quart of water for one-half hour. Strain, and add one teaspoon of honey.

SHU-WEI-TS'AO

English Name: Sage
Botanical Name: *Salvia officinalis*

Sage was so highly regarded by the Chinese that they gave the early Dutch traders twice the amount of their choicest Oriental teas in exchange for it.

This herb is an aromatic astringent and an antiseptic of subtle and penetrating power. It is used alone or in combination with other herbs.

- Place 2 ounces of sage in a container and pour one quart of boiling water over them. Cover with a lid, remove from the heat, and allow the tea to stand for two hours. Strain, and add one tablespoon of honey and a tablespoon of Ts'u (vinegar). Use as a hot gargle for stubborn sore throat or inflammation of the tonsils.
- Simmer 1 ounce of sage in one pint of water for ten minutes, then allow it to stand until cold. Strain, add a teaspoon of

honey, and use as a hot gargle for throat irritation or cool as a mouth wash for ulcerated mouth and ulcers or bleeding of the gums. Excellent for use in daily oral hygiene as it increases the resistance of the mucous membranes to infection. As an added bonus, this sage tea is reputed to be of great help to public speakers because it strengthens and sustains the voice. One tablespoon of the tea is swallowed just before you go to the meeting.

- Mrs. H.C., a correspondent, writes:

    "It might be of interest to readers that during a nasty flu attack lasting five weeks, my throat was so bad I could only croak, and could hardly be heard. I suddenly remembered reading that sage tea was good for sore throats. To my astonishment and great relief, within half an hour of gargling with sage tea my throat was nearly back to normal and I could be heard quite clearly on the telephone. As I live alone, this means a lot to me. Now, when I have a bad throat I use the gargle and it goes back to normal in no time."

- For the condition of tonsillitis, prepare a strong sage tea, 2 ounces to one quart of boiling water. Remove immediately from the heat, cover, and allow to stand for two hours. Strain, and add a small bit of pulverized alum.

    One woman who tried this sage-alum gargle wrote: "My oldest boy got up with tonsillitis one morning, so I prepared a tea of sage and alum and had him gargle with it several times a day. The next day he was rid of the tonsillitis, where other times he would suffer for weeks and could not eat or sleep."

- Here is another formula Chinese herbalists often prescribe for tonsillitis: Place 1 ounce of sage and 1 ounce of Chin-ssu-ts'ao *(Hypericum chinensis* a species of St. John's Wort) in a container and add one quart of boiling water. Cover, and allow the tea to stand for one-half hour. Strain, and add one teaspoon La-chiao (ground capsicum). Reheat, and gargle with it frequently.

- Dr. Bartram of England presents the following:

    "For laryngitis and pharyngitis an infusion of sage can be made by placing a handful of the leaves in a pint of boiling water, and covering until cool to prevent the escape of volatile properties. Excellent for catarrh. One wineglassful can be taken, after straining, between meals, three times daily."[3]

TRADITIONAL CHINESE HERB COMBINATIONS

The following Chinese formulas consist of different herbs scientifically blended and prepared into extract powders. They are available in convenient capsule form, and used for treating various respiratory ailments.

Pueraria Combination

Constituents: Pueraria, ma-huang, cinnamon, peony root, ginger, jujube, licorice.

Uses: For the common cold symptomized by headaches, chills, shivering, fever, but no sweating.

Bupleurum and Pueraria Combination

Constituents: Bupleurum, pueraria, scute, licorice, peony root, chiang-huo, angelica, platycodon, jujube, ginger, gypsum.

Uses: For severe forms of the common cold with nasal dryness and headaches.

Cyperus and Perilla Combination

Constituents: Cyperus, perilla, citrus, ginger, licorice.

Uses: Mild cases of the common cold for persons of a delicate constitution with gastrointestinal weakness.

Pinellia and Magnolia Combination

Constituents: Pinellia, magnolia bark, perilla, hoelen, ginger.

Uses: Influenza, pleurisy, bronchitis, and bronchial asthma.

Blue Dragon Combination

Constituents: Ma-huang, licorice, cinnamon, peony root, ginger, pinellia, schizandra, asarum.

Uses: Nasal drip, rhinitis, persistent cough and wheezing with large amounts of watery sputum, headaches,

---

[3]*Grace Magazine*, Autumn 1960.

fever, but no sweating. Used for colds, bronchitis, bronchial asthma, and hay fever.

Hoelen and Schizandra Combination

Constituents: Hoelen, schizandra, licorice, ginger, apricot seed, pinellia, asarum.

Uses: Considered especially effective for bronchitis, emphysema, and bronchial asthma in the elderly or those of a delicate constitution. Symptoms may include asthmatic wheezing, coughing, pallor, fatigue, and difficulty in breathing when climbing stairs.

Bupleurum and Scute Combination

Constituents: Bupleurum, scute, pinellia, jujube, ginseng, licorice, coptis, ginger, trichosanthes seed.

Uses: Bronchitis, pleuritis, and intercostal neuralgia.

Pueraria Nasal Combination

Constituents: Pueraria, cinnamon, ma-huang, rhubarb root, licorice, peony root, coix, platycodon, cnidium, shih-kao, jujube, magnolia flower, ginger.

Uses: Sinusitis, chronic rhinitis, nasal congestion, and snoring.

Bupleurum, Cinnamon, and Ginger Combination

Constituents: Bupleurum, cinnamon, ginger, trichosanthes root, scute, ostrea testa, licorice.

Uses: For the common cold in the elderly or persons of a delicate constitution with pallor, mild fever, insomnia, wheezing, nervous exhaustion, and diarrhea.

Cinnamon Combination

Constituents: Cinnamon, licorice, ginger, peony, jujube.

Uses: Common cold with low vitality, headaches, fever, spontaneous sweating.

HSIA-KU-TS'AO

English Name: Self-Heal
Botanical Name: *Prunella vulgaris*

This plant contains astringent and styptic properties and is used as a cold mouth wash for bleeding gums or as a gargle or mouth wash for ulceration or inflammation of the mouth and throat. Prepare a tea by adding 1 ounce of the leaves to one pint of boiling water. Remove from the heat, cover, and allow to stand for ten minutes. Strain.

PIEN-HSU

English Name: Knotgrass
Botanical Name: *Polygonum aviculare*

A strong tea prepared from Pien-hsu held in the mouth for five minutes relieves toothache and arrests bleeding gums. Prolonged use is said to harden loose, spongy gums, make the teeth less sensitive, and help prevent tooth decay.

Place 1 ounce of the herb in a saucepan and add one pint of boiling water. Cover and allow to stand until cold. Strain.

FAN-PAI-TS'AO

English Name: Cinquefoil
Botanical Name: *Potentilla reptans*

In ancient China, cinquefoil was used in magic for casting spells and as a love-divining herb.

Cinquefoil makes a fine gargle or mouth wash. Chinese herbalists employ it for its astringent properties to arrest bleeding gums and to fasten loose teeth. Used as a daily mouth wash, it builds strong healthy gums.

Place one teaspoonful of the herb in a cup and add boiling water. Cover with a saucer and allow the tea to stand for 30 minutes. Strain.

HU-CHIN-TS'AO

English Name: Violet
Botanical Name: *Viola odorata*

The violet plant contains salicylic acid, mucilage, resin, sugar, an aromatic principle, a glucoside, and an alkaloid. It is also a rich source of vitamins A and C.

A gargle or mouth wash prepared from violet leaves is used for inflammation, swelling, and ulceration of the mouth and throat and is also reputed to relieve the pain of cancerous growths, especially in these areas.

Fresh violet leaves are more potent; however if they are not easily obtainable, the dried may be used. Prepare as a strong tea, 6 ounces of the leaves to three pints of boiling water. Cover tightly, remove immediately from the heat, and allow the infusion to stand for twelve hours. Strain. Use as a gargle or mouth wash and, in addition, drink one small teacupful of the brew every two or three hours.

The reputation of the violet plant as a means for relieving the pains of cancer is fairly widespread. For example, when Catherine Booth, wife of the founder of the Salvation Army, was dying from cancer, an appeal was made for violet leaves since they alone could ease the agonizing pain. And of special interest are the studies of Dr. Jonathan Hartwell of the Cancer Institute of the National Institutes of Health. In citing the violet, Dr. Hartwell says: "The violet plant, as far back as 500 B.C., was used in poultice form as a cure for surface cancer. It was used in the eighteenth century in England for the same purpose. And now only months ago, a letter from a farmer in Michigan tells us how he used the violet plant as a skin cancer remedy. When the remedy was tried on a cancerous mouse here at the Institute, we found that it did damage the cancer ..."

Summary

1. Select Chinese herb remedies loosen stubborn phlegm, reduce fever, fight infection, soothe irritated air passages and lungs, make breathing easier, and help bring an end to dragged-out respiratory miseries.
2. Persistent coughing is very debilitating since it causes sleepless nights and distressing days. The remarkable properties of specific Chinese herb formulas can relieve your coughing miseries and enable you to get your proper sleep and rest.
3. External herbal applications relieve chest tightness and muscular aches and pains due to colds.
4. Select herbal inhalants are soothing and healing to the air passages. They are very helpful for coping with nasal congestion, head colds, croup, nasal drip, and similar conditions.

5. Chinese herb gargles and mouth washes are important accessory treatments because they remove germs from your mouth and throat and help speed your recovery. They are ideal for oral hygiene since they build mouth and gum health and increase resistance of the mucous membranes to infection.

4

GINSENG—CHINESE HEALTH HERB

Plaudits for Ginseng

For thousands of years the oldest civilization on earth has insisted that the root of a plant known in the Far East as Jenshen (ginseng) is the remedy *par excellence* for preventing or treating an incredible variety of ailments—and further, that it contains near miraculous powers which build energy and zest, sharpen the vision, improve hearing, increase the efficiency of the brain, restore virility, and prolong life. Other Oriental peoples have always fully agreed with the Chinese claims for ginseng, but it took an extraordinarily long period of time before the people of Western lands bothered to give these claims a second thought. Over the years missionaries in China, old-time family physicians, writers, and others tried to stimulate an interest in the Oriental usage of ginseng, and these attempts continued to grow.

• The late Sir Edwin Arnold, famed student of Oriental philosophy and author of *The Light of Asia*, wrote: "According to the Chinese, Asiatic ginseng is the best and most potent of all cordials, stimulant tonics, stomachics, cardiacs, febrifuges, and above all, will best renovate and reinvigorate failing forces. It fills the heart with hilarity, while its occasional use will, it is said, add a decade to human life. Have all these millions of Orientals, all these many generations of men who boiled ginseng in silver kettles and praised heaven for its many benefits been totally deceived?"

• Some decades ago, a United States Consul of Korea submitted an official report stating: "From personal experience and observation I am assured that Korean ginseng is an active and strongly healing

JENSHEN
(Ginseng)

medicine. Western people appear to regard the virtues of ginseng claimed by Orientals rather contemptuously—as imagination or based on superstition. The evidence is that the mystical value attached itself to ginseng after its virtues had been practically ascertained."

• In his field notes, Father Jartoux, a missionary in China, described ginseng as an invigorator, rejuvenator, and longevity plant.

• S.E. Zemlinsky, author of a book on the medical botany of Russia, wrote: "Ginseng is not only a very popular Chinese medicine for longevity but is used in all parts of Asia. Its use is to prolong life, youth, virility, and health."

• A former Vice-Consul in Korea stated: "As to the merits of Korean ginseng, the Chinese at any rate had no doubts. Where vitality was becoming extinct from age or strength had been reduced by long illness, ginseng was employed with equal faith and success."

• Early in the century, Dr. A.R. Harding tested the Chinese claims for ginseng and reported that, much to his astonishment, he found that no matter what ailments his patients suffered from, they recovered more quickly when taking ginseng than when any other medication was given.

• The late Dr. H.S. McMaster wrote: "Ginseng is a mild nonpoisonous plant, well adapted to domestic as well as professional uses. The medicinal qualities are known to be a mild tonic, stimulant, nervine, and stomachic. It is especially a remedy incident to old age."

Growing Habits

Asiatic ginseng grows wild in deep shaded mountain forests of the Far East. It shuns direct and heavy sunlight, and its leaves are uniquely arranged to receive only a weak amount of light evenly. While other plants gather their nutrients in the root, leaves, flowers, and buds, the nutrients of ginseng are concentrated mainly in the root. At one time it was believed that ginseng could not be cultivated, but today we find that it is successfully grown in many lands.

More Precious than Gold

During various periods of Chinese history, ginseng was worth many times its weight in gold. Sometimes an emperor would send an ounce or more of the root to a distinguished friend who was suffering from a serious ailment that had not yielded to other medications.

Usually the gift included a small double kettle for preparing the precious ginseng. The inner kettle was made of silver, and the outer kettle was made of copper. Between the two there was a space for holding water. Cut ginseng root and water were placed inside the silver kettle, and a small amount of rice and water was placed in the cup-like cover of the silver vessel. The kettle was then set on a ring which circled the top of the outer copper vessel, and the space between the two kettles was filled with water. The apparatus was then placed on the fire.

When the preparation was ready, the patient ate the rice and drank the ginseng tea at the same time. Usually the patient took the formula every morning before breakfast and sometimes in the evening for about eight days. Ordinary tea was forbidden for one month.

Ginseng Synonyms

It is interesting to note that the many synonyms which the Orientals have attached to ginseng indicate the herb's traditional use or the high esteem in which it is held—Long Life Root, Man's Health, Queen of the Orient, Root of Life, Promise of Immortality, Divine Herb, Wonder Root, Flower of Life, Wonder of the World, and Man-Plant. The latter synonym actually refers to the shape of the root, which sometimes resembles the form of the human figure. Because of this resemblance, the Chinese composed the name ginseng from two words meaning "man-plant," and many Oriental legends refer to this human-like form of the root.

Ginseng in Modern Times

Today, in the space age, ginseng root is still widely used among Oriental peoples, and now, at long last, the popularity of the plant is rapidly spreading to other lands. In the publication *New Scientific Discoveries in Regeneration*, we read:

> The latest discovery from China is ginseng, the rejuvenation herb, considered by the Chinese as a panacea of all diseases. It is believed by its enthusiasts that ginseng overcomes disease by building up general vitality and resistance, and especially by strengthening the endocrine glands, which control all basic physiological processes, including the metabolism of minerals and vitamins.

The life span of former Korean President Syngman Rhee, who died at the age of 90, was attributed by Koreans to his long use of ginseng. Generalissimo Chiang Kai-Shek, the former leader of Nationalist China, was said to be a regular user of the long-life root. Madame Nhu reportedly took along a supply of ginseng on her trip to New York back in 1963.

In Australia ginseng is used to remedy a number of different ailments and to help perpetuate youthfulness and prolong life. The Russians use it to build mental strength, general vitality, and resistance and to treat various disorders. Some years ago, Dr. Finn Sandburg of Switzerland said, "Whenever I am in Singapore I have lunch with Han Suyin, author of *A Many Splendored Thing* and other best selling novels. As Elizabeth Comber, M.D., she practices medicine in Johore Bahru, near Singapore, prescribing mostly European and American drugs for her patients, but when she is sick herself, the only remedy she uses is ginseng root."

British Celebrity Lauds Ginseng

Back in 1979, Barbara Cartland, renowned author of numerous romantic novels, gave her opinion on the value of ginseng in an article she wrote for a British publication[1]. Here are a few excerpts:

> I find ginseng so wonderful that it is difficult to think how we managed without it. It prevents jet lag, sharpens the brain, and this is borne out by the Chinese contention for generations that it is important for all circulatory diseases.
>
> There is certainly a great deal of proof to show that ginseng will combat impotence and the onset of senility. Travelers in China, from Marco Polo onwards, have been extremely impressed with the virility of Chinese men of advanced years and the Chinese themselves readily admit that it is partly the use of ginseng which is responsible.
>
> I believe that the enormous amount of work I am able to do at 78, and that I have attained the world record with over 20 books for the last four years, is principally due to ginseng.
>
> I am also convinced that when one is taking ginseng one feels happier and enjoys life a hundred percent more than one did before.
>
> It is always very difficult to estimate the physical effect of herbal medicine on people, but however much ginseng may be disparaged I am convinced, like the Chinese, that it has a magical ingredient which our bodies and minds need.
>
> As there are no side effects I can only suggest that those who feel rundown, tense, and worried should let ginseng give them the physical good health and mental vitality which we all seek in our lives.

In a later article[2] in 1981, Barbara Cartland again refers to the value of ginseng. She says:

> Last year, entirely because I was taking ginseng every day, I broke the world record by writing 24 books. This year I brought out my 300th book on my birthday!
>
> When people ask me why, it is because I no longer feel tired.
>
> I take ginseng first thing in the morning and find I can do an enormous amount of work during the day and still not feel exhausted in the evening, which at my age is remarkable.

---

[1] *Grace Magazine*, Spring 1979.
[2] *Grace Magazine*, Autumn 1981.

There are no side effects to ginseng and there is no doubt in my mind that it does not only make you feel well, but its name which means 'All Healing' is a correct one. It also can prolong life.

Ginseng in the United States

In the United States, a 23-year-old student, working hard on his thesis for a degree, told his friends, "I took ginseng last May and I never felt any fatigue this summer."

Another student found that smoking marijuana caused his memory to become sluggish. He quit smoking pot, but three months later when his memory still hadn't shaped up, he consulted a Chinese herbalist. The herb doctor put him on ginseng, stating that it is an effective brain tonic and that it also acts as an antidote to certain types of toxic drugs. After taking ginseng extract for six weeks, the young student happily reported that his memory was better than ever.

In another case, a man 73 years of age was troubled with nervousness, indigestion, and brain fog. After a two months course of ginseng, he became calm, more mentally alert, and was no longer bothered by stomach distress. He says he continues to take the ginseng tonic to retain the benefits.

A 75-year-old woman complained of cold hands and feet, general debility, pains in the bones, depression, and memory lapses. She took ginseng for one month and noted some improvement. Encouraged, she continued taking the herb preparation and after four months her symptoms completely disappeared.

Scientific Evaluation of Ginseng

Although ginseng is still largely ignored by most Western scientists, intensive pharmacological and clinical investigations of the Oriental root have been carried out by Soviet scientists. Many ginseng studies have also been undertaken by other qualified researchers covering such countries as China, Korea, Japan, and Germany. A special Ginseng Committee combining the efforts of all Russian scientists and practical workers engaged in this field has been in operation since 1949 and is subordinate to the Far Eastern Center of the Siberian Division of the USSR Academy of Sciences. During these past many years, the Committee held 23 sessions in which Soviet and foreign scientists participated. The Committee published seven volumes of works and a two-volume collection of the minutes of the Committee sessions.

To briefly summarize, the results of these intensive studies have established that ginseng relieves atherosclerosis, acts as an antidote to various types of drugs and toxic chemicals, produces a good effect in a number of disorders of the central nervous system, helps to normalize the blood pressure and various other bodily functions, favorably effects the activity of the sex glands, protects the body against radiation, stimulates and improves the work of the brain cells, increases physical stamina and endurance, has an anti-rheumatic effect, improves vision and hearing acuity, and is a good adjuvant in diabetes mellitus, diseases of the liver, impotence, and several other diseases.

Dr. I.I. Brekhman, one of the leading scientists of the Soviet team, says that although the list of diseases in which ginseng is effective may be a long one, the root is not a panacea, a "cure-all." He explains that, "Ginseng, being a good tonic, a roborant, increases the resistance of the organism and helps it to overcome many diseases of various origins." He adds that ginseng strengthens almost the entire bodily defense mechanism and refers to this fortifying power of ginseng as a "universal defense action."[3]

Research by Soviet and other foreign scientists has established that ginseng is harmless and acts only by improving physiological processes. "No bad effects are observed after taking it," the report states.

Ginseng and Longevity

The "universal defense action" of ginseng in preventing or treating a wide variety of ailments may be one of the reasons for the herb's traditional reputation as a longevity plant. Scientists tell us that disease is one of the principal causes of premature aging and a short life span. A list of some 90 diseases was submitted to a number of prominent physicians, along with a request to indicate the percentage of deaths from those illnesses which could have been prevented. Calculations based on returns showed that through a possibly timely prevention, more than a dozen years could have been added to life.

---

[3]Lucas, R., *Ginseng: The Chinese 'Wonder-Root'* (Spokane, Washington: R & M Books, 1972),p.40.

Another factor believed by scientists to be partly responsible for the symptoms of aging is the gradual decline in the output of sex hormones that usually begins in the middle years of life. In youth these glands are healthy and active and are directly related to the general health and to the prolonged appearance of youth. If the sex glands are nourished, the precious hormones would once again be produced at higher levels similar to those produced by younger people. In short, the new supply of hormones would help delay the symptoms of old age. Soviet researchers have reported that, "Ginseng favorably influences the functions of the endocrine glands, in particular the hypophysis cerebri, the adrenal cortex, and the genital [sex] glands."

Several Varieties of Ginseng

There are several varieties of ginseng. To mention a few, the Chinese and Korean ginseng is known botanically as *Panax schinseng*, the North American variety as *Panax quinquefolium*, and the Japanese variety as *Panax japonica*. The generic name *Panax* is taken from the word for panacea, meaning "cure-all."

The Chinese and Koreans describe the various grades of their ginseng in poetic terms. For example, the Red Korean Ginseng roots are graded as follows:

> *Whole Roots*
> Heaven Grade (1st class)
> Earth Grade (2nd class)
> Good Grade (3rd grade, called Man-Grade)
>
> *Tails*
> Big Tail
> Middle Tail
> Scrap Tail
> Slender Tail

The term "tails" refers to the smaller root divisions that grow out from the main body.

Available in Many Forms

Ginseng root is available on the market in many forms—whole, cut, bulk powder, powder in capsules, fluid extracts, tea bags, concentrated fluid extracts, and tiny envelopes of powdered instant ginseng. (There are also ginseng compounds and blends, but these are included in the following chapter.)

The only way to find out which particular form of ginseng root is best for you is to give it a fair trial. Ginseng is not a synthetic drug, it is a harmless yet potent natural herb. Directions for using the various ginseng products are listed on the labels. However, individual differences of each person should be considered. For example, some people may find they need greater amounts in order to obtain the benefits, while others find that smaller amounts are sufficient. And a few people may find that if they take ginseng just before going to bed, its stimulating properties tend to keep them awake. This is remedied by taking the preparation earlier in the day.

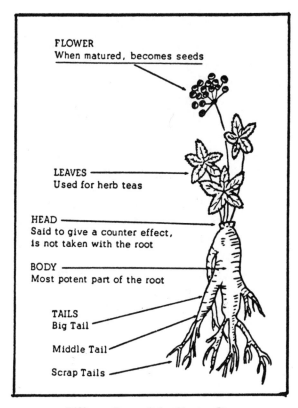

Different Parts of the Ginseng Plant

Further Tips on Ginseng

For best results, acid fruits, acid fruit juices such as orange, grapefruit, and so on, and vitamin C should be avoided for three hours after taking ginseng since they neutralize the beneficial effects of the herb.

If you decide to try ginseng, be sure to purchase your supply from a reliable firm. There have been instances where partially developed roots, stringy fibers, or "culls" of ginseng were shipped into this country. Linda Clark, nutritionalist, reported one such case where the owner of a store and his assistant used ginseng faithfully every day, but saw no benefits. The product they were using turned out to be a "cull" of some ginseng from which most of the strength had been removed before it was shipped to the U.S.

Summary

1. Ginseng has a long history of usage among Oriental peoples for treating disease, preventing illness, and prolonging life.
2. Extensive research on ginseng by modern scientists, covering such countries as Russia, Korea, Japan, and others, has established that many of the Chinese claims for the therapeutic power of ginseng root are true.
3. Whereas the nutrients of many other plants are distributed throughout the leaves, roots, stems, flowers, and buds, the nutrients of ginseng are mainly concentrated in the root.
4. Ginseng is not a synthetic drug, it is a natural herb.
5. There are many different forms of ginseng available on the market. The only way to find out which form is best for you is to give it a fair trial.
6. For best results, acid fruits, acid fruit juices, and vitamin C should be avoided for three hours after you take ginseng.
7. If you decide to use ginseng, deal only with a reputable firm.

5

ORIENTAL HERB TONICS AND BLENDS

There are a number of Oriental herb products available on the market which bring good results as healing agents or health tonics according to many people who have used them.

As space does not permit a comprehensive listing of all the various compounds, tonics, and blends, only a few examples will be given, as follows:

PEKING ROYAL JELLY

Royal Cure?

According to palace insiders, a secret Chinese folk remedy is being used by Britain's royal family. For centuries this carefully guarded secret has been known among generations of British royalty, but the remedy was finally revealed when news leaked out that Princess Diana was taking it. Other sources then discovered that for years it has been used daily by other members of the family.

Reportedly, the Queen, the Queen Mother, Prince Phillip, Princess Diana, and Princess Anne, all take royal jelly which is imported from China. According to a palace confidant, the Queen takes extra amounts of royal jelly when she has lengthy and exhausting engagements to fulfill, or when she must spend time outdoors in very bad weather. The remarkable stamina of the Queen Mother is attributed to her use of royal jelly. Prince Phillip takes it to relieve the pains of his arthritic wrist. Its calming effects on the nervous system reportedly worked wonders for Princess Di who took the remedy to alleviate morning sickness. Princess Anne has used it as a strengthener during competition in equestrian events.

What Is Royal Jelly?

Royal jelly is a substance produced by young worker honey bees which is fed to the larva from which the queen bee develops. The queen rules the hive and receives royal jelly throughout her life. She performs an incredible amount of work and may lay as many as one-quarter of a million eggs in one season. Worker bees (no royal jelly for them) perform industriously for two to six months then die, but the queen bee lives as long as eight years.

Constituents in Royal Jelly

Researchers have analyzed royal jelly and found that it contains proteins, several types of natural sugars, unsaturated fats, a number of enzymes, and is tremendously rich in pantothenic acid, nucleic acid, and vitamin B6. When lab animals were given only one of the last three nutrients in larger-than-normal amounts, their life span increased by approximately one-third. When generous quantities of all three nutrients were given, their life span increased by nearly half. Pantothenic acid has been found to relieve painful burning feet and the pain of neuritis. Some people have reported increased energy and considerable memory improvement after taking this important nutrient.

Scientific Experiments with Peking Royal Jelly

Experiments on lab animals with the use of Peking royal jelly were conducted by specialists of the Peking Medical School Third Hospital, the Peoples' Hospital, the First Hospital of Peking, and other Chinese research institutes. Results showed that the use of royal jelly prolonged the animals' life span, increased their survival rate, and also resulted in greater resistance to disease.

Extensive medical studies with the use of royal jelly for humans have also been conducted in China, Europe, and other lands. From these results we learn that royal jelly:

• Helps relieve conditions of arthritis, peptic ulcers, and liver ailments.

• Acts as a tonic and "balancer" for anyone feeling below par.

• Retards premature senility.

• Stimulates the appetite in cases of anorexia nervosa (a condition that causes people to starve themselves).

• Helps in some cases of menopausal problems and sexual frigidity in women, as well as some forms of impotence and sexual weakness in men.

• Provides protection during the flu season.

• Has helped nervous patients to respond with a more stable nervous system and a higher degree of stamina for mental and physical work.

• Has relieved some cases of skin problems.

• Improves the memory.

• Has been recommended for urinary incontinence.

How Royal Jelly Is Used

Peking royal jelly comes in small vials (miniature bottles), which are packed ten to a box, along with ten miniature straws. A larger size is also available, 30 vials and miniature straws to a box.

The tiny bottle is shaken thoroughly, and the contents sipped through the straw once daily, in the morning or at bedtime. The bottles should be stored in a cool, dark place.

Other grades of royal jelly (not Peking) are sold in capsule form. The amount to be taken daily is cited on the individual labels of these products.

Some Users Report

• "Royal jelly is marvelous and has the approval of my osteopath. I have been very pleased with the results in improvement of health and vitality."—C.J.C.

• "I'm convinced that royal jelly has a youthifying effect. I took it daily and felt a decided improvement in health. After a year I noticed my hair seemed thicker and the skin on my face, smoother. Friends and relatives have noticed it too. I plan to keep taking royal jelly."—Mrs. R.D.

• "My husband and I had a hectic journey in Morocco. We were taking royal jelly throughout our trip and never felt tired."—Mrs. J.M.B.

• "I developed hot, stabbing pains in the first joint of my index finger. After about three months of taking royal jelly, I've had no further pain whatsoever."—Mr. A.E.

JIN SAM JUNG

This is a bottled extract containing a Korean ginseng root, ginseng extractive, honey, and royal jelly. The merits of ginseng and royal jelly have already been cited, so let us briefly consider the nutritive value of honey.

It is well known that honey is a quick source of energy. Edward Bach, M.D., always advised his patients to eat honey to relieve tiredness and exhaustion.

In ancient times, many people believed that the regular use of this natural substance insured health and longevity. Modern studies have shown that honey is an excellent tonic and reconstructive for convalescents, dyspeptics, and the aged. Because of its lubricating action, honey has a gentle and slightly laxative effect. Some medics have reported it to be a good heart tonic and also to be helpful for relieving nervous insomnia.

Reported Uses of Jin Sam Jung

• Mrs. J.S., a housewife, writes: "Jin Sam Jung has had a wonderful effect on my mother who is 70 years of age. She has more energy and vitality, walks a mile every day, does all her own shopping and housework, and doesn't feel a bit tired."

• Mr. L.V., age 72, was troubled by weakness in the knees, and nervous prostration. Normally an active, independent man, the necessity to rely on others to help steady him when he walked was almost more than he could endure. He was given Jin Sam Jung daily for three months. His family reported that "His symptoms have disappeared, and he is his jolly self again."

• Mr. R.P., a business executive, writes: "I went to the doctor because I was feeling tired all the time and thought I might be anemic or have low blood pressure. After I was given a complete physical the doctor told me there was nothing to worry about, that I was in good health. He said the tiredness was probably due to tension resulting from the family problems I had told him about, and that since the problems were now all settled, my energy should return again in a short time.

"However, as the weeks drifted by, I still felt 'beat.' One day I passed a health food store and became interested in various herbs and herb products that were displayed. I bought two bottles of Jin Sam Jung and took some of the extract faithfully every day. By the time I had finished both bottles I had plenty of energy and felt like a new man."

• Mrs. J.D., a waitress, suffered from painful corns and bunions. She said: "The pain wasn't so bad during the first few hours of my daily work shift but those last two hours were torture. I tried special shoes and used foot baths every night, but still the pain toward the end of each work day persisted. My family constantly urged me to switch to a typing job, but I loved my work and hated the thought of quitting.

"Then about two months ago, a friend of mine gave me an article on Chinese herbs, which I found quite interesting. I decided to try an extract called Jin Sam Jung, and after using it for a few weeks I was delighted to find that my corns and bunions were far less painful, and I no longer dreaded the last two hours of my work day. I continue to take the extract daily since I find it not only keeps the pain reduced to a minimum but also gives me a feeling of more energy and pep."

• A woman in her forties was troubled with irregularity, nervousness, and indigestion. She also complained of broken sleep which left her exhausted. She took one bottle of Jin Sam Jung and claimed good progress. After using three more bottles, she reported a marked change for the better. Her bowels were back to functioning normally and her digestion had improved. She added that she was sleeping well and felt refreshed.

• Mr. A.D. writes: "Jin Sam Jung was recommended to me and I bought some from an herb company. It has helped me immeasurably. My headaches and nervous tension are a thing of the past. It also seems to clear your mind (as well as strengthening your nerves) and allows you to think more clearly. This is important to me since I attend college and need an alert mind and calm nerves, especially during exam time."

RENSHENWANGJIANG

Synonym: *Song Bao Su* (Double Treasure Element)

The first part of the Chinese name *Renshen*, means panax ginseng, and the second part *wangjiang* means royal jelly. It is also known as *Song Bao Su, Song* meaning double, *Bao*—treasure, and *Su*—element, which describes the product as "Double Treasure Element." In English this compound is called *Chinese Red Panax Ginseng Extractum with Royal Jelly*. It is manufactured in Hangchow, Zhejiang Province of China.

Orientals consider this product to be the highest quality of its kind. It consists of pure royal jelly collected in the spring, and six-year-old red ginseng roots which grow on the Changpai Mountain of Northeastern China.

Song Bao Su is carefully prepared in well-equipped Chinese pharmaceutical firms with essence of red ginseng extracted and concentrated through air-tight processes, and with fresh royal jelly sterilized and filtered by scientific methods. This product is a national award winner in China where it is considered effective for the following:

- General debility, malnutrition, poor appetite, neurasthenia, infirmities due to long illness, and hypometabolism.
- Its use reportedly strengthens the kidneys, enriches vital energy, and invigorates the function of the spleen.
- Helpful in the treatment of rheumatism, bronchial asthma, hepatitis, anemia, gastric ulcers, and falling hair.
- When taken regularly it acts as a general health tonic which assists memory and concentration, and helps prevent premature senility.
- Increases bodily resistance to some of the major effects of aging, such as degeneration of the blood system which causes heart attacks and strokes.
- Helps the body's resistance to harmful, long-term effects of the stresses and strains of modern living.

How *Song Bao Su* Is Used

Song Bao Su comes in vials, ten to a carton with ten miniature straws. Each tiny bottle is shaken thoroughly before using, and the contents sipped through the straw. One to two bottles are used daily, one in the morning before breakfast and/or one at bedtime. The bottles should be stored in a cool, dry place, and protected from the light.

KOREAN GINSENG COMPLEX

This is a blend of ginseng root powder and assistant ingredients of royal jelly, PABA, and vitamin E. It is sold by various herbal firms and is carried in health food stores.

PABA

PABA (para amino benzoic acid) is a member of the vitamin B complex. It is often referred to as the anti-gray-hair vitamin, and studies have shown that some of the gray hair of persons given PABA was restored to the original color in 70% of the cases.

Researchers have reported that extreme fatigue, skin rashes, or eczema can result from a deficiency of PABA. It is for this reason that the addition of PABA to the diet often helps to increase energy and to clear up or prevent eczema. And indications are that its use may also help to prevent old age texture of the skin.

Vitamin E

Vitamin E is called the "fertility" vitamin because of the favorable effects it reputedly produces on the organs of reproduction. Studies have shown that it is helpful for building muscle tone and strength and that it is a good tonic to the heart. Studies have also revealed that lack of this vitamin can cause the hair to become dull and fall out and may also result in loss of sexual interest, enlargement of the prostate gland, miscarriages, and sterility.

Reported Uses of Korean Ginseng Complex

• Mrs. C., age 49, a nervous woman, developed a rash on the back of both hands. As a typist and receptionist, the appearance of her hands was important to her and she was fearful the rash would persist. She began taking Korean Ginseng Complex daily and in two weeks reported that the rash was fading. Use of the Korean product was continued and Mrs. C. stated that a short time later the rash completely disappeared. She adds that she was surprised to find that she had also lost her nervousness.

• Mr. A.C., age 60, complained of fatigue and frequent attacks of acute pains across the forehead and down to the eyes. His eyes had been tested, but nothing was found wrong. And no medical treatment had so far given him permanent relief from the attacks of acute pain. Mr. C. said he found that loud talking or wearisome conversations would trigger the pain and leave him extremely exhausted.

He decided to try Korean Ginseng Complex and four weeks later reported that the improvement in his condition was encouraging. He continued using the product, and one month later he said: "I can now engage in lengthy conversations, no matter how wearisome, without the pain commencing. And even if the pain does start, it is only very slight and quickly subsides. And although I still find such conversations somewhat tiring, they no longer leave me so terribly exhausted."

• Mrs. R.T., a middle-aged widow, suffered from headache, fatigue, depression, and periods of sleeplessness. She also complained of twinges of rheumatism during the cold winter seasons. Two months after taking Korean Ginseng Complex she told her friends: "I felt the benefits almost right away. It has meant so much to me to be relieved of the pain, depression, and insomnia. I love my work as a music teacher and now I enjoy it all the time."

KOREAN GINSENG HERBTON

This compound comes in tablet form. It consists of white ginseng root, red ginseng root, golden seal, comfrey, passion flower, eyebright herb, rose hips, fenugreek seed, slippery elm, hawthorne berry, red raspberry, licorice root, and dandelion. It is used as a general tonic. One or two tablets are swallowed with a glass of water after each meal, or the tablets may be dissolved in hot water and taken as a tea.

POLLEN

During World War II, Lt. Col. Tratheway of the U.S. Air Force spent nine months in a Japanese prison camp in Burma. He was weak, emaciated, and had lost 90 pounds.

One night he managed to escape but became lost in the jungle, and after about three days of wandering aimlessly about, and with gangrene in his feet, he collapsed. He was found by natives of a Chinese jungle tribe who treated him for several weeks with a diet rich in pollen and honey. They also prepared a mixture of pollen and honey and applied it to his feet.

After a few weeks his health and strength improved and he was able to walk. When he finally reached Calcutta, an English physician told him it was the pollen and honey that had saved his life and the use of his feet.

Tratheway stated that the staple diet of the Chinese jungle tribe consisted of cakes made of pollen and honey. He reported that both the children and adults appeared to be in perfect health.

What Is Pollen?

Pollen is a fine powder which forms inside the blossoms of flowering plants. It ranges in color from golden yellow to dark brown, and is gathered by honey bees and deposited in the hive.

From earliest times man has regarded the use of pollen as a remarkable source of health and longevity. It is mentioned in the Scrolls of the Orient, and the ancient texts of Rome, Persia, Egypt, Greece, and other lands.

Constituents in Pollen

Scientific analyses have shown that honey bee pollen contains an abundance of vitamins, minerals, enzymes, coenzymes, fats, and hormone components, as well as having a very high protein and amino acid content. Two European universities termed pollen one of the richest food substances, saying that it is "without equal in nature."

Pollen and Longevity

Some years ago Dr. Nicolai Tsitsin, a Russian scientist, was engaged in research on longevity. Letters were sent to 200 people who claimed to be over 100 years old, asking their exact age; how they had earned their living most of their lives; and what had been their principal food. Dr. Tsitsin received 150 replies. He reported: "We made a very interesting discovery. The answers showed that a large number of them were bee keepers. But all of them without exception said their principal food had been honey." He then discovered that in each case, "It wasn't really pure honey these people ate but the waste matter in the bottom of the bee hive." Dr. Tsitsin went on to explain that these people were all poor and sold the pure honey in the market, and kept only the residue for themselves. Further investigation revealed that only a very tiny portion of the residue was honey—the rest was almost all pure pollen.

Further Scientific Research on Pollen

In later years, other scientists from various countries began experiments in which pollen was administered to their patients. Dr. Remy Chauvin of France stated: "The first attempts at its use for symptoms of old age have proven most encouraging." He also found that pollen produced an increase in strength and weight during convalescence, and that it increased the red blood cells of anemic children. He also reported that pollen destroys harmful bacteria in the intestines, and relieves constipation. In addition, he stated, "Interesting observations were registered in cases of flatulence as well as colonic infections. Patients suffering from chronic diarrhea which even resisted antibiotic treatment showed improvement." It was carefully noted that no ill effects were suffered by the many persons who took pollen regularly over a considerable period of time.

• Dr. Naum Petrovich Joirich, Chief Russian Scientist at the Far East Institute in Vladivostok, reports that bee pollen has regenerative and health boosting properties. He says, "Long lives are attained by bee pollen users; it is one of the original treasure houses of nutrition and medicine. Each grain contains every important substance that is necessary to life."

• Dermatologist Lars-Erik Essen, M.D. of Hälsingborg, Sweden, treats his acne patients with a specially prepared pollen lotion. He reports that the lotion not only helped clear up the acne conditions but found that it is also an effective skin rejuvenator for elderly people. He states: "Through transcutaneous nutrition, pollen has a profound biological effect, preventing premature aging of the cells and stimulating growth of new tissue. It offers effective protection against dehydration, smooths away wrinkles, and stimulates life-giving blood supply to all skin cells."

• Experiments by French scientists, Drs. E.L. Man and Louveau, also demonstrated that pollen can reverse aging of the skin, wrinkles, and blemishes.

• Cancer specialist, Dr. Sigmund Schmidt of Bad Bothenfels, advises, "Eat pollen. Pollen contains all the essential elements for healthy tissue and could be a cancer preventative."

• In the opinion of British scientist, Dr. G.J. Binding, "Pollen is the finest, most perfect food, a giant germ killer in which bacteria simply cannot exist." He adds that pollen not only gives increased resistance to infection, but also builds strength and energy.

• Dr. Peter Nernuss of Austria regards bee pollen as the strongest preventative food known, and will fortify the body against a variety of ailments. Other European researchers regard the use of adequate amounts of pollen as the best protection against pollutants in food, air, water, and environment. It reportedly mitigates or eliminates the toxic and/or destructive effects of lead, DDT, carbon monoxide, mercury, strontium 90, cadmium, nitrates and nitrites, some drugs, and X-rays.

Pollen Power for Strength and Endurance

Honey bee pollen is being used in increasing numbers by athletes to improve energy, stamina, and over-all performance. Increases in strength of 40-50% in athletes who take pollen has been reported by the British Sports Council.

In Finland, track coach Antti Lananskis says that most of the athletes in that country take pollen food supplements. "Our studies show that it significantly improves their performance. There have been no negative results since we have been supplying bee pollen to our athletes."

Tom McNab, British Olympic track coach, reported: "At least 90% of our athletes are taking bee pollen tablets daily. Most claim that it improves their performance and gives them greater stamina and more energy." He also noted, "A beneficial side effect, which I attribute to bee pollen, has been the diminution of the number of colds which the athletes experienced. Freedom from such complaints is a major factor in any training program." Mr. McNab concludes, "Bee pollen is the most effective, vitalizing food available to athletes today."

A two-year study at Pratt Institute of New York involved 24 athletes and their ability to recover stamina and endurance after vigorous exercises. After each workout, records were kept on respiration, muscle and skin condition, pulse rate, and sweating. All the athletes who took bee pollen during the study experienced speedier recovery time, improved lung capacity, greater endurance, and improved over-all performance. Remi Korchemny, the study supervisor and one of the foremost experts on keeping body energy at maximum level, says, "What bee pollen does for athletes it can do for anyone."

A Variety of Bee Pollen Products

Honey bee pollen is sold commercially in different forms; e.g., granules, capsules, liquid extracts, chewable tablets, and non-chewable tablets. Since each variety of these products differs from every other, the amount to be taken also differs. Therefore it is best to follow the directions given on the cartons or bottles regarding the daily intake.

Since every person is different, some people experience results with the use of bee pollen within 30 days; whereas, others may take from 60 to 90 days before noticing any benefits. Long-standing problems may take a year or more.

Note. Allergic reactions to taking dried honey bee pollen are said to be very rare. However, anyone experiencing such reactions should immediately discontinue use of pollen.

Various Ways of Taking Pollen

There are a number of different ways in which honey bee pollen may be taken. Here are a few suggestions: The capsules or non-chewable tablets may be swallowed with a glass of water, milk, vegetable, or fruit juice. The granules may be eaten direct from the spoon, or mixed with honey or sprinkled over cereals, yogurt, ice cream, or any vegetable or fruit juice.

Pollen—A Geriatric Wonder Food

Some Chinese herbalists suggest a special method for using honey bee pollen for elderly people whose bodies have been debilitated by many years of inadequate nutrition and ill health. According to the Chinese view, such conditions indicate that the whole organism is out of Yin-Yang balance; blood, glands, and organs are not working in harmony. As a result, when elderly people have been depleted of important nutrients for a prolonged period of time, the herbalists advise introducing the abundance of pollen's nutrients into the body gradually, as this gives the body time to adjust. The Oriental method is cited as follows:

First Week
> Each day, one teaspoon of pollen granules is taken with breakfast.

Second Week
> Each day, one teaspoon of pollen granules is taken with breakfast and one at lunch, making a total of two teaspoons daily.

Third Week
> Each day, one teaspoon of pollen granules is taken at breakfast, lunch, and dinner, making a total of three teaspoons daily.

From this point on, the amount of pollen taken can be adjusted more or less according to individual needs. Some elderly people may find they are doing well on the three teaspoons per day, and should continue on that amount as a daily maintenance dosage. Others may feel they need more, in which case the intake of pollen can be slowly and gradually increased until health is improved, then that amount continued daily as a maintenance dosage.

Overexposure to outdoor pollution such as the monoxides in heavy traffic, or exposure to chemical fumes or other stresses of life, may require the use of more pollen. In such cases chewable pollen tablets may be taken off and on during the day as needed, in addition to the maintenance dosage of the granules.

The Chinese insist that only the highest quality of honey bee pollen should be used, if results are to be expected.

The Key to Good Quality Pollen

While all honey bee pollen contains a similar wide range of valuable nutrients, most experts agree that the best quality of its nutritional value depends on climate and type of flora found in a given area. The key to the best quality pollen is said to lie in the higher desert-type areas. The climatic conditions should be similar to that of Tibet, Hunza land, Ecuador, and the Caucasus mountains of Russia, all known areas for their long-lived people and where most are eaters of honey bee pollen.

There are similar regions in the U.S. from which honey bee pollen is gathered and sold on the market. The higher-desert/dry elevations of Arizona, and the higher plains of Eastern Montana are two of several examples.

"HEAVEN" GRADE RED PANAX GINSENG EXTRACT

This concentrated liquid extract is made from Chinese red ginseng roots from the northern provinces of China, the areas where the Wild Imperial ginseng is found. It is imported from Tientsin, and regarded by the Chinese as a high-quality health tonic.

The extract is available in two different sizes, miniature bottles (vials) packed ten to a carton, with ten tiny straws; and larger bottles (1.76 fl. oz.) sold individually, each containing a plastic dropper.

When using the larger bottle, 20 to 30 drops of the extract are added to a cup of warm or hot water and drunk as a tea. One to two cups are taken daily.

The tiny vials may be used by sipping the extract through the straw, or the extract may be poured into a cup of hot or warm water and drunk as a tea, once a day.

Summary

1. There are a number of Oriental herb products sold on the market which bring good results as healing agents and health tonics according to many people who have used them.
2. Extensive medical studies in China and other lands have shown that various ailments yield to the use of royal jelly, and that its use also builds stamina and vitality.
3. *Song Bao Su*, "Double Treasure Element," is a national award winner in China where it is valued as an effective remedy and general health tonic, bringing the body's health level up to optimum strength and helping the organs to function more efficiently.
4. Jin Sam Jung and Korean Ginseng Complex are fortified with valuable nutritional supplements.
5. From earliest times, honey bee pollen has been regarded as a valuable food source for promoting health, strength, and longevity.
6. Honey bee pollen is sold commercially in many different forms; therefore, when using any of these products it is best to follow the directions given on the bottles or cartons regarding the daily amount to be taken.
7. Only the best quality of honey bee pollen should be used.
8. Allergic reactions to taking honey bee pollen are said to be very rare; however, anyone experiencing such reactions should immediately discontinue the use of this natural food substance.

6

CHINESE HERB REMEDIES FOR RHEUMATISM, ARTHRITIS, AND RELATED AILMENTS

According to statistics, rheumatism and arthritis are more prevalent than the combined total number of cases of heart disease, cancer, diabetes, and tuberculosis. Other painful conditions such as gout, lumbago, and associated ailments are also quite common.

Definition of Terms

Terms describing the various afflictions may be briefly defined as follows:

When the joints are inflamed, the condition may be called arthritis or rheumatism. If the muscles are involved, the term muscular rheumatism is applied.

When pain extends along the sciatic nerve from hip to toe, the ailment is known as sciatica.

When one or more nerve trunks in other parts of the body become inflamed, the painful condition is described as neuritis.

Pain along the route of a nerve is known as neuralgia.

Lower back pain in the lumbar region is called lumbago.

Gout is a painful affliction caused by excess uric acids in the blood. Attacks occur suddenly and are accompanied by great pain. The big toe is a frequent site.

Inflammation of a bursa is described as bursitis. A bursa is a small, soft tissue sac located between parts that move upon one another, often lying between bones and muscles. A favorite site of bursitis is the shoulder region.

Guideline to Chinese Herb Remedies

Some of the different herb remedies the Chinese employ for the relief of arthritis, rheumatism, gout, and associated conditions are cited in the following list. Along with the use of the herb remedy, Chinese herbalists advise sufferers of rheumatism and arthritis to avoid greasy foods, bread, pork, white sugar, white flour products, and acidy fruits. Meals should include potatoes boiled in their jackets, vegetables, unpolished brown rice, and alkaline fruits. Avocado is especially recommended.

Sufferers of gout are advised to strictly avoid alcoholic beverages, especially beer. Rich foods—such as pies, cakes, and other starchy desserts—are also on the forbidden list.

Those suffering from neuritis are encouraged to include liberal amounts of unpolished brown rice in their diets. This recommendation has a sound scientific basis. Unpolished brown rice contains valuable minerals and vitamins, among which are the major B vitamins, known as the anti-neuritic vitamins. The lack of these essential elements tends to bring on neuritis.

TWO SPECIAL CHINESE HERB FORMULAS

Centuries of experience of compounding herbs has led the Chinese to develop several unique formulas which are reputed to be effective for the treatment of various types of arthritis. Following are two of the herbal combinations most often used.

Coix Combination

One of the most popular of the Chinese traditional herbal formulas is the Coix Combination, named after its principal herb, called Job's Tears (*Coix lachryma-jobi*). In Chinese, the name is I-Yi-Jen Tang. Along with its principal herb, this formula contains six assistant herbs.

The Coix Combination has been highly valued in China for centuries, and has now been approved by the government of Japan for treating the early stages of arthritis and related ailments. Its use covers such conditions as subclinical or subacute arthritis; muscular rheumatism; neuralgia; lumbago; sciatica; rheumatism with pain, swelling, and fever; generalized pains in the joints and muscles; wrist pain due to rheumatism and/or overuse; early stages of osteoarthritis; and shoulder stiffness. The Coix formula is used for people with a strong constitution and good digestion.

Clematis and Stephania Combination

This combination consists of 17 herbs and is used for people with weak constitutions who have difficulty recovering from illnesses. It is known in Chinese as Shu-Ching-Huo-Hsieh-Tang, and has also been approved by the Japanese government as a remedy for arthritis and related ailments.

The Chinese recommend this formula for treating the more severe and chronic cases of the same conditions as those cited under the Coix Combination. In addition, it is especially regarded as a specific for sciatica where the pain is concentrated in the left leg, and is more painful at night.

How the Formulas Are Used

Both herbal formulas are gradually becoming better known in the United States where they are being sold in capsule form, and as a powder for tea.

The Chinese point out that it is important to choose the most appropriate formula for the particular problem. The dosage for either of the herbal combinations is the same, two to three capsules at a time, taken two or three times daily. For optimum results the formula is taken on an empty stomach.

Some people reportedly experience the pain-relieving effects in one hour after using the remedy, and many have enjoyed lasting relief of their condition after taking the formula for a few months.

Note: In some instances when a person first begins taking either of the herbal combinations, a mild digestive disturbance occurs, which generally ceases in just a few days. However, if it persists, the formula should be discontinued.

ZHENG GU SHUI

This tincture is based on a private Chinese folk remedy. Its quality and strict manufacturing processes have earned it a Gold Award and Silver Award given by the Guangxi Regional People's Government and The State Council.

Zheng Gu Shui is used externally as an analgesic liniment. It reputedly relieves the pains of rheumatism, sprains, lumbago, neuralgia, arthritis, and sore muscles.

How the Liniment Is Used

Muscular Fatigue. Rubbing Zheng Gu Shui on the body, or bathing in water with a small amount of the tincture before or after exercises or hard physical labor, is said to help prevent or relieve excessive muscular fatigue. It is very popular among the athletes in China, and five cases of the liniment were reportedly kept on hand for the Chinese Olympic team. Zheng Gu Shui is also becoming very popular among sports participants in the U.S., Europe, and other lands.

Aches and Pains. For relieving the pains of rheumatism, sprains, sore muscles, and similar aches and pains, Zheng Gu Shui is rubbed on the affected areas and allowed to dry.

Note:

1. Areas treated with Zheng Gu Shui must never be bandaged as this would cause excessive stimulation and inflammation of the skin.
2. The liniment should not be used on open wounds, or broken or irritated skin.
3. The bottle of Zheng Gu Shui should be kept tightly capped after use, and stored in a cool place.

Reported Use

• "So many people suffer rheumatism pain. My mother suffered badly all her life, and I spent many a sleepless night myself, till being recommended a Chinese remedy with a name I don't quite know how to pronounce. But on the bottle it is spelled Zheng Gu Shui. It is a liniment, and it worked wonders. I don't know if it would help everyone as it did me, but you can never tell till you give it a try."— R.T.

• "I have always heard that the Chinese have much ancient wisdom for healing people with herbal remedies and acupuncture. Recently I put this to a test myself. The pain from a wrenched shoulder kept me awake nights, so I went to an herb store in our local Chinatown and it was suggested I try Zheng Gu Shui.

"The soothing comfort of this liniment was effective in a very short time, and following a good night's sleep, the improvement was remarkable."—Mr. C.F.

• "After long hours of hard work at our place of business, my wife develops muscle tension with aches and pains in her shoulders and back. Each night at bedtime I apply Zheng Gu Shui to her shoulders and the center of her spinal region, and massage these areas for a few minutes. She goes to sleep within ten minutes—that fast—completely relaxed, all muscle tension and aches and pains gone."—Mr. B.C.

• "I heard about Zheng Gu Shui some years ago from a neighbor who has always had a keen interest in Chinese healing methods. He was with me the day I twisted my ankle when I accidentally stepped in a small hole my dog had dug in the yard. After helping me into the house, he went next door and came right back with a bottle of Zheng Gu Shui.

"My ankle was swollen, stiff, and very painful, and I was worried it would mean I'd be off work for several days. My neighbor applied the liniment all around my ankle, and I kept my foot elevated on a chair. He left the bottle of Zheng Gu Shui with me and the next morning I applied the liniment again to my ankle. That day I was able to go to work, and by evening was walking normally. I could hardly believe it.

"A few months later, I sprained my wrist digging in the garden. It was very tender and painful. I rubbed Zheng Gu Shui on the area and within one hour there was no longer any tenderness or pain on movement.

"Zheng Gu Shui will always have a place in my home."—Mr. P.M.

JENSHEN

English Name: Ginseng
Botanical Name: *Panax shenseng*

Among its many uses, ginseng is valued by the Chinese healers as a remedy for rheumatism. In some instances, this claim has been verified by medical doctors. For example, early in the century, A.R.

Harding, M.D., reported that he found ginseng to be an effective remedy for certain ailments from which his patients suffered, and in reference to the use of the herb for rheumatism he wrote:

> For several years past I have been experimenting with ginseng as a medical agent and of late I have prescribed, or rather added it to, the treatment of some cases of rheumatism. I remember one instance in particular of a middle-aged man who had gone the rounds of the neighborhood doctors, without success, when he employed me. After treating him for several weeks and failing to entirely relieve him, more especially the distress in bowels and back, I concluded to add ginseng to his treatment. After using the medicine he returned, saying the last bottle had served him so well that he wanted it filled with the same medicine as before. I attribute the curative powers of ginseng in rheumatism to stimulating healthy action of the gastric juices, causing a healthy flow of the digestive fluids of the stomach, thereby neutralizing the extra secretion of acid that is carried to the nervous membranes of the body and joints, causing the inflammatory condition incident to rheumatism.

Recently, one M.D. carried out his own research with ginseng and later gave it to his patients. He discovered that in some cases ginseng could help a considerable number of conditions including rheumatism, gout, neuritis, sciatica, and creaking in the joints.

LIU

English Name: Willow
Botanical Name: *Salix alba*

There are many varieties of willow which grow extensively in China, North America, and Europe. In botanic medicine the white willow (*Salix alba*) is cited as one of nature's greatest gifts to man because its bark contains the glucoside *salicin*, a scientifically proven pain reliever. Salicin, as obtained naturally from the willow was officially in the *U.S. Pharmacopeia* from 1882 - 1926, and in the *National Formulary* 1936 - 1955, but has since been displaced by synthetic drugs such as aspirin.

Willow bark tea is still popular today as a domestic remedy for relieving the pains of muscular rheumatism and various related ailments. The tea is prepared by slowly boiling 2 ounces of the cut bark in two pints of water for 15 minutes. The decoction is then strained and one wineglassful is taken four or five times a day.

A stronger decoction may be made as follows: One or two teaspoons of the cut bark are soaked in a large cup of cold water for four hours. The beverage is then brought to a boil for three minutes, then strained. One cup of the tea is taken warm (not hot) daily, a large mouthful at a time.

CHINESE ANALGESIC PLASTER

This plaster is manufactured in Kwangchow, China, and is prepared according to the dialectic therapeutics of traditional Chinese medicine. It is used externally to produce a local analgesic effect for conditions such as muscle inflammation, bruises, sprains, neuralgia, rheumatic arthritis, and similar ailments.

The plaster is available in boxes of ten pieces, and in cans of one roll. It is used by cutting a piece to the desired size and applying it to the affected part. The pain-relieving effects are said to last for 24 hours.

The container should be kept closed and stored in a cool, dry place.

AI-HAO
(Mugwort)

HAN-CH'IN
(Celery)

HAN-CH'IN

English Name: Celery
Botanical Name: *Apium graveolens*

Celery is used in China not only as a food, but also as a remedy for the relief of rheumatism, arthritis, gout, lumbago, neuralgia, and nervousness. The treatment, which consists of a strong tea made from celery seeds plus plenty of celery in the diet, is said to neutralize uric acids and other excess acids in the body. The tea is prepared by placing two heaping tablespoonfuls of the seeds in two quarts of water. The container is covered, and the decoction is allowed to simmer slowly for three hours. It is then strained, and one cup of the tea is taken hot, three or four times daily.

The use of celery as an anti-rheumatic remedy is also well-known to other Oriental peoples. For example, Dr. Kirschner writes:

> Japanese physicians prescribed celery for rheumatism. For one month the patient was placed on a diet of celery in all forms. When the patient got better, people attributed it to the healing power of celery. Since we Americans know of celery's alkaline reaction in the body and of the valuable minerals (particularly sodium) which it contains in abundance, it is not to be wondered at that great benefit was derived from following such a diet.
>
> That most Americans over-indulge in concentrated, acid-forming starches is generally conceded. This results in deposits of insoluble inorganic calcium. Food chemists have demonstrated that the organic sodium in celery helps keep the inorganic calcium in solution so at least some of it can be eliminated. Thus celery helps in both the treatment and prevention of arthritis.[1]

Reported Uses

• "I had been under conventional treatment for arthritis in my fingers for almost a year, and in spite of this there was no progress. The large knuckle of my right index finger was particularly painful and was so swollen I could hardly bend it to touch my palm. I am single and the sole support of my aged mother, so I was fearful that my fingers might eventually become so crippled I'd no longer be able to work.

---

[1]*Nature's Healing Grasses* (Yucaipa, Calif.: H.C. White Publications, 1960).

"A friend who believes in natural health foods told me that the Chinese have many different herb remedies for rheumatism and arthritis. I decided to try the one in which celery is used, so I drank three cups of the tea daily and used plenty of celery with my meals. I also munched on a stalk of fresh celery while watching TV. I did not remove the dark green leaves from the stalks as I was told they are a very beneficial part of the plant.

"Within one month, the soreness in my fingers had lessened considerably, and the fingers were loosening up a little.

"In less than three months, the large swollen knuckle was reduced almost to normal size, and I found I could bend it and almost touch my palm. I have no more pain. There is no doubt in my mind but that a few more weeks on the celery and I will be completely healed."—Miss E.H.

• "For more than a year I suffered painful arthritis and could walk only with a limp. Then several months ago my wife heard about a remedy using celery for arthritis. She explained it all to me, and also about the diet, so I agreed to give it a try. In addition to giving me two cups of hot celery seed tea daily, my wife also gave me two glasses of fresh celery juice a day, which she made with her juicer.

"I noticed relief from pain in a very short time, and after being on the celery for four months I could walk without a limp. I still drink two cups of celery seed tea every day and will continue to do so."—T.G.

AI-HAO

English Name: Mugwort
Botanical Name: *Artemisia vulgaris*

This plant is the common mugwort, found in most parts of China where it is known as Ai-hao, or simply Ai. In Chinese commerce it is sold principally in three forms—Ai-yeh, the dried leaves; Ai-t'iao, the dried twigs tied in bundles; and Ai-jung, which is made by taking the best dried leaves and grinding them in a stone mortar with water, removing the coarsest particles and refuse, then drying and powdering what remains.

Mugwort is employed extensively in Chinese medicine. At one time it was also used in China as a charm during the Dragon Festival where it was hung up in the main room of the house as a protection against evil influences. The herb was so highly venerated that the Chinese rebel, Huang Ch'ao, ordered his soldiers to spare the lives of anyone in whose home mugwort was found.

Mugwort Fomentations

Fomentations of mugwort are used to relieve torticollis (neuritis of the neck muscles), a condition symptomized by a spasm or contraction of the muscles on one side of the neck which causes the head to be tilted. One quart of boiling water is poured over 1 ounce of mugwort, the container is covered, and the infusion is allowed to stand for 15 minutes, then strained. A cloth is dipped into the tea, quickly wrung out, applied to the area as hot as can be comfortably tolerated, and covered with a dry towel to retain the heat. When the cloth completely dries, the same procedure is repeated three or four times. This routine is followed daily and must be continued for lasting results.

CHINESE DRAGON BALM[2]

This Chinese herbal balm has a fascinating background. In the sixth century, A.D., Emperor Tang Ming was married to Empress Yang Quai Fay, who was renowned as an expert dancer. Her Imperial courtesans were known to dance for the Chinese Royal Family, both day and night during their reign. In order to treat frequent incidents of muscular soreness from this strenuous activity, the Empress ordered the Imperial doctors to concoct an ointment using only Chinese herbal ingredients.

The formula was so effective that it was considered by the Royal Family to be an all-purpose panacea for relieving the pains of rheumatism and arthritis, as well as lumbago and other muscular aches and pains. At this time, the Imperial army also used the analgesic balm during frequent outbreaks of the Tibetan Rebellion, for treating foot blisters, insect bites, and sore, aching muscles.

---

[2]Note: Chinese Dragon Balm is not to be confused with Tiger Balm which is a different herbal product.

Over the centuries that followed, the formula has been used by all classes of Chinese people, and is now available in the U.S. It is called Dragon Balm. The dragon in China symbolizes the power of the Emperor in the Imperial Dynasties, and is an indication of the ointment's effectiveness.

Dragon Balm is composed entirely of Chinese herbal ingredients, containing no animal byproducts or synthetic chemicals. It is used as an analgesic ointment to relieve headaches, and to ease muscular aches and pains due to overactivity, strains, colds, fatigue, or rheumatism. It may also be used as an inhalant for nasal congestion.

Reported Use

"I tripped over the telephone cord and the phone fell off the end table and landed on top of my foot. X-rays showed that no bones were broken, but I suffered hours of throbbing pain as I refused to take pain-killers. After several days the pain and soreness gradually left. But every once in a while as the months passed, my foot would suddenly start paining me and would continue for a day or two. My daughter sent me a jar of Chinese Dragon Balm and told me to try it. I found it to be excellent as it takes the pain away very quickly. And I would like to say that I just love the natural herbal odor of this Chinese product."—M.P.

PEKING ROYAL JELLY

According to Dr. E. Barton-Wright, a British biochemist, arthritis is essentially a vitamin-deficiency disease caused by the lack of pantothenic acid in the diet. He reported 100% success in treating 160 arthritic patients with pantothenic acid, with absolutely no harmful side effects. He pointed out that although pantothenic acid is found in most foods, it is easily destroyed by heat, cold, water loss, and storage. He added that processing food destroys many unstable vitamins, such as pantothenic acid. In rheumatoid arthritis which affects the joints, he uses a combination of pantothenic acid and royal jelly.

HUA-SHEN-YU

English Name: Peanut oil

Peanut oil is used warm as a massaging oil to reduce joint inflammation and pain of arthritis. The joints are massaged three times a day. The remedy works slowly, but is said to bring very good results if continued.

Reported Use

"In reading Jess Stearn's *Cayce: The Sleeping Prophet,* I noted with much interest his reference to arthritis and the use of pure peanut oil. As a rheumatoid arthritic I have found it to be of great benefit to my condition. After using peanut oil as a massaging oil for several years I have to agree with Cayce's belief that it not only lubricates but heals as well. I am sure that had I known about the oil in this use, I would have been spared much misery. Why isn't the use of peanut oil to reduce joint inflammation and pain in arthritis better known? Does the medical profession spurn it as a home remedy?"[3]

PEI-MA

English Name: Castor Oil Bush
Botanical Name: *Ricinus communis*

---

[3]*Grace,* Spring 1973.

This plant is native to India but is extensively cultivated in China where it is esteemed as an ornamental shade tree, and highly valued as a medicine.

Castor oil taken internally is a well-known laxative for temporary constipation. However, what is not so commonly known is that the *external* use of the oil has been employed with good results in some cases of arthritis, rheumatism, and other forms of aches and pains. Consider the following:

- Mrs. A.R. writes:

   "The third finger of my right hand had been very stiff and difficult to manipulate. I massaged it every day with castor oil and improvement came gradually. Now, after many weeks it is normal again."

- Mrs. D.L. reports:

   "Hot castor oil has done more for my rheumatism than anything I have ever tried or used for it. I massaged the oil on my legs and arms every day and it took all the pain away."

- Here is another interesting account submitted by Mrs. F.G. of England:

   "I feel I must write to you what has been a joyful cause of a minor miracle. I read of the external uses of castor oil. I was determined to do something about a big toe-nail which for three years after a fall, had been black and dead and so ugly that I dared no longer wear open-toed sandals in summer.

   "The result is that after applying castor oil daily, the nail has not only turned a healthy white/pink again, but has started to grow. At least three-quarters of the nail was dead, now three-quarters is clean and new. I am absolutely thrilled and know that if I had not read about this I would never have had such wonderful results.

   "I hope my use of castor oil will help someone else with the same problem."

Summary

1. Chinese experience has shown that various herb remedies can relieve rheumatism, arthritis, lumbago, bursitis, and other painful conditions.

2. Along with the use of a Chinese herb remedy, sufferers of rheumatism, gout, arthritis, and neuritis are advised to follow a special diet.
3. Coix Combination and Clematis & Stephania Combination are two unique Chinese traditional herb formulas reputed to be very effective for treating various types of arthritis.
4. Specific herbs in the form of oils, balms, liniments, plasters, or poultices are used externally for the relief of aches and pains.
5. Chinese Dragon Balm is not to be confused with Tiger Balm which is a different herbal product.
6. The quality and strict manufacturing process of Zheng Gu Shui liniment has earned it a Gold Award and Silver Award.
7. Areas treated with Zheng Gu Shui should not be bandaged, nor should the liniment be used on open wounds, or broken or irritated skin.

7

CHINESE HERB REMEDIES FOR URINARY DISORDERS

Nature's Marvelous Filtering System

Science informs us that each of our two kidneys contains one million microscopic filters consisting of specialized tissue. The blood circulates through the entire body and carries nutrients as well as waste products of our everyday living processes (the collective name for these processes is *metabolism*). When the blood reaches the kidneys, remarkable mechanisms go to work to sort out the various constituents of the fluid. Substances needed by the body—such as water, useful proteins, and so on—are restored to circulation, and the waste products and other unwanted factors—such as surplus nutrients, surplus water— are passed to the central collecting ducts, called the ureters, to be led to the urinary bladder where they are expelled (via the urethra) during urination.

If placed end to end, the capillaries of both kidneys would stretch 35 miles! Each kidney weighs about one-half pound, and these two hardworking organs process between 400 to 500 gallons of blood a day. These figures indicate the magnitude of the task performed by the kidneys. Without this process of purification, the body would continue to accumulate poisonous amounts of harmful substances that would eventually lead to death.

Thus we see that the kidneys are vitally important organs, performing a task necessary to maintaining a healthy life. Sufficient liquid intake (from four to six pints of water and similar fluids a day) plus good hygiene and a well-balanced diet will help ensure good service from the 2 million filters of the kidneys.

A Word About Kidney and Bladder Stones

Undoubtedly, some of the most painful kidney and bladder troubles are caused by gravel and stones. Excess elements in the system form a nucleus or starting point for gravel and stone formation. Some of the solids, instead of being held in solution and then expelled from the system, deposit in the kidneys or bladder where they gradually accumulate to form gravel. Gravel, sometimes referred to as "sand," is composed of minute particles of kidney stones. Before these deposits of gravel become too large in size, they may be expelled from the body with little pain or discomfort. But when they remain in the kidneys or bladder and continue to accumulate and form stones of a larger size, they cause agonizing pain when they move. For example, the passage of a stone down the ureter from the kidney cuts or tears the delicate lining membrane of the ureter, causing much suffering. When the stones are in the bladder, they are called *vesical calculi;* and when they are in the kidneys, they are called *renal calculi.*

Kidney and bladder stones are complex disorders involving a number of factors. For example, there are many different types of stones. They may be composed principally of either alkaline constituents or acid substances. Some have calcium as a base, some have uric acid, some have oxalic acid, and so on. Calcium and oxalic acid, both normal substances of the urine, may combine to form urinary calculi.

No doubt you've heard of oxalic acid in relation to certain foods such as chocolate, rhubarb, cocoa, spinach, chard, and beet tops, which are all noted for their high oxalate concentration. If you consume large amounts of such foods without increasing your intake of certain nutrients which help reduce the oxalate concentration, you run the risk of kidney stone formation.

A dietary deficiency of vitamin B_6 and magnesium oxide has been found to result in kidney stones. Other factors also enter the complex picture—heredity, metabolic disorders, and others.

Reduced intake of calcium is usually advised for people who have a tendency to form stones. And according to two Harvard medics, Drs. Prien and Gershoff, 10 mg of vitamin B_6 and two capsules of magnesium oxide (140 mg each capsule) should be taken every day.

They report that vitamin B_6 cuts down the amount of oxalates in the urine, and the remaining oxalate that does reach the urine is rendered more soluble by the action of magnesium.

A Word About the Bladder

The bladder is a temporary storage sac for urine which must be voided from time to time. When its elastic walls have been stretched to a certain point, a nerve impulse relays a sensation of the need to urinate. The sphincter, a ringlike muscle which controls the opening and closing of the bodily opening, surrounds the urethra (the tubular structure leading from the bladder to the outside) and is under conscious control. However, very young children often have the problem of enuresis (bed-wetting), because they are unable to control urination during sleep, sometimes due to nervousness, tension, or other causes. Similarly, in the elderly, bladder control may be impaired or the sphincter muscle weakened, and incontinence (involuntary voiding of urine) may result.

Cystitis

Cystitis is an inflamed condition of the bladder and is generally associated with catarrh of the urinary system. Mucous membrane lines the passages to and from the bladder as well as the bladder itself. If the mucous membrane becomes inflamed, it produces excess mucus in the attempt to keep harmful germs and salts from injuring the system. This, together with pus formed as the body tries to destroy the invading germs, may cause the urine to become cloudy and slightly thicker than normal. The condition is symptomized by a dull aching pain in the lower part of the abdomen which increases with pressure when the urine is retained in the bladder for awhile. In very acute cases, pain is also felt towards the small of the back. The desire to urinate frequently is experienced, but the urine is voided with great difficulty and pain, sometimes only in dribbles.

The pain and difficulty in urinating slowly increase, and may eventually become so severe that the patient suffers intense agony each time he tries to pass water, and finally a catheter must be employed. In the condition of cystitis, the urine is generally very acid, whereas normal urine is only slightly so. Retention of urine can also be caused by various disorders other than cystitis. Enlarged prostate gland in the male, for example, can cause difficulty in urinating, often becoming so severe that a catheter must be used.

Various Causes of Cystitis

Because the female urethra is very short (less than 2 inches), the condition of cystitis is much more common among women than men. Approximately three out of every four women suffer from cystitis at some time during their lives, and in some cases the condition becomes chronic.

Physicians mention several possible causes of this painful ailment. One common cause is the allergic reaction to the use of perfumed soaps such as bubble baths, and to scented toilet paper. Prescription antibiotics can trigger an attack as it kills off some of the beneficial bacteria in the body while fighting off an infection. Clothes that are tight-fitting produce a warm atmosphere between the legs, which creates a breeding ground for bacteria. Another common cause is invasion by the colon bacillus.

Health Tips for Cystitis

The following health measures recommended by physicians and herbalists should be included with any treatment used for cystitis. These suggestions not only help prevent cystitis from recurring after it has been successfully treated, but also help reduce the chances of ever getting the painful ailment to begin with.

1. Cleanliness and strict hygiene are necessary at all times, especially after urination and bowel movements. After moving your bowels, wipe yourself from front to back—i.e., away from the vagina—as this will prevent bacteria from reaching the urethra. Wash the area once or twice a day with plain water and a clean cloth.
2. Drink plenty of fluids, especially water, several times a day, as this helps to flush your system of harmful bacteria.
3. Avoid spicy foods, alcohol, and coffee which can irritate the bladder.
4. Wear only cotton underwear, or any other type made of natural fibre material. Change the underwear every day.
5. Empty your bladder before engaging in sexual intercourse, as this will prevent pressure on the bladder.

6. Avoid the use of perfumed bubble baths and scented toilet paper.
7. Never refrain longer than necessary from emptying your bladder when nature calls.
8. Avoid wearing tight garments that can prevent air from circulating around the area of the vagina.

CHINESE HERB REMEDIES FOR URINARY DISORDERS

In addition to the disorders cited (gravel, stones, cystitis, enuresis, incontinence), there are many other ailments of the urinary system. For example, urethritis (inflammation of the urethra), bladder inflammation or irritability, ureteritis (inflammation of the ureter), nephritis, and so on. (Nephritis is an inflamed condition of the kidneys, and there are many forms of this disease.)

The number of herb remedies the Chinese have for treating urinary disorders are legion. Under the circumstances space will not permit a complete coverage; therefore, let us consider a few of the many Chinese formulas and some of the urinary ailments for which they are used.

KUEI

English Name: Juniper Berries
Botanical Name: *Juniperus communis*

This evergreen shrub reaches from 4 to 6 feet in height and grows on hills, rocky slopes, and edges of woods. It is common to the Northern Provinces of China, but is also found in many other parts of the world.

The berries of the Juniper tree have a pleasant aromatic odor, and scientific analyses have shown they contain a combination of wholesome, active properties. In some areas of the Far East and other lands, the berries are used as a balsamic incense. A handful placed on a warm stove fills the home with a lovely fragrance that masks strong, lingering cooking odors. At one time it was believed that burning Juniper berries regularly would purify the air of sick rooms and prevent the spread of infection.

In Chinese medicine the berries are employed for relieving kidney and bladder complaints and for strengthening and imparting tone to the urinary passages. They are also reputed to be helpful in treating conditions of urethritis and cystitis. In addition, the Chinese value the berries as a remedy for other disorders, such as loss of appetite and flatulent indigestion, for which purpose they eat from three to six berries at a time. These berries are said to be agreeable to the weakest stomach. It is also claimed that the distressing back pains of lumbago are quickly relieved by the use of a Juniper berry remedy.

Juniper Berry Formulas

For various urinary conditions the Chinese may use the berries in any one of several different forms. For example, they may use them as a tea prepared from the berries alone, as a combination tea made with the berries and other select herbs, as a Juniper berry wine, or as an oil obtained from the berries (Juniper berry oil).

Simple Tea. One tablespoonful of crushed Juniper berries is placed in a saucepan, and four cups of water are added. The saucepan is covered with a lid, and the tea is brought to a boil and boiled slowly down to two cups. One cup of the strained tea is taken during the day, and a second cup is taken at bedtime.

This simple tea is considered a good kidney remedy.

Juniper Berry Wine. To prepare the wine a large handful of Juniper berries is placed in a gallon of any kind of good quality wine. The bottle is capped and allowed to stand for three weeks. During this period the bottle is shaken thoroughly once a day. At the end of three weeks the berries are strained off and thrown away.

The Juniper wine is used as a kidney and stomach tonic. One small wineglass of the wine is taken a day.

Juniper Berry Oil. Commercial oil of Juniper berries sold on the market is obtained chiefly from the ripe fruit. (Juniper berry oil must not be confused with *Juniper wood oil,* which must never be used internally.)

Medicinally, the oil of Juniper berries is regarded as a powerful remedy for ailing kidneys. In addition to relieving various types of kidney complaints and reducing bladder irritation, the oil reputedly tones up the entire urinary system. It is also said to increase the flow of urine and is therefore helpful as a stimulating diuretic in certain dropsical conditions.

Juniper berry oil reputedly is so active, especially on the kidneys, that it must be used only in very small amounts, from three to eight drops on a little sugar two or three times a day.

Oil of Juniper berries and oil of rosemary mixed together in equal amounts and taken in five- to ten-drop doses (on a little sugar) three times a day is considered a superb remedy for lumbago.

The mixed oils may also be used externally as a liniment for the relief of lumbago pains.

Combination Herb Tea Formulas

For relieving conditions of cystitis, urethritis, gravel, stones, bladder and kidney inflammation, scalding urine, and various other kidney and bladder complaints, Juniper berries are combined with other select herbs and prepared and used as follows:

One ounce each of Juniper berries, Buchu *(Barosma betulina)*, Clivers *(Galium aparine)*, Uva-ursi *(Arctostaphylos uva-ursi)*, Parsley Piert *(Alchemilla arvensis)*, Sage *(Salvia officinalis)*, and Marsh-mallow leaves *(Althaea officinalis)* are pulverized, then thoroughly mixed together and stored in a capped jar. One teaspoonful of the mixture is placed in a cup and boiling water added. The cup is covered with a saucer, and the tea is allowed to steep (stand) for ten minutes and is then strained. One cup of the tea is taken three times daily (once before each meal). In more stubborn cases one cup is taken every three hours. (If necessary, another supply of the herb mixture may be prepared and stored inside a jar for further use.)

In conditions of cystitis, an accessory treatment is used in addition to drinking the combination herb tea. This consists of fomentations of hot cloths (cloths dipped in hot water and wrung out) applied frequently to the bladder area. The fomentations are continued for a few days. Hot sitz baths taken daily are also recommended.

Note: To give us some indication why the various herbs were selected for the combination tea formula, let us briefly consider the medicinal action attributed to each of the herbs.

(Juniper Berries.) Medicinally, the Juniper berry is classed as a diuretic and carminative. The principal constituent in the Juniper berry is a volatile oil. It is the same aromatic oil that is released when Juniper remedies are prepared that gives the berries their effectiveness and healing qualities. It is also the same fragrant oil that evaporates into the air when the berries are placed on a hot stove.

(**Clivers.**) The medicinal action of Clivers is cited as diuretic, tonic, alterative, and aperient. It is reputed to be a helpful agent in conditions of the bladder and scalding urine.

(**Uva-ursi.**) This contains a glycoside called *arbutin* and owes much of its marked diuretic action to this substance. During its excretion by the kidneys, *arbutin* exercises an antiseptic effect on the urinary mucous membrane. Uva-ursi is therefore considered to be of value in various conditions of the urinary tract such as cystitis, urethritis, and so on. Uva-ursi is also said to be a strengthener of the sphincter muscle, and as such is useful in conditions of "night rising" and incontinence. For this particular purpose, the herb is used alone and prepared as an instant tea, one teaspoonful of the powdered herb to one cup of boiling water. One cup of the tea is taken every morning and evening.

(**Parsley Piert.**) This herb is not related to the common parsley, however its medicinal action is somewhat similar. It is classed as a diuretic and soothing demulcent. In olden times the herb was called "Parsley Breakstone," and to this day the plant has retained its reputation as a helpful remedy for gravel, kidney and bladder stones, and other urinary complaints.

(**Buchu.**) Buchu is cited medicinally as a diuretic and astringent. It is considered one of the best herbs for diseases of the bladder. It is said to normalize the flow of urine, produce a restorative effect on the bladder, relieve irritation, and reduce acid. It is also considered to be a very useful agent in treating conditions of cystitis and gravel.

(**Marshmallow.**) Marshmallow has a mucilaginous and demulcent action which is very soothing to irritable or inflamed urinary organs and passages. Its lubricant properties also reputedly heal the membranes which may have been cut by rough edges of gravel.

(**Sage.**) Sage is regarded as a helpful agent in purifying the kidneys. In pharmaceutical writings sage is listed among the antiseptics.

PIEN-HSU

English Name: Knotgrass
Botanical Name: *Polygonum aviculaire*

Knotgrass is used in Chinese medicine for many different ailments and is especially valued as a helpful remedy for gravel and kidney and bladder stones. The tea is also regarded as a preventative where there is a tendency to develop gravel or stones.

Knotgrass is prepared as a tea. One ounce is added to one pint of boiling water. The container is covered, and the tea is allowed to stand until cold. One cup of the cold tea is taken three or four times a day.

Another Chinese formula consists of mixing ½ ounce each of knotgrass and horsetail grass *(Equisetum)*, prepared and taken the same as the previous recipe.

CHI-TS'AI

English Name: Shepherd's Purse
Botanical Name: *Capsella bursa pastoris*

This herb was given the common name of Shepherd's Purse because its seed pods somewhat resemble an old-fashioned leather purse. It is generally distributed throughout the world and has been used medicinally as an astringent, diuretic, and urinary tonic in Chinese herb practice since earliest times.

A decoction of the herb is employed for soothing and toning up the urinary passages. It is used in conditions of scalding urine, urethral irritation, and catarrh of the bladder and ureters. It reputedly brings prompt relief in cases where mucus is voided with the urine.

The decoction is prepared by adding 2 ounces of Shepherd's Purse to one and one-half pints of water, and slowly boiling the mixture down to one pint. It is then strained and taken cold, one teacupful four or five times daily until results are obtained.

Combined Formulas

As a stimulant diuretic for conditions of water retention, a mixture of 1 ounce of Shepherd's Purse and ½ ounce each of Couch Grass *(Triticum repens)* and Knotgrass are placed in a container, and two pints of boiling water are poured on. The container is covered and is allowed to steep (stand) for 30 minutes, then it is strained. One cupful is taken four times daily.

For conditions of mucus or gravelly deposits in the urine a tea is prepared with one quart of boiling water poured over a mixture of ½ ounce each of Shepherd's Purse, Sage, Marshmallow leaves, and Peach leaves. The porcelain container is covered, and the tea is allowed

YU-SHU-SHU
(Corn—Showing Corn Silks)

CHI-TS'AI
(Shepherd's Purse)

CHU-YANG-YANG
(Clivers)

KUEI
(Juniper Berries)

to stand for one-half hour and then strained. One teacupful is taken four or five times daily. This remedy is also used for the relief of scalding urine.

INN SAI

English Name: Parsley
Botanical Name: *Apium petroselinum*

Parsley tea reputedly produces a soothing effect on the lining of the urinary passages. It is said to bring great relief to the kidneys and bladder whenever there is irritation, congestion, inflammation, or weakness of these organs. It is also claimed to be helpful in conditions of kidney and bladder calculi.

Chinese claims for the remedial effects of parsley have received some scientific support. Considerable research on the plant was conducted by R.D. Pope, M.D. who reported that parsley is "excellent for the genito-urinary tract, of great assistance in the calculi of the kidneys and bladder, albuminaria, nephritis, and other kidney trouble."[1]

Parsley tea is prepared by placing a fresh bunch of parsley in a saucepan and adding two pints of cold water. This is brought to a boil and simmered not more than ten seconds. The vessel is covered, removed from the burner, allowed to stand until cold, and then strained. Four to five cups of the tea are taken daily until results are obtained. (The cold tea may be reheated and taken warm.)

Although the leaves of parsley are the part of the herb most commonly used to prepare the tea, the beverage may be made from the dried roots if one prefers. In this case, a heaping tablespoonful of the dried, cut roots are boiled slowly in one quart of water for 15 minutes. The decoction is allowed to stand until cold, strained, and taken in cupful doses four times daily.

Reported Uses

I was incapacitated by what was diagnosed as toxic poisoning accompanied by a tough case of pyelitis [infection of the outlet

---

[1]Kirschner, H.E., *Nature's Healing Grasses* (Yucaipa, Calif.: H.C. White Publications, 1960), p.97.

of the kidney]. For two years I helped support a general practitioner and a neurologist. At the end of that time I could not walk across the room without help, and I had lost 50 pounds in weight and my pocketbook was a mere shadow of its former self.

During a friendly visit an acquaintance asked me if I had tried parsley tea for the urinary condition. As I had never done this, he gave me these instructions: 'Take a fresh bunch of parsley, as obtained in most markets, untie it and wash it in cold water. Place in a dish and cover with scalding hot water. Cover to keep warm. When cold, pour off the liquid, and drink during a twenty-four hour period. Repeat daily until cured.'

I've recommended this to many people. They never fail to get a cure, regardless of whether it is a kidney or bladder complaint. I've never known it to require more than three weeks for a cure, and have known several cases where only three days was necessary. My own case required between two and three weeks for a cure, and there has been a lapse of 35 years without a recurrence.

A few months ago, I heard that a friend was having kidney trouble. Without further investigation I sent her the above instructions. About a month later I received a two-page letter stating that she had been under a doctor's care for six months with two hospital confinements. She received my letter on the day that she returned from the last hospital trip, and was ready to try anything once, and she did. In three days, her urine was perfectly clear, and she was ready to resume her household duties in her mobile home. In a week's time, she was covering the park to catch up on her social obligations and tell the world of her wonderful cure.—H.K.W.[2]

SHU-WEI-TS'AO

English Name: Sage
Botanical Name: *Salvia officinalis*

The botanical name for sage *(Salvia officinalis)* is derived from *salvere,* meaning "to be in good health." This herb is classed medicinally as a natural antiseptic.

A tea made with equal parts of sage and peppermint leaves is said to help purify the kidneys. One pint of boiling water is poured into a vessel containing ½ ounce each of sage and peppermint leaves. The

---

[2]*Prevention,* Emmaus, Pa., October, 1970, p.14.

vessel is covered with a lid, and the tea is allowed to stand until cold. One cupful is taken two or three times daily.

Reported Uses

One woman reports that she suffered from a kidney infection for more than a year. She says:

"My doctor treated me with antibiotics which helped for a while, but the infection returned. I finally had so many treatments with antibiotics that they no longer worked at all.

"Then one night my son brought home an Oriental friend whose father was an herbalist. The young man knew all about Chinese herbs and told me to try a tea of sage and peppermint. The next day I bought the herbs and began drinking the tea. I took two cups a day for three months, and my kidney infection is all gone."

CHIH-MA

English Name: Flaxseed
Botanical Name: *Linum usitatissimum*

The flax herb is extensively cultivated in China for its seeds and oil. Medicinally, a tea made from the seeds is considered valuable for relieving irritation or inflammation of the urinary passages and organs, especially bladder irritability.

The prepared infusion has the consistency of a soothing mucilage. It is made by placing 2 ounces of the seeds in a container and pouring one quart of boiling water over them. The preparation is covered with a lid, allowed to stand for ten minutes, and then strained. A small pinch of powdered licorice is added. If the tea is too thick for drinking, dilute it with water.

In acute cases, one cup of tea is taken every two hours; in milder cases, three to four cups of the warm tea are taken daily.

HU-LU-PA

English Name: Fenugreek
Botanical Name: *Trigonella foenum-graecum*

The seeds of the fenugreek plant have been used as a medicine in China since the Tang dynasty. A tea prepared from the seeds is recommended as a soothing demulcent for irritation of the bladder, and it reputedly has helped some people troubled with the condition of "night rising" (getting up too often during the night to urinate).

Fenugreek seed tea is prepared according to the same directions as those given for flaxseed tea, except that the licorice is omitted. Three to four cups of the warm fenugreek tea are taken every day.

HSI-KUA

English Name: Watermelon
Botanical Name: *Citrullus vulgaris*

The common watermelon was introduced into China from Mongolia in the 10th century. Several varieties are grown in the Far East, but the black-seeded variety is the most highly favored.

Watermelon seed is classed as a diuretic and considered a good kidney and bladder cleanser for women. Two tablespoons of the seeds are boiled for five minutes in one pint of water. The container is then covered, and the brew is allowed to stand until cold. One teacupful of the strained tea is taken three or four times a day. Watermelon is eaten frequently during the watermelon season.

Reported Uses

Mrs. J.R. writes: "For about ten years I suffered from a bladder infection. During this time I cooperated fully with my family physician, and we tried many antibiotics, drugs, and sulfas. In spite of this I would suffer a recurring bladder infection about four or five times a year. Then a neighbor told me about watermelon seed tea. Since I felt it was a perfectly harmless remedy and I had nothing to lose even if it didn't help, I gave it a try. What a suprise to find that it worked! I take the tea about three times a week, and I have not had a recurrence of the bladder infection in 16 months. I also eat plenty of watermelon itself when it's in season and save the seeds for year around use."

Note: The Chinese do not recommend the watermelon remedy for men, as they claim too much melon builds "moisture pressure" in the male body and causes pressure on the prostate gland.

YU-SHU-SHU

English Name: Corn
Botanical Name: *Zea mays*

Corn as a food crop was introduced into China from the West. When prepared as corm meal it is considered to be a nutritious gruel and an excellent diet for convalescents. Common Chinese names for Indian corn include Pa-lu and Liu-su.

The part of the corn plant used in Chinese medicine consists of the fine silky threads of the stigmas of the flowers of maize (corn). These filaments hang from the point of the husk and are called "corn silk" (known botanically as *Stigmata maidis*). Chinese herbalists cite the medicinal action of corn silk as a diuretic, stimulant, and demulcent.

A tea made with dried corn silks reputedly imparts a soothing effect to the bladder, kidneys, and urinary passages whenever there is irritation or inflammation of these organs. It is said to be helpful in relieving acute and chronic cases of cystitis and bladder irritation caused by phosphatic and uric acid gravel. Another beneficial effect credited to corn silk tea is that of normalizing the flow of urine.

The tea is prepared by placing one heaping teaspoon of finely cut dried corn silks in a cup and adding boiling water. The cup is covered with a saucer, allowed to stand until cool, and then strained. The tea may be taken frequently every day.

A stronger tea may be made as follows: Place two heaping tablespoons of dried corn silks in a porcelain container and pour one pint of boiling water over them. Cover with a lid, allow the tea to stand for one-half hour, then strain.

With either method the tea may be taken in cupful doses frequently every day.

Combined Formula

For conditions of bladder drip, gravel, incontinence, scalding urine, or a burning sensation accompanied by a frequent desire to urinate, 1 ounce of dried corn silks and ½ ounce each of couch grass *(Triticum repens)* and uva-ursi *(Arctostaphylos uva-ursi)* are mixed together and placed in a porcelain container. One quart of boiling water is poured on the herbs, the container is covered, and the tea is allowed to stand for 20 minutes and then strained. One cupful is taken three or four times daily.

Reported Uses

• Mrs. G.M. is one of many people who has found corn silk to be an effective remedy. She writes:

"Some years back (I am now 83) when I was living in St. Louis there seemed to be something dreadfully wrong with my kidneys. Three doctors, having taken an X-ray which showed the lower half of one kidney completely black, decided that I must have an operation, at least an exploratory one.

"Deciding not to have the operation, I took my family to the country, bag and baggage, and drank corn silk tea instead of water for a year. Upon my return to the city, one of the doctors called upon me and asked, 'How are you?' I answered, 'Just fine! And you are going to laugh when I tell you I have been drinking corn silk tea.' He said, 'Well, that is nothing to laugh at—that is where they get their kidney medicine.' Another X-ray showed an entirely clean kidney. Now I swear by corn silk tea."

Following are three more interesting reports on the use of corn silk tea:

• "My husband broke his hip, and his lying in bed all the time caused his kidneys to become sluggish so he did not urinate as much as he should. A Chinese herbalist suggested he drink corn silk tea, and this fixed him up just fine."—Mrs. R.V.

• "Each summer when we husk our sweet corn we save all the silks and dry them thoroughly. These we place in an airtight jar, and when we need to we take a portion and make a tea of them. This is so good for any kind of kidney trouble. The tea will regulate the amount of urine if there is too much or too little. It can be taken any time since it is absolutely harmless."—Mrs. R.L.C.

• "For several weeks I suffered from scalding urine, bladder drip, and a painful bladder. After trying many things without success, I finally obtained complete relief from a Chinese herb formula, a tea made with a combination of corn silk, uva-ursi, and couch grass. It was remarkable!"—Mr. C.R.

Some Medical Opinions of Corn Silk Tea

Research into medical literature spanning many years shows that the Chinese claim for the effectiveness of corn silk tea has been shared by a number of Western physicians. For example, in the last century *The Medical News* (1881) recommended the use of corn silk tea as a remedy for bladder complaints and the condition of cystitis. In the same year an article by Professor L.W. Benson appeared in the *Therapeutic Gazette,* in which he reported that he found the corn silk tea remedy both gentle and effective. Dr. John Davis, a physician of Cincinnati, reported that a decoction of corn silk combined with dried pods of beans was the most active of all diuretics he had ever employed in his practice.

In later years, Dr. Neiderkorn of Lloyd's cited the following uses of corn silk:

> *Stigmata maidis* [corn silk] is indicated in cystic irritation, due to phosphatic and uric acid concretions. In these cases, the urine is usually scant and of a strong odor. The remedy not only relieves the bladder and urethral irritation, but tends also to prevent the formation of gravel and calculi. It is an important and favorite remedy in the treatment of urinal disorders of the aged, especially where the urine is strong and scant, and throws a heavy sediment. Stigmata should always be thought of in inflammatory kidneys, where it is evident that the inflammatory trouble is due to the presence of concretions.

Dr. S. Clymer adds:

> Where there is a tendency to the formation of gravel, or where it is known to exist, give:
>
> Tincture Stigmata maidis (corn silk) . . . . 1 oz.
> Tincture Triticum repens (couch grass) . . . . ½ oz.
> [The two tinctures are mixed together in a small bottle]
> Dose: 10 to 60 drops of the mixture in a little hot water, as
>   required.
> Dose of Stigmata maidis, in other conditions, is 10 to 60
> drops.[3]

---

[3]Clymer, R. Swinburne, *The Medicines of Nature* (Quakertown, Pennsylvania: The Humanitarian Society Reg., 1960), p.111.

The 17th edition of the *U.S. Dispensatory* listed the uses of corn silk as follows:

> Zea (corn silk) has been highly recommended by various surgeons as a mild diuretic, useful in acute and chronic cystitis, and in bladder irritation of uric acid and phosphatic gravel...It has been affirmed by M. Landreux to be a useful diuretic and even cardiac stimulant in the dropsy of heart disease. It has been commonly used in the form of an infusion, 2 ounces to one pint of boiling water, taken almost *ad libitum* [as much as one wishes]; but the fluid extract, dose 1 to 2 fluid drachms [in a little warm water] every two to three hours is an excellent preparation.

CH'IAO-MAI

English Name: Buckwheat
Botanical Name: *Fagopyrum esculentum*

Buckwheat honey is among the various Chinese remedies used for bedwetting. From one teaspoonful to a tablespoonful of buckwheat honey, taken at bedtime, has proved effective in many cases. Consider the following examples:

• "My seven-year-old son was a bedwetter until he was given a tablespoonful of buckwheat honey at bedtime."—Mrs. F.H.

• "A teaspoonful of buckwheat honey, taken at bedtime, cured our neighbor's four-year-old daughter of bedwetting. Some of our relatives have children who wet the bed, so we told them about the honey remedy. It has worked wonders for all these children."—Mrs. L.T.

• "Our ten-year-old son was a bedwetter. We tried everything we could think of to help, but nothing worked. Because of his problem he could not go to summer camp with the other boys, nor could he accept invitations to stay overnight at his friend's house. We became very concerned since we could see that his bedwetting condition was gradually affecting his personality, causing him to become shy and withdrawn.

"Then someone at my husband's office told him about a Chinese remedy of using buckwheat honey for bedwetting. We gave our son a tablespoonful of honey that night, and it was like a miracle to find the bed dry in the morning. We have given him the honey every night for three months, and he has never wet the bed in all that time."—Mrs. J.B.

MUI

English Name: Cranberry
Botanical Name: *Vaccinitium macrocarpon*

Our common cranberry is called "Mui" by the Chinese because it resembles a small plum or tiny peach in shape. Drinking the freshly pressed juice of ripe cranberries is regarded as a helpful remedy for relieving some types of infections of the kidneys, bladder, and urinary tract. It is also employed in some cases of bedwetting.

If fresh cranberries are unavailable, bottled commercial cranberry juice is used. Four to 6 ounces of the juice are taken three times a day for kidney, bladder, and urinary infections. This is repeated daily for at least two or three weeks, or longer if necessary, until results are obtained.

In conditions of bedwetting, 4 ounces of the juice are taken once a day, around three or four o'clock in the afternoon.

Reported Uses

• "My 12-year-old son wet the bed every night for as long as I can remember. I heard that Chinese herbalists sometimes recommended cranberry juice for bedwetting, so I gave him 4 ounces every day, and it completely stopped his bedwetting."—Mrs. D.G.

• "For eight months I suffered a bladder infection and visited two different urologists. In spite of their treatments, the infection persisted. My daughter suggested I try a Chinese herbalist since these people seemed to have much healing wisdom. The herbalist told me to drink a glass of cranberry juice three times a day for two or three weeks, and I followed his instructions to the letter. At the end of two weeks I had my bladder tested by a urologist, and the infection was gone."—Mr. C.S.

• "Our teenage son wet the bed twice a night for the past two years. He had a kidney infection and passed cloudy, discolored water. A small fortune was spent on medical treatments with little relief, so our family doctor finally advised that we take the boy to a specialist.

Before the date of the appointment with the specialist, a friend told me that cranberry juice had cleared up her daughter's urinary infection and bedwetting problem.

"I bought a bottle of cranberry juice and gave my son 4 ounces about mid-afternoon. That night he didn't wet the bed. He has taken the juice daily for a year now and has slept dry every night except once. His kidney infection cleared up after he was on the juice for three weeks. The appointment with the specialist was never kept. Our family doctor checked my son and gave him a clean bill of health."—Mrs. C.T.

Science Evaluates Cranberry Juice

According to an article in *The Times Record,* Dr. George B. Ceresia of the Albany College of Pharmacy reported that of 60 adults with definite symptoms of urinary tract infection, all received beneficial results when treated with 16 ounces of commercial cranberry juice daily for a period of three weeks. Twenty-two of the patients were considered cured in that the bacteria count was sharply reduced, while others obtained varying degrees of improvement. Dr. Ceresia's experiments also showed that the juice of cranberries aids in the effectiveness of drugs used to relieve urinary disorders.

HU-TS'UNG

English Name: Onion
Botanical Name: *Allium cepa*

Herbalists classify the medicinal action of the onion as diuretic and expectorant. The water in which onions are boiled is used as a tea to eliminate retention of fluid in the system.

CHU-YANG-YANG

English Name: Clivers
Botanical Name: *Galium aparine*

In botanic medicine, the action of clivers is cited as diuretic, alterative, tonic, and aperient. Its use is recommended by herbalists in conditions of bladder complaints such as scalding urine, gravel, and calculi. It also reputedly purifies the blood, reduces obesity, and induces quiet, restful sleep

Two ounces of the herb are steeped in a quart of warm water for two hours. The infusion is then strained, and 2 to 4 ounces of the tea may be taken either warm or cold, three or four times a day.

Or the fluid extract of the herb may be used. Dr. Boericke, M.D. recommends the fluid extract in half-dram doses in a cup of water or milk, three times daily.

LAN-TS'AO

English Name: Queen-of-the-Meadow, Gravel Root
Botanical Name: *Eupatorium purpureum*

Queen-of-the-Meadow is a purple-flowered herb which grows in damp meadows and marshes, and can be seen skirting along moist banks. Since it is principally used for renal and vesical calculi, it is commonly called gravel root. For these conditions, or as a diuretic for water retention, 2 ounces of the roots are boiled slowly in two pints of water, down to one pint. One cupful of the strained decoction is taken twice daily, a large mouthful at a time. Of the fluid extract, half to one teaspoonful in a small glass of water, two or three times a day.

MAI-HU

English Name: Couch Grass
Botanical Name: *Triticum repens*

Herbalists classify the medicinal action of couch grass as diuretic and demulcent (soothing agent). It is used for cystitis, catarrh of the bladder, irritation of the urinary passages, and to dissolve gravel.

A tea is prepared with 1 ounce of couch grass to two pints of boiling water, reduced to one pint, which may be freely taken in small teacupful doses. Of the liquid *extract,* half to one teaspoonful is given in a glass of hot water, two or three times a day.

A Medical Opinion of Couch Grass

Dr. Swinburne Clymer refers to the remedial value of couch grass as follows:

Couch Grass
(Triticum repens)

The kidney, bladder, and gravel remedy. It is soothing in cases of irritation of the kidneys, bladder, urethra, and is especially valuable in gravel, many experienced physicians claiming that its timely use has dissolved small calculi. In incontinence of the urine with intense burning sensation and constant desire to urinate, it is splendid in its results. Dose of the *tincture,* five to 30 drops in hot water. To help calculi to pass, the maximum dose of 40 to 60 drops in hot water should be given.

CHINESE TRADITIONAL HERB COMBINATIONS

Chinese traditional herb therapy employs the following formulas for treating various urinary disorders. The herbs in these preparations are carefully selected and balanced for maximum potency, and are available in capsules.

Capillaris and Hoelen Five Combination

Constituents: Capillaris, hoelen, cinnamon, polyporus, atractylodes, alisma.
Uses: Chronic and acute cystitis with discomfort after urination, or urinary retention.

Lotus Seed Combination

Constituents: Lotus seed, ophiopogon, ginseng, hoelen, plantago, scute, astragalus, lycium, licorice.
Uses: Urethritis, cystitis, enlarged prostate, cloudy urine, urinary gravel, no appetite. Considered especially effective for persons of a delicate constitution, prone to nervousness.

Peony and Licorice Combination

Constituents: Peony, licorice.
Uses: For severe pain from kidney and gallstone colic.

Hoelen Five Herb Combination

Constituents: Hoelen, alisma, polyporus, atractylodes, cinnamon.

Uses: For the early stages of acute nephritis (non-bacterial inflammation of the kidney), cystitis, scanty and cloudy urine, and urethritis.

Polyporus Combination

Constituents: Polyporus, hoelen, alisma, gelatine, talc.

Uses: Considered very effective for painful or difficult urination, decreased urinary volume, irregular urination, and a sensation of residual urine. Treats cystitis, urethritis, urinary calculi, and gallstones.

Minor Bupleurum Combination

Constituents: Bupleurum, scute, ginseng, pinellia, jujube fruit, ginger, licorice.

Uses: Chronic nephritis. This formula is often taken with Hoelen Five Herb Combination or with Polyporus Combination.

Summary

1. The two kidneys are Nature's marvelous filtering system, performing a task essential to maintaining a healthy life.
2. Sufficient liquid intake, plus good hygiene and proper diet, helps insure good service from the 2 million filters of the kidneys.
3. Some of the solids, instead of being held in solution and then expelled from the system, deposit in the kidneys or bladder where they gradually accumulate to form gravel or stones.
4. Kidney and bladder stones are complex disorders involving a number of factors.
5. When stones are in the kidney they are called renal calculi; when they are in the bladder they are called vesical calculi.
6. Cystitis is an inflamed condition of the urinary bladder, accompanied by pain and difficulty in urinating, often becoming so severe that a catheter must be employed to withdraw the urine.

7. Because the female urethra is very short, the condition of cystitis is much more common among women than men.

8. Certain health measures should be followed to help prevent the condition of cystitis from recurring after it has been successfully treated. Such measures also reduce the chances of ever getting the painful ailment to begin with.

9. In addition to disorders such as cystitis, gravel, or stones, there are many other ailments that can affect the urinary system.

10. Specially prepared herbal formulas known as Chinese traditional herb combinations are available in capsules, for use in treating various urinary problems.

8

CHINESE HERB REMEDIES FOR MEN'S AILMENTS

The Prostate Gland

According to scientific estimates, some difficulty with the prostate gland affects almost every American man over the age of 50. Some medical authorities place the age even lower. For example, referring to the estimates of many physicians, Robert M. Overton, a leading chiropractor, wrote: "For many years the medics have propounded the fact that all men over 40 should expect prostate trouble. It appears they are correct." (Because prostate trouble is a rather common occurrence in men as they grow older, it does not mean that younger men are immune to the problem.)

Although most males of adult age have heard of prostate trouble, and many suffer from it, few really know much of anything about it. Under the circumstances, it would be helpful to acquaint ourselves with at least a few basic facts regarding the important prostate gland and the various ailments that can affect it. Without going into lengthy, minute details and technicalities, the following information should suffice.

The prostate gland is situated at the neck of the bladder and is normally about the size of a chestnut. This gland plays some part in the reproduction of the species and is said to add a thin alkaline secretion to the seminal fluid. The urine exits from the bladder and empties through the long narrow tube called the urethra, which carries the urine out through the penis in a man. It is the same urethra through which seminal fluid is ejaculated during sexual intercourse. Since the sex glands must empty their secretions into the narrow tube, it is obvious that the urethra must be intimately connected with these glands. This is the reason why a disorder or malfunction of the prostate (which is a sex gland) is most frequently connected with urination.

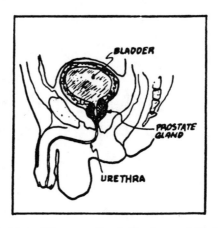

Position of Prostate Gland, Urethra, and Bladder

Enlarged Prostate

When the prostate gland enlarges, it presses against the neck of the bladder which it surrounds, constricting the urethra and preventing the bladder from completely emptying itself. According to medical authorities, one of the earliest signs of a swollen prostate is difficulty in urinating. The stream of urine may become weak and not as forceful as it normally should be. You may experience a sense of not completely emptying your bladder. The residual urine—that is, the urine remaining trapped in the bladder—causes the bladder to fill up more quickly than before, and you find that frequent voiding during the day and the night becomes necessary.

If the condition is not treated, infection usually occurs, causing throbbing pain and sometimes mucus discharges.

Because of its anatomical position circling the urethra, if the prostate continues to enlarge, a complete stoppage of urine results, which is known as stricture. This condition is extremely painful and can often only be relieved by insertion of a catheter (a rubber or plastic tube) into the urethra for withdrawal of the urine from the bladder. It should be pointed out, however, that retention of urine may be caused by disorders other than enlarged prostate. Cystitis, for example, can cause difficulty in urinating, often becoming so severe that a catheter must be used. (If the serious condition of complete urine stoppage is not treated, it can be fatal.)

Prostate Infection

Symptoms of prostate infection generally include backache, extreme impairment of sexual potency, burning on urination, and sometimes a slight discharge.

John Eichenlaub, M.D. gives directions for a home-test in determining whether the condition is prostate infection or urethritis (inflammation of the urethra). He writes: "One helpful home-test is the three-glass procedure. Pass a few drops of urine in one glass, almost all of what remains in another glass, and the last teaspoonful in a third. Cloudiness in the first glass only usually points to urethritis, while cloudiness in both the first and third glasses almost always means prostate infection."[1]

Prostatitis

Inflammation of the prostate gland is called *prostatitis*. The condition may be symptomized by infection and/or pain in the bladder region, frequency of urination, blood in the urine, and so on. Dr. Ask-Upmark of Sweden describes prostatitis as it occurs both in "acute form and as a chronic disease, in which acute exacerbations [flareup of a condition; relapse of a disease] are highly characteristic. The local symptoms can most simply be described as those of cystitis; i.e., a continued urge to void, and discomfort on urination. Prostatitis has, however, certain typical features. Firstly, the discomfort on urination consists far more of pain than of burning. Secondly, this pain is often referred to the tip of the penis, approximately as in the presence of an advanced vesical calculus (stone). Thirdly, the patient may have a sensation of fullness in the rectum, which can reasonably be ascribed to bulging of the swollen prostate gland into it. This makes the patient try to relieve his discomfort by (unsuccessful) defecation [bowel

---

[1] *A Minnesota Doctor's Home Remedies for Common and Uncommon Ailments*, (Prentice-Hall, Inc., Englewood Cliffs, N.J., 1960), p.162.

movement]. These local symptoms are accompanied, in the acute stage, by systemic disturbances in the form of fever..."

CHINESE REMEDIES FOR PROSTATE AND OTHER MALE DISORDERS

Following is a partial list of herb remedies the Chinese use for treating various ailments that can affect members of the male sex.

JENSHEN

English Name: Ginseng
Botanical Name: *Panax schinseng*

Ginseng, a herb prized as a near panacea for varied illnesses, is also highly valued as a treatment for sexual impotence. Its history shows that it was used to pep up fading virility by Chinese men for thousands of years. According to reports that have filtered through from the Far East, men who have passed the spring and summer of their lives take ginseng regularly and are able to satisfy their romantic desires as though they were young again.

Professor Lakhovsky, a Russian biologist residing in Paris, studied the ginseng plant and found that the herb, particularly the wild Manchurian variety, has a beneficial effect on the sexual and other endocrine glands, which increases their hormone-producing activity. He believes that the increase of these various hormones is responsible for the rejuvenating effect claimed by Chinese physicians and accepts these claims as valid.

P.M. Kourenoff, in his book, *Oriental Health Remedies,* writes:

Asked by the author which of the Chinese-Tibetan remedies he considered best for the treatment of sexual impotence, the late Dr. S.N. Chernych of San Francisco stated, 'Ginseng! Oriental healers are successfully curing patients of sexual impotence by the use of ginseng, and sexual impotence is one of the most difficult disorders. I can state from personal experience that the Oriental physicians have cured several men whom I and several other doctors tried to help.'

The author can verify this from his own personal observations in the city of Harbin, Manchuria, during the years 1920-1923. Harbin was crowded with civilian refugees and interned units of the Russian National (White) Army. Most of these ex-soldiers had served in the First World War, and later in the Civil War. Nerve-shattered and ill, many of these veterans were suddenly stricken with sexual impotence.

They stormed the offices of regular doctors of medicine, and receiving no help, finally turned to the Chinese healers. It is reported that all of them were cured by the Chinese practitioners, chiefly with the use of ginseng, occasionally supplemented by, or combined with other substances. Three of six persons known to the author were completely cured by ginseng alone.

When all else has failed to restore sexual vigor, ginseng can be counted on, if there is any hope at all.

Ginseng—A Strengthener of Endocrine Glands

Chinese healers insist that ginseng does not stimulate the sex glands into unnatural activity, but that it is a *restorer* of the normally healthy sexual function that has become "weary."

The power of ginseng as a sex improver has been confirmed by a team of Soviet scientists who have been studying the Oriental herb for a great many years. They have established that the root has a beneficial influence on the sex glands and other endocrine glands, and their findings also show that the effects do not lead to premature exhaustion of the organism, for the herb is definitely not a strong stimulant. Dr. I.I. Brekhman, a member of the Russian team, reports that ginseng "acts only by improving physiological processes. No bad effects are observed after taking it."

How Ginseng Is Used

Ginseng's remedial effect on conditions of sexual impotence is not instantaneous. The Chinese maintain that the herb is not classed as an aphrodisiac in the popular concept; that is, it does not stimulate the sex organ into unnatural activity, but works by rebuilding and restoring healthy functioning. Therefore, men who have used the root regularly over a period of time agree that its strengthening effect on the reproductive system is slow and gradual.

Ginseng is used in various ways. For example, some men drink the tea or chew portions of the root. Others prefer to take it in powdered form contained in gelatine capsules or to use the bulk powder added to soups, broths, or coffee. Still others use it in the form of an elixir or tincture measured by drops or a teaspoonful, while others prefer either a fluid extract or a blend. When the fluid extract or tincture is used, the dose is added to a small glass of water.

Reported Uses

• "My friend's brother was about 35 or 40 years old, and he had recently remarried. The girl he wedded was about 21 or 22 years old. He worked as a milkman and had to get up quite early. By the time evening rolled around he was too tired to be in an amorous mood. After a couple of months of this, his wife had become very unsatisfied. My friend bought a supply of Chinese ginseng, the best quality he could find. It was in powdered form in capsules, and he gave them to his brother to try. After about a month of taking the capsules, his brother said he had obtained wonderful results and was very satisfied. He took one capsule each night at first, but after a couple of weeks he felt that this was too much so he cut it down to about three a week and says it is working very well. He said it saved his marriage."—Mr. D.S.

HU-LU-PA

English Name: Fenugreek
Botanical Name: *Trigonella foenum-graecum*

Fenugreek has been widely cultivated in many countries throughout he world. According to Chinese writings it was introduced into the southern provinces of China from some foreign country and has always been an important and popular ingredient in Oriental curry recipes for lamb and other dishes.

The botanical name *foenum-graecum* means "Greek hay." In the Far Eastern and Mediterranean countries, the herb and seeds were mixed with hay and fed to cattle as an animal sex and general health conditioner. Perhaps the ancients got the idea of including the seeds in their own diets after noticing the improvement in the animals.

Eventually, fenugreek seeds were included in medical botany listings and pharmacopoeias and have been used as a medicine in China since the Tang dynasty. From that time, among the many medicinal uses, fenugreek seeds have been held in high regard by the Chinese as a tonic to the reproductive system, reputedly producing a beneficial effect on the generative (sex) organs. In addition, mild cases of hydrocele are said to sometimes be benefited by taking the seeds in powdered form. (Hydrocele is a condition in which fluid collects in a sac surrounding the testicle. Surgery may be necessary if the fluid is not absorbed.)

Constituents in Fenugreek Seeds

Fenugreek seeds contain protein and, according to a report in *Biological Abstracts,* "new free amino acids," the building blocks of the human body. Another substance found in the seeds is *trigonelline,* which the *U.S. Pharmacopoeia* describes as the methylbetaine of nicotinic acid—the pellagra preventative factor. (Pellagra is a serious disease resulting from nutritional deficiencies.) The seeds also contain an aromatic oil rich in vitamins A and D and similar in composition to cod liver oil.

The oil in fenugreek seeds could possibly account for their ancient reputation as a sex rejuvenator for the animal or man deficient in vitamins A and D. For the past 40 years the damaging effects on the male organs resulting from vitamin A deficiency in the diet have been under scientific study. Experiments on laboratory animals showed marked reduction or complete loss of sperm as a consequence of vitamin A shortage. Scientists in Denmark reported on experiments in which boars were fed a diet low in vitamin A. On this diet the animals' sperm count dropped. Daily injections of vitamin A in dosages varying between 6,000 and 8,000 units gradually restored the sperm count to normal.

Another possible sex-rejuvenating property contained in fenugreek is *trimethylamine.* Scientific studies show that it acts as a sex hormone in frogs, causing them to prepare for mating.

How Fenugreek Seeds Are Used

The Chinese advise that fenugreek seeds be used daily in powdered form, adding the powder to soups, broths, vegetable or fruit juices, or sprinkling it over foods. Fenugreek seeds are also available in tablets which may be used instead of the powder. From eight to ten tablets are taken daily.

The Chinese point out that individual needs should be considered. Some people find the powder works best, while others find they get better results by using the tablets.

INN SAI

English Name: Parsley
Botanical Name: *Apium petroselinum*

The Chinese claim that parsley tea has proven helpful in relieving some cases of prostate pressure. The tea is prepared and used according to the same directions as those given for parsley in the previous chapter on urinary disorders.

The reputation of parsley as a valuable herb for urinary ailments and prostate trouble is not held by the Chinese alone. The use of the tea as a remedy for such disorders is widespread and well known in many parts of the world. For example, Mr. R.B. wrote:

"A year ago I met a doctor who took a trip to the Netherlands. There he discovered what the people use for all urinary tract troubles. Would you believe it? It is the lowly plant called parsley, taken two or three times a day, steeped as a tea, quite strong. The doctor came back and started to recommend it to his patients.

"Ever since I started to take parsley I got relief, both from bladder irritation and prostate pressure. Now, after over a year, I feel so grateful I want to pass the information on to others who suffer as I did."

Another example is that reported by Cyril Scott, popular British author of several books and articles on natural healing. He mentions the use of parsley by a man in his sixties:

"This person was in great distress because he was unable to pass water. The doctor was called in, and a catheter had to be used several times. The doctor told him he was suffering from prostate trouble and would have to undergo an operation. But it was then discovered that he had sugar in his urine, and it would be dangerous to operate while the diabetes condition was present. In consequence, injections of insulin were given. Finally, the patient's osteopath advised him to try parsley tea. The result was astonishing!"

Scott goes on to say that the patient could urinate freely. He adds, "After he first drank the parsley tea, a lot of offensive substance came away in his urine. But the latter soon became normal, and the erstwhile patient is now in fine fettle, and able to play his rounds of golf with enjoyment. There is no more thought of an operation."

CH'E-CH'IEN

English Name: Plantain
Botanical Name: *Plantago major*

Plantain is a familiar perennial "weed" in China and other lands and may be found anywhere along roadsides and meadows. The botanical name is derived from *planta,* a foot, and *ago* a wort, in allusion to the shape of the broad leaves as they lay on the ground.

Medicinally, plantain has a very ancient reputation in China and is given as a tea for general debility, spermatorrhea, and sexual asthenia (loss of sex power). It is also said to promote fertility.

Among its many constituents, plantain provides a considerable quantity of potassium. According to nutritionalists, this mineral is very important to the health of the body. A lack of it may cause varied conditions such as a weak heart, dropsy, enlarged glands (such as the prostate), upset stomach, or swollen testicle.

As a tea plantain is generally combined with other substances, such as flaxseed *(Linum usitatissimum),* for example. To prepare the formula, 1 ounce of plantain seeds are boiled in 1 ½ pints of water down to one pint, then strained. One ounce of flaxseed is placed in a container, and a pint of piping hot water is added. The brew is covered with a lid and allowed to stand for one-half hour, then strained. (If too thick, dilute with a little water.)

When ready, the two teas are mixed together in one container and three or four cups are taken daily. The tea may be reheated and taken warm or hot. (Flaxseed contains the valuable vitamin F, a nutrient important to the health of the prostate.)

YEN-MAI

English Name: Oats
Botanical Name: *Avena sativa*

The medicinal action of oats is that of a stimulant, nerve-cell nutrient, and nerve tonic. They are considered valuable as a remedy for strengthening and restoring nerve force to the entire system, with a specific beneficial effect on the generative system. They are used in conditions of spermatorrhea, nervous debility of convalescense, nervous exhaustion, and general neurasthenia. They are rated an effective agent in conditions of impotence or sexual debility due to over-indulgence since they are said to produce a tonic effect on the nerve structure of the sexual organs. They are employed for prostatic irritation.

How Oats Are Used

Fifteen drops of the fluid extract of oats are added to a small glass of water and taken three times a day, between meals. If the extract is taken in hot water, the action is said to be faster; if it is taken in cold water, it reputedly has a more extended influence.

For prostatic irritation or early signs of prostate trouble, oats are prepared as a tea in combination with black willow bark *(Salix nigra)* and celery seeds. One ounce each of oats and black willow bark are placed in a container, and 2 ½ pints of water are added. This is brought to a boil and simmered slowly for 15 minutes. It is then strained, and the hot tea is poured over 1 ounce of celery seeds. The container is covered, and the brew is allowed to stand until cold and then strained. One teacupful is taken three or four times daily.

HU-LU

English Name: Pumpkin
Botanical Name: *Cucurbita maxima*

Pumpkin seeds have been used for their beneficial effects on the prostate gland. This is an age-old folk remedy which has been handed down from one generation to another.

Dr. W. Devrient of Berlin has taken an interest in the use of pumpkin seeds for treating prostate gland disorders. In an article titled "Androgen Hormonal Curative Influence of a Neglected Plant," he says:

> There is a disease-preventative plant, little noticed until now, whose rejuvenating powers for men are extolled with praise by popular medicine both in America and in Europe. Experience reveals that men in those countries where the seeds of this plant are copiously eaten throughout a lifetime remain amazingly free of prostatic hypertrophy [prostate trouble] and all its consequences.

Dr. Devrient reports that:

> Investigations by G. Klein at the Vienna University revealed the noteworthy fact that in Transylvania, prostatic hypertrophy is almost unknown. Painstaking researches result in the disclosure that the people there have a special liking for pumpkin seeds. A physician from the Szekler group in the Transylvanian mountains confirmed this connection as an ancient healing method among the people. Dr. Bela Pater, of Klausenburg, later published these associations and his own experience in the journal *Healing and Seasoning Plants*.

In conclusion, Dr. Devrient writes:

> My assertion of the androgen-hormonal (the male hormone) influence of pumpkin seeds is based on the positive judgment of old-time doctors, but also no less on my own personal observations throughtout the years. This plant has scientifically determined effects on ontermediary metabolism and diuresis (urination), but these latter are of secondary importance in relation to its regenerative, invigorative, and vitalizing influences. There is involved herein a native plant hormone which affects our own hormone production in part by substitution, in part by direct proliferation.
>
> Anyone who has studied this influence among peasant peoples has been again and again astonished over the effect of this plant in putting off the advent of old age. My own personal observations in the course of the last eight years, however, have been decisive for me. At my own age of 70 years I am well able to be satisfied with the condition of my own prostate, on the basis of daily ingestion of pumpkin seeds, and with that of my health in general. This beneficial result can also be found among city patients, who are prudent enough to eat pumpkin seeds every day and throughout life. But one must continue proving this to the city dweller. The peasants of the Balkans and of Eastern Europe know of the healing effects of these seeds already from their forefathers.

Valuable Nutrients in Pumpkin Seeds

Pumpkin seeds contain an abundance of valuable nutrients and are one of the richest natural sources of the mineral zinc. Chemical analyses of the healthy prostate gland and of spermatozoa (the male "living seed") show very high concentrations of zinc; whereas, the amount of zinc found in the sick prostate is low. So it seems likely that this mineral is extremely important to the health of the reproductive system. Studies reported by Dr. Meyer show that in certain lands or regions where there is a widespread deficiency of zinc, the sex organs do not develop properly. Describing a group near Cairo, Egypt, Dr. Meyer wrote: "Their external genitals were remarkably small with both atrophic testes and small penises; and they had no facial, pubic, or axillary hair..."

HAI-TSAO

English Name: Seaweed
Botanical Name: *Algae*

Seaweeds are known under the collective name of algae. Over 435 varieties have been discovered and these are generally grouped into three kinds, depending on color—the brown, the red, and the green

One of the most commonly known of the brown seaweeds is kelp *(Fucus vesiculosis)* which is also called bladderwrack. These are long whip-shaped plants which range from 5 to 10 feet in length (along the Atlantic Coast) to the giant kelp of the Pacific which reach a length of several hundred feet. In the Southern hemisphere these plants form submarine forests of enormous size.

Professional guides in the land of Tibet always carry a small supply of kelp with them. When ascending to heights at which the air becomes rarefied causing difficult breathing and labored straining of the leg muscles they take a pinch of dried kelp and reportedly feel a burst of new energy.

Seaweed as Food and Medicine

The use of seaweed as food and medicine is not new. Shen-ung wrote of their value as early as 3000 B.C. During the time of Confucius a poem about a housewife cooking seaweed appeared in *The Chinese Book of Poetry* written between 800 and 600 B.C. In that era, seaweed was regarded as such an exquisite delicacy that it was offered as a sacrificial food for the gods. In the *Pen Tsao Kang Mu,* published in China in the sixteenth century, algae is recommended for the treatment of goiter.

The ancient empire of Japan has also known of the value of seaweeds for a very long time and the harvesting of marine crops is a thriving industry in that country today. The people of Japan refer to seaweed as "Heaven Grass," so great is their regard for its nutritional and remedial value. Diving girls (ama) of coastal villages probe marine gardens of offshore lagoons, where the algae used for food and medicine abounds. These young women are graceful, hardy divers with superb figures and have become a proud Japanese tradition.

Remedial Use of Kelp

Kelp contains an abundance of vitamins, minerals, and trace elements. Because of its rich content of iodine, kelp is well-known in many lands as a remedy for preventing or treating goiter. However, some practitioners have reportedly found it to be helpful in normalizing a weak or enlarged prostate gland, and certain other male disorders. For example, Dr. Eric Powell of England says:

> The action of kelp on the prostate is to improve the nutrition of the organ and the circulation of the blood through the tissues. 'The blood is the life' and, in common with all other organs, the health of the prostate depends on the normal circulation of chemically balanced blood through its substance. Again I say that the value of kelp in this connection has been proven by the excellent results obtained; but it is necessary to take the food-remedy for some time, and also wise to keep it up.

A man in my district was saved a nasty opration by taking kelp, and he was nearly 70 years of age when he came to me!

Dr. Powell states further:

> For hardening of the testicles and simple impotence this remedy (kelp) may be expected to produce good results if persisted with. It does not overstimulate and cannot harm. No doubt the value lies in the improved local circulation of blood rich in cell salts.
>
> I recall one case of a man with very painful testicles. Kelp removed the pain in a surprisingly short time. Cases of impotent men have been given kelp treatment with varying degrees of satisfaction, but it must be remembered that the causes of impotency are complex and often include the psychological side; so too much must not be expected of kelp or any other remedy in the treatment of this kind of trouble.

HSÜN-TS'AO

English Names: Melilot, Honey Lotus
Botanical Name: *Melilotus arvenses*

This fragrant plant can be found growing in many countries of the world as it has great adaptability to a wide variety of climates and soils. It grows abundantly in the Yangtse provinces of China, and the Chinese use it as a medicine, and burn it as incense. It is also employed in cosmetics.

Used as a tea, the herb is said to be a helpful organ remedy for the penis, when there is weakness of tone, and partial impotence. It is prepared like ordinary tea and one cup taken three times a day.

POLLEN

Honey bee pollen has long been valued in the Orient as a remedy for prostate trouble and other ailments that affect the human male. Today a growing number of medical reports from many different countries of the world are vindicating these Chinese claims for pollen.

Dr. Ask-Upmark of Sweden reported on a case of prostate infection that he had been unable to completely cure in five years of orthodox treatment. One day the patient decided on his own initiative to take pollen tablets as he felt he needed something to strengthen his general condition. He took six tablets daily, and Dr. Ask-Upmark says the improvement was like a miracle. The patient had only one recurrence of the trouble, and that was due to the fact that he neglected to take the pollen tablets for two weeks. Once he began taking the tablets every day again, he experienced no further prostate trouble.

Later, Dr. Ask-Upmark treated 12 cases of inflammation of the prostate gland with a dosage of five to six pollen tablets daily, taken first thing in the morning. Ten of the 12 patients showed remarkable improvement. Of the two cases that did not, one was due to another medical complication. The other enjoyed the sport of salmon fishing and would go wading up to his knees in very cold rivers. Dr. Ask-Upmark believed this wading practice aggravated the prostate condition, and since the patient would not give it up, the pollen treatment was ended.

Dr. L.J. Denis, a urologist in Antwerp, Belgium, selected ten patients who suffered prostatitis but in whom no evidence of infection was detected. They all experienced discomfort when urinating, and four had pain in one of the testicles, groin, or perineum, and three complained of loss of sexual desire. The ten patients were treated with four pollen extract tablets daily. At the end of the treatment, the patients said they had improved and no longer complained of their symptoms.

Professor H. Palmstierna, Dr. Gösta Leander, and Professor Gösta Jonsson of Sweden reported on 179 cases of chronic prostate inflammation. Patients treated with a special pollen preparation, together with conventional treatment, gave 60 to 80% of the cases better results than with conventional treatment alone. Over the years their studies included over 1,100 cases with the same successful results.

Professor Heise of the Urological Clinic of Magdeburg treated nine prostate patients with pollen extract, one tablet three times a day. All had similar symptoms; e.g., lowered libido, difficulty in urinating, painful orgasms, bacterially positive emissions, difficulty during coitus, and some showed manifestations of impotence. Dr. Heise reported that when the course of treatment had ended, all the patients had responded with definite improvement. He concluded that it would be commendable if treatment with pollen preparations were to be incorporated into recommended therapeutic practice.

Pollen and Royal Jelly

Professor Izet Osmanagic, head of the Gynecological Department at the University of Sarajevo, reported the result of his trials with a strong blend of pollen and royal jelly on 40 men, aged 20 to 52. He found that 75% of the men suffered from poor sperm production and partial impotence. All the patients had had sterile marriages for two or more years.

The patients took two capsules of the pollen blend daily and when the course of two or three months of treatment ended, each had taken a total of either 80 or 120 capsules.

After one month, more than half of the patients had improved in their sexual and general condition, and the majority showed improvement of sperm production. Two of the men were happy to announce that their wives were pregnant.

Summary

1. According to reliable medical estimates, prostate trouble is a rather common occurrence in men as they grow older.
2. Trouble with the prostate can take the form of painful infection, inflammation (prostatitis), or enlargement of the prostate.
3. One of the earliest signs of an ailing prostate is difficulty in urinating. If the prostate continues to enlarge, complete stoppage of urine may result, and the use of a catheter for withdrawal of the urine will be required.
4. Retention of urine may be caused by disorders other than enlarged prostate. Cystitis, for example, can cause difficulty in urinating, often becoming so severe that a catheter must be employed.
5. A simple home-test explained by a medical doctor can help determine whether a condition is prostate infection or urethritis (inflammation of the urethra).
6. Prostatitis can occur in acute form and as a chronic disease. Although the local symptoms are most simply described as those of cystitis, inflammation of the prostate has certain typical features.
7. The Chinese have a number of herb remedies from which to choose for treating various ailments and sexual inadequacies that can effect members of the male sex.
8. The Chinese herbs and herb products cited in this chapter as being helpful in conditions of impotence and sexual debility do not stimulate the organs into unnatural activity, but work by providing the nutrients needed to restore normal, healthy functioning.

9

BUILDING FEMALE HEALTH WITH CHINESE HERBS

There are a number of different ailments—for example, vaginal irritation and discharge, menstrual difficulties, vomiting during pregnancy, and so on—that can affect the human female. In addition, the stress of menopause can leave a woman prone to a swarm of insidious symptoms, such as hot flashes, a kind of rheumatism known as "menopausal arthritis," or that dismal depression popularly called "menopausal melancholia."

The change-of-life also means change in the thyroid gland and the sex glands. Puffiness of the face, a little gain in weight, dry skin, falling hair, and slow pulse can indicate that the thyroid especially is finding it a little rough going. Domestic stress does not help matters, and the woman of the house finds it increasingly difficult to check the tide of irritability, at an age when the children are sufficiently grown to be especially critical. The busy housewife going through the menopause cannot always be sparkling and cheerful.

Oriental Health Wisdom for American Women

Chinese girls are taught early in life about the value of specific herbs, for the female body. And they are also taught a few words of warning passed down from generation to generation about the adverse effects of anything cold on the female system.

As one prominent Chinese herbalist explains:

"You will find many American girls in their twenties with arthritis already all through their bodies. I will tell you what the cause of that is—American people don't know how to take care of themselves, especially in the case of women and girls. When they have their monthly period, they eat and drink all kinds of ice cold things, take cold showers, and go swimming and skiing. All of the coldness gets into the body. That's one thing. All right, there's another thing—the American girls wash their hair and go to bed with the head damp or put their hair up in wet curls just at bedtime. Again, the cold goes into their body. They don't start suffering from the effects of this repeated practice until they are older, maybe twenty-five, usually thirty or thirty-five years old.

"And when they have a baby, a few days later they are up running around in the cold, rainy weather. Now, when a woman in China gives birth to a baby she stays inside the house for sixty days, drinks special broths to strengthen her body, eats and drinks everything warm—no cold drinks at all. It is our way of what you Americans call 'preventive medicine.'"

CHINESE HERBS FOR FEMALE DISORDERS

To improve female health the natural way, let us consider some of the Chinese herb remedies that have been developed over the centuries.

DONG QUAI

English Name: No equivalent.
Botanical Name: *Angelica polymorpha*

In different parts of China, according to the variations of dialect, this Oriental plant is either called Dong Quai or Tang Kuei. Botanically the herb is known as *Angelica polymorpha*, but is often mistaken by Westerners as either common angelica *(Angelica archangelica)* or Lovage *(Lisgusticum)*.

The root is the part of the Dong Quai plant that is used in Chinese medicine. The roots occur in different shapes and colors, generally whitish-grey or yellowish-grey, or, in the case of old roots, an odd dark color. Some roots have only a few rootlets. Others have a fat body with many rootlets, but these are considered to be of poor quality. Some roots are processed and squashed flat like a leaf, while others are sold in bundles like asparagus.

The best quality of Chinese Dong Quai root has a strong pungent aroma and taste, whereas weaker qualities have a faint odor and taste. It is said that Korean Dong Quai is very mild and consequently can be taken more often during the day.

Only the hips of the root, up to the head, are in general use. The upper half is considered a great blood builder; the tails of the roots are employed under the direction of Chinese herbalists for emergency purposes only, to dissolve blood clots resulting from serious accidents and for expelling afterbirth that has failed to appear. A liniment prepared with the tails mixed with other herbs and steeped in Chinese wine is used as an external application for removing the discoloration of black and blue marks.

Boon to Women

Dong Quai root is famed in Chinese medicine for its affinity for the female constitution. It is highly valued as a remedy for building blood, nourishing the female glands, regulating monthly periods, and correcting menopausal symptoms, including hot flashes and spasms of the vagina. It is also used in anemic conditions in mothers after childbirth but is never given to women during pregnancy. Dong Quai has been found to bring relief in a number of cases of menopausal rheumatism. It has also proven very helpful in amenorrhea (stoppage of normal monthly periods, scanty periods) and deficient secretion of uterine mucosa.

How Dong Quai Is Used

Capsules containing Dong Quai in powdered form, prepared only from the hips and head of the roots, are available. The capsules may be swallowed with a glass of warm water or broken open and the contents added to hot soups or broths. Since its taste somewhat resembles that of celery, it adds to, rather than detracts from, the flavor of various food dishes. Chinese herbalists advise that for best results, little or no fruit should be eaten while you take Dong Quai, nor should any other strong root teas, such as ginseng for example, be taken for two or three hours after. Vegetables should be included in the diet; however, since many vegetables are very Yin (weak), a slice of ginger root (Yang) should be cooked with them to restore proper balance.

Reported Cases

• "I am a woman thirty years of age and run my own mail order business. For a long time I had been suffering from chronic female tiredness and low energy. One day I bought a bottle of Chinese Dong Quai capsules in a health food store, and after taking them for a few days I noticed a decided pickup in energy. I could do a whole day's work without fatigue. I take Dong Quai faithfully because I feel it is a valuable food product which supplies some nutrients and vital elements otherwise missing from my diet."—Mrs. J.W.

• "Let me tell you the good which Chinese Dong Quai has done for me. I used to suffer terrible cramps the first day of my monthly period and couldn't be on my feet, but just had to sit around all day with a hot water bottle on my abdomen. Dong Quai capsules completely relieved me of these terrible cramping miseries, and I feel like a normal human being again."—Miss C.G.

• "I took estrogen for three years for my 'change of life,' but after using Chinese Dong Quai for a few months I no longer needed the estrogen."—Mrs. B.C.

• "Chinese Dong Quai is a superb remedy for retarded menstruation."—Miss L.T.

• "My daughter suffered from menstrual irregularity accompanied by cramps and headaches. Her social life was necessarily restricted during her monthly periods, and this caused her to become very depressed. After taking Chinese Dong Quai capsules, her periods became pain-free, and she is her cheerful, active self again, month in and month out."—Mrs. B.R.

• "I hope many more women will benefit from the use of Chinese Dong Quai as I have. For over two years I suffered the misery and inconvenience of severe menstrual cramps and premenstrual tension. Since taking Dong Quai, my last three periods have been normal and my emotions more balanced. You cannot imagine what a blessed relief this has been for me."—P.J.

• "In my opinion hot flashes have upset more women's lives than bad marriages. I found the condition not only miserable to endure, but terribly embarrassing as well. One night while sitting at a table in a fine restaurant with a gentleman, my face suddenly became so flushed, I had to fan myself with the menu! I felt like crawling under the table! The hot flashes happened many other times too, around other people, with everyone pretending not to notice.

"My doctor recommended estrogen, but I heard it can cause side effects so I refused it.

"One day I came across an article on Chinese herbs and read where Dong Quai was used for symptoms of the menopause, and other female problems, so I decided to try it.

"When I bought two bottles of the capsules at a Chinese herb shop, I was assured they were safe, effective, and had no side effects. I was also told that nature works slowly, so the results would be gradual. Two capsules were to be taken three times a day.

"Within a few weeks of using the remedy, the hot flashes became less severe and less frequent. Encouraged by these results, I bought another supply of the capsules and continued taking them. Finally the hot flashes were a thing of the past, and I could hardly believe it! I will always be very grateful to the Chinese for this remarkable herb remedy."—M.V.

FU-P'EN-TZU

English Name: Red Raspberry
Botanical Name: *Rubus strigosus*

The common raspberry grows in many parts of the world, including the uplands of the central and western provinces of China. Its Chinese name, Fu-p'en-tzu, means "a turned-over bowl," in reference to the shape of the fruit. A number of other names are given, some of which apparently refer to the foreign origin of the plant.

In Chinese medicine a tea prepared from raspberry leaves is recommended as a female tonic and restorative. It is employed to help prevent miscarriage, to relieve the severe labor pains of childbirth, and to treat urethral irritation and menstrual difficulties. One cup of the tea, prepared as an ordinary tea, is taken three or four times a day for profuse or painful menstruation and for urethral irritation.

To ease the pains of childbirth and to help prevent miscarriage, 1 ounce of dried raspberry leaves is placed in a porcelain container, and one pint of boiling water is poured over. The tea is covered with a lid

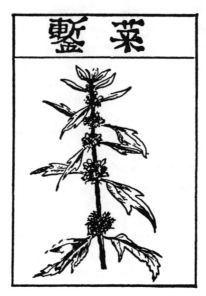

TSAN-TS'AI
(Motherwort)

FU-P'EN-TZU
(Red Raspberry)

MA-PIEN-TS'AO
(Vervain)

and allowed to stand until cold, then strained and reheated. One small cupful is taken half an hour before each meal.

Modern Support of the Ancient Chinese Claims

• Dr. Kirschner states:

"Herbalists have long prescribed raspberry leaf tea during pregnancy. Medical men laughed at this 'superstition.' Then came the confession by a woman physician, Violet Russel, M.D., who wrote in the London medical journal *Lancet*: 'Somewhat shamefacedly, I have encouraged expectant mothers to drink this infusion. In a good many cases labor has been easy and free of muscular spasms.'"

Dr. Kirschner gives these instructions: "During confinement, a pint of raspberry leaf tea is taken daily. Ordinary dosage is 10 to 20 ounces of the hot tea made from an ounce of the dried leaves steeped in 20 ounces of boiled water. Sweeten with honey."[1]

• *Potter's New Cyclopaedia of Botanical Drugs* cites the following: "Dr. Thompson and Dr. Coffin recommended the drinking of raspberry leaf tea by pregnant females for giving strength and rendering parturition easy and speedy. It should be taken freely before and during confinement."[2]

• In reference to the use of raspberry leaf tea, Dr. Fox wrote: "It is an excellent remedy in painful and profuse menstruation and to regulate the labor pains of women in childbirth. A teacupful of strong red raspberry leaf tea, in which the juice of an orange has been pressed, taken three times a day during the last months of pregnancy, will render labor easy when the hour of parturition has arrived."

• The following information appears in a Canadian book on herbs:

Red Raspberry Leaves: A good source of vitamins A, B, C, G, and E. They are rich in calcium, phosphorus, iron, and an unknown factor that prevents miscarriage. I know of several cases where this was proved beyond a doubt. A woman had four miscarriages, and despaired of ever bearing a child. Several doctors told her that she could never become a mother. On advice given by close members of my family, she took to drinking

---

[1]*Nature's Healing Grasses*, p. 97.

[2]Wren, R.C., *Potter's New Cyclopaedia of Botanical Drugs* (London: Sir Isaac Putman & Sons, Ltd. 1956), p. 193.

raspberry leaf tea every morning during pregnancy. She gave birth to a lovely girl, and in 18 months she had another. The labor in both cases was practically painless.[3]

• J.H. Oliver, a medical herbalist of England, wrote: "A lady doctor who had been practicing for many years in a maternity home, and had helped thousands of babies into the world, told us she had always insisted on the prospective mothers taking raspberry leaf tea, and she scorned the idea of ever losing a case. Since we started this campaign we have received scores of letters from grateful parents. One lady told us she was reading the paper only a few minutes before her baby was born."

• The following interesting account appeared in a health publication:

> A number of people find it difficult to relax when nervous or in pain, women particularly, especially during childbirth. The birth of my own first child was prolonged and frightening, mainly due to my fear and inability to relax the necessary muscles.
>
> Three years later, when I was pregnant again, I dreaded the coming ordeal. I had not, as yet, discovered the benefits of herbs. One day I was admiring a sow and litter with a neighboring farmer and remarked on the dreadfulness of producing such a large family. He laughed and told me that he always gave his sows an herbal remedy of raspberry leaf tea to help them when farrowing, and also thought that many ladies could benefit from the same herb.
>
> I was willing to try anything to allay my fears, and purchased a packet of raspberry leaf tea from a local herbalist. At first I did not care for its unusual flavor but in no time I grew accustomed to it, and schooled myself to take it regularly. The months passed and the day came when I knew my baby would soon arrive. I was filled with an apprehension, which I soon found was quite unnecessary. My fears vanished when I found myself responding quite involuntarily to the muscular contractions with very little discomfort, and was amazed when the baby came into the world with such ease. My crowning achievement was a lovely little daughter whose quick arrival forestalled a surprised doctor who remembered my last drawn out ordeal.
>
> The practical experience with herbal treatment has strengthened my belief in the potential cures that are obtained from herbs. I have since learned that Dr. Grantley Dick Read advocated the use

---

[3]James, Claudia V., *Herbs and the Fountain of Youth* (Edmonton, Alberta, Canada: Amrita Books, 1959), p. 68.

of raspberry leaf tea as an aid to easier childbirth in some of his studies of natural childbirth.

So the farmer's recommendation proved successful; only someone who has suffered pain because of unrelaxed muscles can know the advantage of discovering a reliable source of help, and a simple one, too.

I am fully convinced that I found such a remedy in raspberry leaf tea, and by taking it regularly throughout the latter months of pregnancy ensured myself of an easier birth.[4]

Fragarine

It is interesting to learn that during World War II the drug *fragarine* was discovered by obstetricians for use in allaying severe pains of childbirth. Fragarine is the active principle extracted from raspberry leaves and appears to relax the uterine muscles. It was reported, however, that midwives ignored the new drug and continued to brew raspberry leaf tea for their patients.

Other Raspberry Leaf Formulas for Female Disorders

1. To relieve menopausal or menstrual "nerves," 1 ounce each of dried raspberry leaves and dried lime flowers *(Tilia europoea)* are mixed together. One teaspoonful of the combined herbs is placed in a cup, and boiling water is added. The cup is covered with a saucer, and the tea is allowed to steep for five minutes and then strained. One cup is taken three times daily.

2. For the condition of leucorrhea (a distressing complaint consisting of a whitish or creamy discharge from the mucus glands of the uterus) the following herbal formula is used. One ounce each of the *fluid extract or tincture* of raspberry leaves, gentian root *(Gentiana lutea)*, comfrey *(Symphytum officinalis)*, uva-ursi *(Arctostaphylos uva-ursi)*, golden seal *(Hydrastis canadensis)*, are mixed together in one bottle. One teaspoonful of the combined fluid extracts or tinctures is taken in a little water three times daily after meals.

Accessory Treatment. In addition to taking the above formula, the cleansing process of an herbal douche is used. A mixture of 1 ounce each of raspberry leaves, white oak bark, *(Quercus alba)*, witch hazel

---

[4]*Fitness*, January 1963.

leaves *(Hamamelis virginiana),* black currant leaves *(Ribes nigrum),* and cranesbill *(Geranium maculatum)* is boiled slowly in two quarts of water for 20 minutes and then strained through a cloth. The straining process should be continued until the liquid is perfectly clear, and when the solution is cooled to a tepid warm it is used as a douche.

When the tip of the douche bag is inserted, the lips of the female organ are held snugly together with the fingers around the base of the tip. The herbal solution is then allowed to flow in, and as it does so it opens and washes thoroughly all the deep folds and crevices. When a slight stretching sensation is experienced, the lips of the female organ should be released, allowing the herbal douche to flow back out again freely. As this occurs, the vagina returns to its natural folds again. This process is repeated several times, until the herbal solution has been used up. A fresh batch should be prepared and used every other night until the condition has cleared up. Some cases respond favorably after only one or two douches; others require longer treatments of a week or ten days and even longer. However, once the leucorrhea has stopped the douches should not be continued.

TSAN-TS'AI

English Name: Motherwort
Botanical Name: *Leonurus cardiaca*

This plant is native to the Far East and Europe, but has been naturalized in other lands. For centuries it has been valued by the Chinese as a remedy for various ailments, especially for weakness and disorders of the female, hence its common name of "motherwort." It reputedly has a good effect on the womb and tones and strengthens the uterine membranes and other female organs. It is used as a remedy for inflammation or irritation of the uterus and also for suppressed or retarded menses.

Motherwort is prepared as a tea. One pint of boiling water is poured over 1 ounce of the herb. The container is covered, and the tea is allowed to stand for one-half hour, then strained. One hot cupful is taken four times a day.

Combined Formula

For nervous disorders that are peculiarly female, such as menopausal "nerves" and irritability, ½ ounce each of motherwort, passiflora *(Passiflora incarnata)*, lady's slipper herb *(Cypripedium pubescens)*, and valerian *(Valeriana officinalis)* are mixed together and placed in a porcelain container. One quart of boiling water is poured over the mixture, the container is covered, and the brew is allowed to stand for 20 minutes and then strained. One cupful of the tea is taken four times daily.

T'AO

English Name: Peach
Botanical Name: *Prunus persica*

The peach is native to China, a fact which is shown by the Chinese character representing it, which is one of the few unchanged ancient characters. The wood of the tree was used in ancient times for fortune telling. This is indicated by the way the Chinese character is composed—the right hand part meaning "omen," and the left part meaning "wood."

In ancient folklore the flowers of the peach tree were believed to possess supernatural powers that could drive away demons of ill health. Slips of peach wood were used as charms against evil spirits. The slips were worn on the person, attached to the door of the home, or set around the rooms of the house.

Used in Chinese Medicine

Many different parts of the peach tree—such as the bark, leaves, flowers, and so on—are prized in Chinese medicine for treating various ailments. For example, a strong tea made from peach leaves is said to be a very good remedy for relieving or preventing morning sickness (vomiting during pregnancy). Two to four tablespoons of the tea are taken first thing in the morning, and the same dosage is continued, if necessary, every one or two hours, or oftener. It is said that in most cases the remedy acts very promptly to bring relief.

The tea may be prepared the night before. One pint of boiling water is poured over 1½ ounces of dried peach leaves. The container is covered with a lid, and the tea is allowed to stand until cold. It is then strained and stored overnight in the refrigerator. In the morning the tea is reheated and taken warm according to the dosages previously cited.

Other Remedies for Morning Sickness. Here are a few of the many other Chinese remedies that have proven helpful in allaying the morning sickness of pregnancy:

1. A cup of ginseng tea, made from an instant ginseng tea bag, is sipped slowly first thing in the morning. This may be repeated in an hour or so if necessary.
2. Some women have found relief by drinking a tea made by steeping two tablespoons of oats in a pint of boiling water. The container is covered, immediately removed from the burner, and allowed to stand for 20 minutes. It is then reheated, and one teacupful is sipped every one or two hours until results are obtained. This is regarded as a very fine formula.
3. In some cases, sipping a glass of lemon juice in water first thing in the morning has proven helpful.
4. One or two cups of tea made from the leaves or blossoms of the herb yarrow *(Achillea millefolium)* has been known to check the nausea of morning sickness within minutes. The tea is prepared in the usual way—1 ounce is placed in a container and one pint of boiling water added. The infusion is covered, immediately removed from the stove, allowed to stand for 15 minutes, and then strained.

CHIANG

English Name: Ginger
Botanical Name: *Zingiber officinalis*

Ginger is reputed to be of value in relieving suppressed or retarded menstruation. One-half ounce of the powdered root is stirred in one pint of boiling water. One cup of the hot tea is taken three or four times a day (the tea is sipped slowly)

Combined Formula

Ginger combined with other herbs is used for the relief of ovaritis, a condition fairly common among women. Symptoms generally include tenderness or pain on the lower side of the abdomen just above the groin. One or both sides may be affected.

Usually the pain begins two or three days before menstruation and persists through the menstrual period, then gradually ceases or suddenly stops when the period has ended. If the condition continues every month, it is chronic and can affect the general health.

As a remedy for ovaritis, ½ ounce of ginger root and 1 ounce each of motherwort, feverfew *(Chrysanthemum parthenium)*, and pleurisy root *(Asclepias tuberosa)* are mixed together and boiled slowly in one quart of water for 15 minutes. (Keep the container covered.) The decoction is then strained, and a half teacupful is taken warm every two hours during the day. As the condition improves, the dose is reduced to three times a day. The treatment should be continued (generally three or four months) until the periods are normal.

JENSHEN

English Name: Ginseng
Botanical Name: *Panax schinseng*

For leucorrhea, 1 ounce each of ginseng, black cohosh *(Cimicifuga racemosa)*, gentian *(Gentiana lutea)*, and golden seal *(Hydrastis canadensis)*, all in coarse powder, are mixed together and placed in one quart of brandy. The bottle is capped and shaken thoroughly for about one minute, then stored in a cool dry place for ten days. During this ten-day period the bottle is shaken every day for one or two minutes. After the ten days have elapsed, the herbal tincture is strained through a muslin cloth. If any sediment remains, the straining should be repeated until the liquid is clear. Filter papers may be used instead of the muslin, but the straining process will take much longer.

Dose: Two tablespoonfuls of the herbal tincture are taken in a little water three or four times a day.

Accessory Treatment. The same herbal douche is prepared and used according to the directions given in the information covering the herb raspberry.

HAI-TSAO

English Name: Seaweed
Botanical Name: *Algae*

Among its many uses by the Chinese, seaweed is prescribed for menstrual difficulties, and is also said to have a beneficial effect on the uterus. Some Western practitioners agree that seaweed is an effective remedy for treating various female problems. For example, Dr. Eric Powell refers to the use of kelp as follows:

"The organ which develops into the prostate gland in the male becomes the uterus in the female; hence, it is natural that we should find kelp to be a most useful agent for toning up a weak uterus. Of the ten vegetable remedies I employ for weakness of this organ, kelp is one of the best, especially when the sufferer is troubled with associated nervous disorders and depression.

"I also find that kelp tends to normalize the periods in weakly women, and does much to banish the depression sometimes associated with the appearance of the menses.

"For ovarian disorders, kelp does as much as it accomplishes for weakness of the uterus. Quite often the two troubles go together and what aids one organ directly affects the others.

"For ovarian pain, irregular menses, depression, and even in some cases of anemia, kelp will be found most helpful. The food-remedy should be taken for several weeks or months, and the normalizing process, although slow, is in harmony with natural law and usually produces satisfactory results in due course. There is good reason to believe that the constant use of kelp may prevent growths and ovarian cysts, but it is not held out as a cure for such conditions."

SHU-WEI-TS'AO

English Name: Sage
Botanical Name: *Salvia officinalis*

Sage is a perennial plant reaching about 2 feet in height, bearing blue flowers variegated with purple and white. The leaves are of a grayish-green color, sometimes tinged with purple or red. All parts of the herb have a strong aromatic odor and a warm, slightly bitter taste, due to a volatile oil contained in the tissues.

In former times, sage was regarded as a sacred herb of such magical healing powers that it was often referred to as *Salvia salvatrix* (Sage the Savior).

Remedial Use

Among its many uses as a domestic remedy, sage tea is employed for relieving menopausal symptoms. The tea is prepared as an infusion, 1 ounce of the dried herb placed in a container and one pint of boiling water poured on. The tea is allowed to stand for ten minutes, then strained. When cold, one to two cupfuls are taken each day, a mouthful at a time.

Case History. Mrs. J.B.L. writes:

"I thought I'd drop you a line to spread the news that I have tried sage tea with success for hot flashes. I put one teaspoon of sage in a cup of boiling water, let the tea stand for five or ten minutes, then strain it. I drink the tea cold, sip by sip, at night before bedtime.

"Another method I heard about is to drink two cups of the tea spread over the day.

"I told two of my lady friends, who are sisters, about the sage tea because both were complaining about the trouble they wre having with menopause. One refused to try the remedy at first because she said she didn't believe it would really work. But when she saw the good results her sister got, she began drinking the tea herself and had to admit that it surely did help."

MA-PIEN-TS'AO

English Name: Vervain
Botanical Name: *Verbena officinalis*

The "Holy Vervain" or verbena is not to be confused with the lemon-scented verbena of gardens. It is, rather, a common plant with no aroma which bears small purple flowers.

Vervain reputedly contains natural properties which strengthen the womb and its appendages. It is said to cleanse and tone the lining of the womb and uterus and to free certain obstructions that interfere with efficient liver functioning.

Chinese herbalists have been aware of how dilation of arteries of the brain, which results in torturous migraine headaches or chronic headaches, can sometimes be traced to uterine and ovarian derangement. Although any one of a number of other causes could be the culprit of migraine, in those cases in which certain female disorders are responsible the herb vervain has often proven helpful.

To prepare the tea, instant vervain tea bags may be used or a quart of boiling water may be poured into a porcelain bowl containing 2 ounces of vervain. The bowl is covered with a lid, and the tea is allowed to steep for ten minutes and then strained. The whole quart is taken in teacupful doses throughout the day.

Reported Uses

● Mrs. M.B., who suffered vicious attacks of migraine headaches, writes: "I had to lie in bed in complete darkness for two whole days, and whatever tablets I took made no difference whatever.

"But life had to go on, and if I got up before my time the sickness was intensified. My husband would have to stay at home away from work, but there was nothing he could do except be at hand, downstairs. He had to prepare his own meals. To me, food was impossible.

"I used to enjoy having friends at the house and joining social activities, but I dared not face it any longer. Some friends thought I was making a lot of fuss about nothing.

"It was only after six years of torture that I discovered the effective relief in a simple infusion of vervain *(Verbena officinalis)*, an herb popular as a health tonic on the continent and elsewhere, which can be obtained in small sachets sufficient to make a teacupful. I took several teacupsful daily."

CHINESE TRADITIONAL HERB COMBINATIONS

Chinese traditional herb therapy employs the following formulas for treating various female disorders. The herbs are carefully selected and balanced for maximum potency, and are available in capsule form.

Tang Kuei and Evodia Combination

Constituents: Tang kuei, evodia, ophiopogon, pinellia, cnidium, ginseng, cinnamon, gelatine, moutan, ginger, peony, licorice.

Uses: Menstrual irregularities, infertility, lack of vitality, body chills, leucorrhea, and menopausal disorders.

Gentian Combination

Constituents: Gentian, tang kuei, alisma, scute, rehmannia, akebia, plantago, gardenia, licorice.

Uses: Vaginitis, urethritis, leucorrhea, cystitis, and genital pruritis (external itching of the vagina), in women of strong constitution and good digestion.

Tang Kuei Eight Herbs Combination

Constituents: Tang kuei, cnidium, smilax, akebia, hoelen, lonicera, citrus, rhubarb.

Uses: Considered effective for women of a delicate constitution with subacute or chronic leucorrhea accompanied by moderate inflammation and congestion.

Bupleurum and Peony Combination

Constituents: Bupleurum, peony, tang kuei, white atractylodes, hoelen, licorice, moutan, gardenia, ginger, mentha.

Uses: Menopausal disorders and menstrual irregularities. Associated symptoms are headache, irritability, hot flashes, constipation, backache, and fatigue.

Tang Kuei, Evodia and Ginger Combination

Constituents: Tang kuei, evodia, ginger, cinnamon, asarum, jujube, licorice, akebia, peony.

Uses: Painful or difficult menstruation, with chills and poor circulation.

Cinnamon and Hoelen Combination

Constituents: Cinnamon, hoelen, moutan, persica, peony.

Uses: Ovaritis, (inflammation of the ovary), inflammation of the oviduct, leucorrhea, excessive or difficult menstruation. Used for women of a strong constitution.

Pinellia and Magnolia Combination

Constituents: Pinellia, magnolia bark, hoelen, perilla, ginger.
      Uses: Menopausal anxiety, depression, irritability, or other
            strong emotions.

Ginseng and Tang Kuei Ten Combination

Constituents: Ginseng, tang kuei, peony, atractylodes, hoelen,
            cnidium, rehmannia, astragalus, cinnamon, licorice.
      Uses: Fatigue, weakness, anemia, and persistent leucorrhea
            after childbirth or miscarriage.

Tang Kuei and Gelatine Combination

Constituents: Tang Kuei, gelatine, cnidium, peony root, artemisia,
            rehmannia, licorice.
      Uses: Anemia due to prolonged and profuse menstruation.

Summary

1. There are a number of different ailments that may affect the human
   female.
2. Menopause can leave a woman prone to a variety of unpleasant
   symptoms such as hot flashes, menopausal blues, and menopausal
   arthritis.
3. The change-of-life also means change of sex glands and thyroid
   gland.
4. Chinese girls are taught early in life the value of specific herbs to
   improve female health the natural way. They are also taught a few
   words of warning about the adverse effects of anything cold on the
   female system.
5. Dong Quai root has been famed for ages in Chinese medicine for its
   affinity for the female constitution.
6. Only the upper parts of Dong Quai, from the hip to the head of the
   root, are used as a domestic remedy.
7. For best results, little or no fruit should be eaten while you take
   Dong Quai, nor should any other type of strong root teas, such as
   ginseng, be taken for two or three hours after. Vegetables should be

included in the diet and should always be cooked with a slice of ginger root to maintain proper Yin-Yang balance.

8. There is a good variety of harmless Chinese herbs or herb formulas from which to choose for treating or relieving a wide range of female disorders.

10

CHINESE HERB REMEDIES
FOR BOWEL COMPLAINTS

Mrs. L.L. suffered from internal "piles," symptomized by rectal itching and burning, a dull aching sensation, and pain up inside the rectum, with occasional bleeding. The pain increased during a bowel movement and became intensified when there was constipation. She reported:

"Surgery was advised, but I dreaded the knife, so I began checking into different forms of natural healing methods. My search led me to a Chinese herbalist, who gave me a box of capsules containing the powdered root of an herb he called *Collinsonia*, which I understand is also commonly called 'stone root' herb."

"He explained that *Collinsonia* was one of the most highly valued Chinese herb remedies for piles. He went on to say that generally two capsules taken twice daily between meals until results are obtained are sufficient for most cases. But since my condition was a bit worse than average, he advised that I take two capsules three times a day between meals, and that as soon as definite improvement was noted, I should cut the dosage down to two capsules twice daily until cured. To immediately ease the rectal pain, burning, itching, and occasional bleeding until the healing treatment of *Collinsonia* could clear up the condition, he gave me a box of soothing herbal suppositories prepared from witch hazel and pilewort herb *(Ranunculus ficaria)*. A suppository was to be inserted night and morning and after each bowel movement.

"The herbalist also instructed that I keep my bowels open and suggested several helpful natural aids such as a baked apple or stewed prunes for breakfast. He cautioned me to avoid any fruit that had small seeds, such as figs, and also to avoid nuts since these things are not easy to digest and will often aggravate the condition of piles. However he added that nuts would be all right to eat provided they were finely ground and mixed with honey for use as a spread.

"Hygiene was also stressed. Coarse or scented toilet paper was not to be used. I was also instructed to bathe the anus with warm water after each bowel movement, dabbing dry with a soft towel set aside for this purpose.

"I followed all his instructions faithfully, and the results were just wonderful. Within several weeks, my condition was completely cured and has remained so from that time on (about two years). One unexpected and astonishing result was that the capsules of powdered *Collinsonia* root, in addition to curing my pile condition, also brought about marked improvement in the varicose veins in my legs!"

What Are Piles?

The word "piles" is the common name for the medical term *hemorrhoids*. It is a very annoying ailment which has plagued many people of all ages and either sex, although it is rare in the very young. The pain may range from simple discomfort to excruciating agony.

Medics inform us that piles are caused when the upward flow of blood through the rectal membrane is obstructed. Impeding the flow of blood up through the portal vein allows the remaining blood to congest in the veins of the rectum. If the condition continues, the walls of the veins lose their tone and become distended. This distension of blood vessels can be external, often causing the piles to protrude below the rectum. The condition of external piles can be seen and felt on the outer rim of the anus. The hemorrhoid can range in size from that of a small pea to that of a walnut. As much discomfort can often be experienced from a small external pile as from a large one.

The distension of blood vessels can be *internal* when the mucous membrane inside the rectum is the only part affected. With the condition of internal piles there is invariably a group of veins and arteries involved. The blood vessels are in a varicosed condition and are able to expand or contract according to the amount of blood which is congested in the rectum at any particular time.

If the internal pressure becomes great, the small veins of the rectal membrane can burst, causing a discharge of blood. This discharge relieves the congestion and brings prompt relief to the sufferer, but unfortunately such bleeding can sometimes be so frequent and profuse that the victim develops anemia. (Bowel movements may irritate the swollen veins of internal or external piles and also cause them to bleed at times.)

Many Causes

There are a number of different causes of obstruction of the upward flow of blood, which results in piles. One obvious cause is constipation. But this does not mean that costiveness must automatically lead to piles. If blood circulation in the rectum is strong and the walls of the rectal veins are firm and elastic, constipation will not lead to piles, unless there is also a circulatory obstruction in the vein abdominal flow. But if there is weakness in the rectum, the pressure of excrement contained there and in the lower part of the descending colon would tend to flatten the blood vessels by distending the membranes.

Examples of other causes are straining due to constipation or constant looseness of the bowels, improper diet, other rectal troubles, or constant straining to urinate as in conditions of cystitis. Another important and common cause of hemorrhoids is congestion of the liver. Pressure upon the big portal vein leading to the liver would cause any blood that could not force its way past the constricted part of the vein to be held back in the rectal veins, allowing them to fill up with congested blood to produce piles.

The Action of *Collinsonia* Root

In view of all the facts outlined regarding the causes of piles, we can understand why the Chinese value the *Collinsonia* root as one of their most important remedies for hemorrhoids when we compare the facts to the following information from Ellingwood's *Materia Medica and Therapeutics*:

> Physiological Action: *Collinsonia* stimulates the stomach.
> It is actively tonic in its influence upon the entire function of this

organ, and from this influence its beneficial action is exercised upon the *function of all vital organs. It is conspicuous in its ability to overcome relaxed and out-of-tone conditions of the walls of the veins. It has a direct influence upon atonic and dilated or otherwise impaired conditions of the veins and venous capillaries.* (Italics added.)

The action of *Collinsonia* root as pointed out by Ellingwood covers the basic cause of piles. The liver would benefit if the function of all the vital organs is improved, and most portal vein obstruction in the liver would be relieved. Regarding the action of the remedy upon the atonic and dilated veins, we find that *Collinsonia* identifies itself exactly with the condition the Chinese seek to cure.

Many Different Forms of Piles

In addition to *Collinsonia* root, the Chinese have a variety of other herb remedies for treating the early stages, and sometimes the advanced stages, of general homorrhoid conditions, some of which are covered in the following pages. However, there are many types of piles of a very complicated nature which are beyond the scope of this chapter and which should receive the personal attention of a physician or practicing Chinese medical herbalist. Some examples are piles with prolapse of the rectum, ulcerated piles or piles with ulcerated rectum, internal piles complicated by colitis, piles with fissures, and so on.

Constipation

Simply defined, constipation means that bowel action is irregular, occurring only at prolonged intervals, or that bowel evacuations are excessively hardened and difficult to pass.

Along with food wastes, the bowels discharge cellular debris of body tissues, living and dead bacteria, mucus, and so on. When retained for longer than the normal period in the bowels, this mass of decaying debris offers a habitat and breeding ground for many harmful germs. These heated, putrefying wastes cause bowel discomfort, repulsive breath, sour stomach, headache, and other distresses associated with constipation. Poisons generated by putrefying wastes become a potential hazard to linings of the intestines. A feeling of depression and of "being out-of-sorts" have been blamed on irregularity.

Kellogg was of the opinion that the problem of constipation and associated autointoxication (a condition resulting from absorption into the blood stream of toxic fecal waste products due to chronic constipation) are the causes of most human ailments.

After much study, Professor Metchnikoff, a Russian biologist and Nobel prize winner in physiology, concluded that many diseases which affect mankind are caused by toxic types of bacteria which propagate in the large intestine. He further maintained that such intoxication is one of the chief causes of old age, and that its prevention would not only help man avoid many illnesses, but would also help preserve youth and prolong life beyond the so-called normal span.

"Bathroom Straining." Severe and repeated straining to move hard dry feces may cause fissures and/or piles. Straining at stool, of sufficient intensity and duration, also puts abnormal strain on the heart and threatens the life of any heart patient. According to a paper delivered to a symposium by Dr. Norman Shaftel, even people who have no signs of a heart problem can also dangerously overburden their hearts when straining to move the bowels.

Dr. Shaftel reported that tests showed that straining produced important changes in blood pressure, heart rate, and electrocardiograph patterns in people with no previous history of heart disorder. He said that such changes very closely resemble those which are observed in known heart patients.

Dr. Shaftel strongly recommended that physicians take every precaution to make sure their heart patients do not become constipated. Although he was unable to state just how frequently death had resulted from strained defecation, he did say, "It is not rare."

Writing in the *Journal of the American Medical Association* (September, 1961) Paul M. Zoll, M.D. points out that due to the increase in pressure within the thoracic and abdominal cavity while straining, "a diverticulum of the bowel, or an aneurysm of a major blood vessel of the left ventricle might rupture." He also warns that straining can bring on angina or "prolonged cardiac pain in a patient with extensive coronary disease."

Regularity—An Important Health Measure. Regular, normal bowel movements are important to help keep you feeling youthful and healthy. However, according to some authorities the "laxative habit" does more harm than good because the use of laxatives or cathartics (when taken in large enough doses to relieve stubborn constipation) irritates delicate intestinal membranes and interferes with digestion and absorption. In addition, laxatives may also cause cramps, diarrhea, and fluid depletion. Chinese herbalists agree with these views, and, although they readily admit that even concentrations of certain botanicals such as *senna* and other strong, stimulant type herbal laxatives are undesirable, they are quick to point out that the plant kingdom provides certain specific herbs and a large variety of natural foods that are not actually laxatives, but are *normalizers* and *regulators* of bowel function. They explain, for instance, that it is easier for the bowels to move if you include with your meals foods that contain roughage or bulk. Some examples are brown rice, oatmeal, buckwheat, unprocessed bran, and fruits and vegetables such as spinach, prunes, avocados, pumpkins, papayas, very ripe bananas, baked apples, and so on. By consuming ample portions of such foods and/or using one of a number of select Chinese herb teas, constipation can be overcome the natural way.

Exercise is also stressed. It is well known that people who spend any time in a hospital bed are frequently constipated, due to lack of exercise. Another of many examples is that of people who take long-distance vacation trips, driving steadily in their cars for hours at a time, day after day. Such people often complain of experiencing irregularity during their travels.

Daily exercise—such as a brisk walk, working in your garden, or riding a bicycle—is important to the maintenance of normal bowel activity.

Ample fluid intake is also important—at least six glasses of water should be taken a day, in addition to the liquids you normally consume with your meals. This would amount to well over one quart daily. The Chinese point out that when you do not drink enough fluid, the stool becomes dry, hard, and difficult to pass.

Diarrhea

Diarrhea is a condition of increased frequency and loose watery consistency of the stools. This can be a very serious and dangerous illness since it affects the mechanisms of the whole body. With diarrhea, the food does not remain long enough in the digestive tract to be absorbed. As a result, fats and carbohydrates are lost, and all the functions of these food elements in the body are not performed. All the work of calcium—which includes strengthening the bone and tooth structure, the heart, blood, and nerves—cannot be done since the calcium combines with the undigested fat and is carried away in diarrhea.

Prolonged diarrhea in infants and very young children can cause enough calcium loss to result in rickets; in adults it can cause bone softening. Loss of weight, poor appetite, and irritability are often due to the loss of calcium. Phosphorus, iron, potassium, many other valuable minerals, and the important fat-soluble vitamins A, D, K, and E are also sacrificed. And whenever there is a constant iron loss, anemia follows. A high incidence of respiratory ailments often occurs in patients suffering from diarrhea because their systems are depleted of vitamin A. (This vitamin is important in preventing infections and keeping the tissues healthy.)

In diarrhea cases blood sugar is also low, and the patient is left open to other physical disorders since blood sugar must be maintained at a certain level or exhaustion, weakness, allergies, blackouts, and other problems are likely to occur.

Dr. Carl L. Thenebe, a pediatrician, warns that when severe diarrhea strikes, body fluids, particularly the blood, become depleted of water. Demands are then made upon the cells of the body to make up the deficiency. When these cells become dry, a state of dehydration exists. When the body's water is lost there is, as previously stated, an outpouring of minerals or the electrolytes which are so essential to the life of the cell—calcium, phosphorus, iron, potassium, and so forth.

There are many causes of diarrhea. Dysentery, for example, is an inflammation of the large bowel and is symptomized by cramps, pain, and diarrhea. And there are many types of dysentery, each caused by a specific germ.

CHINESE HERB REMEDIES FOR BOWEL TROUBLES

Following is a list of natural Chinese remedies for coping with constipation, diarrhea, piles, and various other disorders of the bowels.

CHIN-CH'IAO-MAI

English Name: Yellow Dock
Botanical Name: *Rumex crispus*

Dock is the name applied to a wide variety of wayside plants such as Round-Leaved Dock, Water-Dock, and so on. They are found growing in ditches, meadows, and fields and are very common in China and other parts of the world. All docks are considered medicinally useful, but the species known as yellow dock *(Rumex crispus)* is the variety Chinese herbalists value most. This plant is easily recognized by its long, narrow leaves which have crisp, curled edges.

Nature's Aid for Irregularity

A tea made from yellow dock is said to be a gentle, natural aid for anyone troubled with constipation. The tea is not considered a laxative, but rather a normalizer and regulator of bowel function.

The root is the part of the herb used for making the tea. Although hard substances such as roots and barks are generally boiled continuously for a certain length of time in order to extract their active properties, delicate yellow dock root is an exception to this rule and must never be allowed to boil *continuously*. It is simply prepared by placing one teaspoonful of the cut roots in a cup and pouring on boiling water. The cup is covered with a saucer and allowed to stand for one-half hour. It is then strained, reheated, and taken hot. One cup of the tea is taken three or four times a day.

For the sake of convenience, a pint or quart of the tea may be prepared and one cupful at a time reheated for use during the day. One ounce of the cut roots is used to make one pint of the infusion; 2 ounces of the cut roots are used for one quart of the infusion. The cut roots are placed in a container. Using a separate container, bring one pint or one quart (as the case may be) of water to a boil and then pour it into the container which holds the cut roots. The tea is covered with a lid, allowed to stand for one-half hour, and then strained.

Individual Needs

The Chinese point out that the problem of constipation varies with different people, so that the amount of yellow dock tea taken daily depends upon individual needs. For example, some people may find that less than the average three or four cups daily is sufficient, whereas others may need more. The tea is perfectly harmless; it is a natural beverage. (Many people enjoy the bitter taste of yellow dock root tea, but for those who do not, the tea may be sweetened with honey.)

The Chinese also explains that with some people it may take a few days of drinking the tea daily before normal bowel function begins

HU
(White Oak)

CH'IN-CH'IAO-MAI
(Yellow Dock)

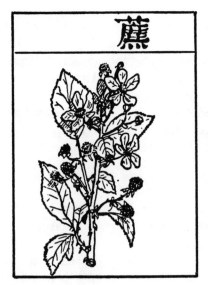

PIAO
(Blackberry)

SHU-KUA
(Papaya)

to take hold. Once it starts, irregularity is usually abolished from then on, so long as the tea is consumed daily thereafter. However, it is suggested that a daily enema should be used until the tea begins producing results. If the bowels still do not move after several days' use of the tea, some other natural remedy may be tried.

In very stubborn cases of constipation, the Chinese recommend that in addition to yellow dock root tea, breakfast should consist of a natural food that helps normalize bowel action, such as a baked apple or a dish of stewed prunes topped with slices of a very ripe banana. Again, individual needs are stressed. When you use a natural breakfast food, only one or two cups of the yellow dock tea may be necessary— or more of the tea may be required. The only way to find out which is best for your own particular needs is to adjust the program accordingly.

Capsule Form

Yellow dock root is also available in powdered form contained in gelatine capsules. Two of the capsules swallowed with a glass of warm water, are taken three times a day. This amount can be adjusted according to individual needs.

Reported Uses

• "I suffered from constipation, and at times my bowels would not move for three or four days. Finally I had to take laxatives. I tried all kinds, but it was always the same old story of griping pains, harshness, and the 'runs.'

"I was willing to try almost anything to get away from using laxatives, so when an acquaintance told me about a Chinese herb remedy called yellow dock tea, I decided to try it. The result was pure magic. I drink one cup of the hot tea first thing in the morning before breakfast and take three more cups during the day. I have done so for the past two years. Right from the second day on, I had regular bowel movements, just as normal as nature intended. There was no griping, looseness, or harshness. Anyone troubled with constipation should know about this Chinese herb tea. It really works beautifully."—C.R.

• "When it comes to regularity, my hat's off to yellow dock root tea. Four cups of the tea taken daily cured my long-standing constipation. I used to get relief only from laxatives or enemas, but that's all in the past now. So long as I drink the herb tea daily, I have good healthy bowel movements."—Mr. T.L.

• "I would like to relate my husband's experience with a Chinese herb tea named yellow dock tea. For over a year, my husband didn't have normal bowel movements and had to use either physics or enemas. Yellow dock tea was the answer to his problem. He took three cups of the tea the first day, and when there was no result by the next two days he increased it to five. That did the trick. He had a natural bowel movement and has continued to have them regularly (about eight months now). He drinks the tea faithfully. Another remarkable thing is that he says the tea does not cause watery stools...the bowel movements are very natural."—Mrs. R.W.

• "My father, who is 72 years old, was troubled with constipation. Although many different laxatives and pills prescribed by the doctor were tried, they didn't really do the job, so finally he had to rely mostly on enemas.

"Thanks to a friend, we heard about yellow dock root tea. My father drank three large cups of the hot tea daily, and on the third day he had a partial bowel movement. He increased the amount of tea, but for several days he still had only partial movements. Nevertheless, he was very encouraged by the results and began following the additional instructions for stubborn constipation cases. He ate a dish of stewed prunes with sliced ripe banana for breakfast and drank the tea during the day. He had a complete normal bowel movement the following day.

"We were all as surprised as he was when he told us about it. As time went on, he found that by eating the natural breakfast food he could cut the tea down to two cups a day and still maintain daily regularity. One time he omitted drinking the tea for a few days because he was curious to see if the breakfast food alone would give the same good results. But he found the best it could do was produce partial movements, so he went right back to including the tea again. The combination resulted in the same complete daily regularity as before and has done so now for three years."—Mrs. C.B.

• "I suffered from miserable constipation and had to strain so hard that I developed painful piles. I hated taking laxatives since they not only irritated the pile condition, but also gave me the "runs." So on those days when I felt I just had to take a physic, I wouldn't go out anywhere for fear I'd suddenly get an urgent call from nature and might not have enough time to make it to a women's restroom.

"One day, instead of taking laxatives I began drinking yellow dock tea. I started with four cups, then increased it to five. Three days later I had a normal bowel movement, not loose or runny, but soft and natural. And there was no sense of sudden urgency to dash to the bathroom, but just nature's gentle way of letting you know, so you'd have plenty of time to heed her call. I was absolutely delighted and found that so long as I drank the tea daily I'd get the same fine results. And since there was no need to strain and I quit using laxatives, my pile condition cleared up within two weeks! I have been drinking yellow dock tea every day for about a year and a half and have never been constipated in all that time."—Mrs. V.R.

• "For years I was troubled with constipation. Five months ago, I threw out all the laxatives and started drinking yellow dock tea daily, and the result has been regular bowel movements ever since."—Mr. S.C.

• "I have just finished my first bottle of yellow dock capsules and must say how pleased I am for the relief they have given me from stubborn constipation. I had tried yellow dock tea but found the taste too bitter, so I switched to the capsules."—C.B.

• "For those who are troubled with constipation, let me say they may be spared this miserable condition if they'll try yellow dock capsules as I did.

"For months I suffered from constipation which gave me dull, throbbing headaches, along with a bloated, uncomfortable feeling. The drugstore laxatives I tried caused terrible griping pains, and loose, runny bowel movements. Then one day my daughter who believes that nature's way is best, sent me a bottle of yellow dock capsules, and told me how to use them. Before long, my bowel movements became normal, and the capsules caused no griping pains whatsoever. How grateful I am to have learned of this gentle remedy. I feel just wonderful."—D.S.

HU

English Name: Common White Oak
Botanical Name: *Quercus alba*

There are more than 40 species of the genus *Quercus* distributed widely over China; however, the identification of Chinese names are somewhat confusing because many of the different characters may apply to the same species or be used in combination with each other or with other characters in different parts of the country.

The species we are considering here is known as the common white oak tree. The acorns cluster in ones and twos and are attached to the twigs by long stems, the leaves having barely any stalks at all.

The bark is the part of the oak used in Chinese medicine, and its action is cited as slightly tonic, strongly astringent, and antiseptic. It is considered a good remedy for diarrhea and dysentery. A decoction is made with 1 ounce of the bark and two pints of water, boiled down to one pint and strained. One cupful is taken every one or two hours until relief is felt.

Capsule Form. Some people have reported very good results in abolishing conditions of diarrhea or dysentery by using white oak bark in powdered form contained in gelatine capsules. Two capsules are swallowed with a glass of warm water three or four times a day.

TS'U

English Name: Vinegar

Other Chinese names for vinegar include Tso, Hsi, and K'uchin. In China, different types of vinegar are made from various natural substances, such as rice, wheat, apples, cherries, peaches, grapes, and certain other fruits.

Among its uses in Chinese medicine, apple cider vinegar is recommended as a wash for pruritus of the anus. This is a chronic condition of itching of the anus (the final 1 or 1½ inches of the rectum). The cause is usually of unknown origin, however, recent evidence has indicated that one of the possible causes is that some people are allergic to fresh or canned citrus juices, and if they are taken in other than very minute quantities, itching of the rectum (pruritus ani) results.

For best results, the vinegar is generally used full strength. However, it may be diluted with a little water. First the anal area is washed with clear water (no soap), then the area is thoroughly dabbed or bathed with a wad of cotton saturated with vinegar. (If the anus has been irritated by scratching, the vinegar will cause a temporary burning or smarting sensation.) The treatment is used once or twice a day until the condition is totally cleared up. Results are claimed to be very fast.

Reported Use

● Mrs. V.R. writes:

"For several months I suffered the unbearable itching of pruritus of the anus, with only mild and temporary relief from medical prescriptions. Then, by good fortune, I heard about a Chinese remedy of bathing the rectal area with vinegar. I soaked a large piece of cotton with ordinary vinegar and applied it to the rectum overnight. It brought complete relief, and there has been no further recurrence of the problem in over eight months. When I first applied the vinegar it smarted quite a bit, but the smarting lasted only for a few moments. It is still hard to believe how quickly this simple remedy worked and how very effective it was."

PIAO

English Name: Blackberry
Botanical Name: *Rubus fructicosus*

The root, leaves, and bark are all classed as astringents, but the root is more strongly astringent than the leaves or bark.

A tea made from blackberry root has long been used in Chinese herb medicine as a remedy for dysentery and diarrhea. The Chinese also maintain that it strengthens the Yin. This is interesting when we consider that diarrhea or dysentery has a weakening (Yin) effect on the body. Therefore, if the remedy corrects these conditions, the patient regains his strength; i.e., the Yin would be strengthened.

Blackberry root must be boiled for a long time in order to extract its astringent properties. For conditions of diarrhea, a decoction is prepared by placing 2½ ounces of the cut roots in one and a half quarts of water. The container is covered, and the decoction is brought to a boil and boiled very slowly (simmered) down to one quart. When cool, one cupful of the strained decoction is taken every two or three hours or one tablespoonful is taken every 15 or 20 minutes, until relief is felt.

For a stronger formula for diarrhea, the decoction is prepared with milk instead of water. (The same amount of cut roots is boiled slowly, in one and a half quarts of milk, down to one quart and strained.) The dosage is the same as it was in the previous recipe.

For dysentery, one ounce each of cut blackberry roots, wild cherry bark, and white oak bark is mixed with the others and boiled slowly, in three pints of water, down to two pints. When cool, one half to one teacupful of the strained decoction is taken several times a day until results are obtained.

MAI-FU

English Name: Wheaten Bran

In China wheaten meal is of a very good quality since only tiny amounts of bran and wheat germ (high-fiber food sources) are removed from the flour, due to the rough mode of grinding the meal. By contrast, for many years the mills of flour industries of Western nations have been removing all the bran and wheat germ from the flour by means of modern refining methods. As a result, a large number of scientific studies indicate that the lack of fiber in our diet has caused a prevalence of certain diseases relatively uncommon in China and other lands where high fiber foods such as bran, wheat germ, brown rice, and so on are still eaten. Some examples of such diseases cited include constipation, gall bladder problems, cancer of the colon, hemorrhoids, diverticular disease, and appendicitis.

How the Chinese Use Bran

As ,a domestic remedy, the Chinese use unprocessed bran in different forms. For example, bran mixed with vinegar is applied externally as a poultice for inflammation, boils, and so forth; a pillow stuffed with bran is used in place of an ordinary pillow for inducing relaxation in cases of insomnia; or bran made into a tea is used for profuse sweating and certain urinary problems. However, a daily ration of unprocessed bran in the diet is especially valued as an effective natural means of preventing or relieving constipation. For this purpose, the Chinese instruct that sufficient fluids—such as milk, soup, juice, or broth—should always be taken with bran. The bran may be stirred in the fluids, or, if the bran is baked into muffins, eating of the muffins should be accompanied by drinking of fluids. The reason for this is that bran has the ability to absorb many times its weight in water or watery fluids, and it is the fluid that makes the type of large, soft stools that pass easily.

Generally, two teaspoonfuls of unprocessed bran are taken three times a day, but some people find that less is sufficient, while others may need more. The Chinese explain that each person must find the amount suitable to his own individual need, and this may be done by starting with one or two teaspoonfuls of bran per day and gradually increasing the amount each day until the desired results are achieved, then continuing daily with that specific amount. White flour and refined sugar should be greatly reduced in the diet.

Centuries of experience have convinced the Chinese that unprocessed bran is not a laxative, but rather a normalizer of bowel elimination, and therefore is of value not only in conditions of constipation, but also in troublesome diarrhea.

However, they point out that some people find that when they add bran to their diet it causes temporary discomfort from flatulence. But in most cases the problem disappears within two or three weeks. And a few people may find that bran disagrees with them. In such cases, other types of natural high fiber foods and/or specific herb teas such as yellow dock may be the answer to their constipation problem. The Chinese add a word of caution that any food source high in dietary fiber, such as bran, should not be used for constipation by patients with intestinal stenosis or adhesions.

Bran sold in supermarkets is generally processed and usually contains sugar. Unprocessed bran (the type of bran used by the Chinese) can be obtained from health food stores and various herb firms.

Some Scientific Findings on the Value of Bran

As early as 1941, Surgeon Captain Cleave of the British Royal Navy began reporting in medical literature on the value of unprocessed bran as one of the best and natural ways to cure or prevent constipation. In the *British Medical Journal* (May 1972), Cleave reviewed some of his past experiences and related that on one occasion while he was serving on a battleship there was a scarcity of fresh vegetables and fruits, and he found "bran invaluable for correcting constipation of the ship's company." He added, "The sailors loved the stuff by comparison with purgatives [very strong cathartics]. I think it is a great tragedy of our present age that, with Medical Research Council workers showing at least 15% of the population to be on regular purgatives, this precious material [bran] is ever lost through the manufacture of white flour."

In a letter printed in a British medical publication, *The Lancet*, Dr. Harold Dodd wrote: "Constipation is an ailment of so-called civilization and it can be greatly relieved by the way we live. I cannot speak too highly of Surgeon Captain Cleave's prescription—one tablespoonful of unprocessed bran daily. It restores to the diet what the miller has taken out. For several years I have practiced and prescribed a dessertspoon of unprocessed bran and one of unprocessed wheat germ daily. It is moistened according to taste with milk, gravy, soup, coffee, or fruit juice. In most patients it ensures a daily formed stool as smooth as with liquid paraffin."

Dr. Neil S. Painter, a London surgeon, and his colleagues engaged in a long-term study in which they gave bran to patients with diverticulosis. They reported the results in an article entitled "Unprocessed Bran in Treatment of Diverticulosis Disease of the Colon," which appeared in the *British Medical Journal* (April 15, 1972). In this study, anywhere from one teaspoonful to nine tablespoonsful of unprocessed bran were taken daily by 70 patients with diverticular disease, each patient adjusting the dose to his own personal comfort. Most of the patients took their bran with milk, soup, or water or sprinkled on cereals, the average dose being two teaspoons three times a day. In addition to the bran, Dr. Painter also placed his patients on a high residue diet—including whole meal bread, vegetables, fruits, and porridge—and advised them to cut down on sugar.

Of the 62 patients who continued the program faithfully every day, 90% were able to relieve or completely abolish their symptoms, which ranged from severe colic to nausea, heartburn, tender rectum, bloated feeling, and constipation. Whereas about 80% of the patients previously had to strain and had stools that were small and hard, their bowels now were regular, their stools were large and soft, and they no longer needed to strain. Patients with the opposite problem also were helped. Prior to using bran, one individual needed to visit the bathroom six times a day, and another did so 12 times a day. However, on the bran diet each had only two bowel movements daily. (Other researchers have reported the same effect, which indicates that bran is a *normalizer* of bowel elimination.)

Dr. Painter reported that his findings also suggest that "the widely held view that so-called 'roughage' irritates the gut is not founded on fact; bran, when moist, becomes 'softage.'"

However, another medic, Dr. Marian T. Troy, adds a warning that if diverticulosis reaches the acute stage of diverticulitis, the dietary advice is different. Dr. Troy explains that this is a very painful inflammatory disease, not a condition, and when it is in the acute state the old fashioned advice of a low-residue or no-residue diet applies. She goes on to say, "If you should suffer a bout of diverticulitis, drink only clear liquids, but no milk. You want your bowels to be empty, to let the inflammation subside, to let any pus in the diverticula drain into the bowel. Do not try to treat a bout of diverticulitis yourself. This is a job for your doctor." She advises that to avoid diverticulosis in the first place, you should eat green vegetables, fresh fruits, and some unprocessed bran every day and cut out highly refined foods.

Other research studies on the value of unprocessed bran were reported in the *Medical World News* (Sept. 6, 1974). These studies pointed to the ability of bran to lower cholesterol and to help prevent cardiovascular disorders—such as occlusive vascular diseases, ischemic heart disease, deep vein thrombosis, and varicose veins—and other conditions related to metabolism, such as diabetes and obesity.

P'ENG

English Name: Canada Fleabane
Botanical Name: *Erigeron canadense*

The medicinal action of this plant is cited as tonic and astringent. It is used in cases of diarrhea and dysentery. It is prepared as a tea. Two pints of boiling water are poured over 2 ounces of cut pieces of the herb. The container is covered, and the brew is allowed to stand for one-half hour and then strained. The tea is taken cold, one cupful every hour or two until relief is achieved.

If a fluid extract of the herb is used in place of the tea, one-half to one teaspoonful of the extract is added to a small glass of cold water, and the mixture is taken until results are obtained.

The Chinese were not the only ones who valued Canada Fleabane for conditions of diarrhea. The North American Indians and early settlers also used the herb for the same condition. In the *Journal of Allergy* (September, 1955), J.A. Blue, M.D. reported that when Indians and early settlers suffered the sometimes serious problem of diarrhea, they relied on a tea made from Canada Fleabane. In reference to the herb, Dr. Blue said that experiments showed that it worked when diarrhea "proved so baffling and defied the best modern remedies to relieve it."

YU

English Name: Slippery Elm
Botanical Name: *Ulmus fulva*

There are many varieties of elm. Slippery elm is a small tree with rough branches and long leaves rough with hairs on both sides. A yellow "wool" covers the leaf buds. Flowers are stalkless.

The inner bark is the part of the tree used in Chinese medicine and is considered one of nature's most excellent demulcents and nutritives. It is employed for its ability to absorb foul gases in the body. It is also used for its gentle, soothing action in cases of enteritis (inflammation of the intestinal tract) and colitis (inflammation of the large bowel). There are many types of colitis. Some are mild, others are very severe.

Because of its soothing, mucilaginous nature, the use of slippery elm reputedly assures easy passage during the process of bowel evacuation. In addition it acts as a buffer against irritation and inflammation of the mucous membranes and is considered helpful in conditions of dysentery and diarrhea.

One cup of the tea is prepared from the powdered bark and a pinch of powdered golden seal and is taken three times a day. As an accessory treatment for bowel inflammation, dysentery, and other diseases of the bowels, a second batch of the tea is prepared in the same way and used as an injection with a rectal syringe (after the tea has been cooled to luke warm).

Further Instructions

The powdered bark of slippery elm is difficult to mix without forming lumps. To solve this problem, the tea is prepared by placing two teaspoonfuls of the powder in a jar and adding one-half cup of cold water. The jar is capped, and the mixture is shaken thoroughly. The mixture is then poured into a porcelain container, and one pint of boiling hot water and a pinch of powdered golden seal is added. The solution is thoroughly stirred until the powders are well mixed and dissolved.

The same procedure is followed when you prepare another batch for use as a rectal injection. If the solution is too thick to flow freely through the syringe, the tea may be diluted with a little more water.

SHU-KUA

English Name: Papaya
Botanical Name: *Carica papaya*

The papaya is a tropical, melon-like fruit which is produced in clusters by the *Carica papaya* tree. In the tropics, where the papaya tree has been valued as a food and medicine for ages, fascinating stories and legends are told of the tree. In certain regions it is regarded by the natives as a mystical plant because in some ways it appears to possess human attributes—producing male and female flowers in separate plants, while the fruit, like the human embryo, develops in about nine months.

The papaya tree was introduced and cultivated in South China and other parts of the Far East less than a century ago. Its Chinese name, *Shu-kua*, means "tree melon." Other Chinese names include *Wan-shou-kau*, "longevity fruit"; *Fan-kua*, "foreign melon"; and *Mu-kua*, which is another way of saying "tree melon."

Constituents of Papaya

The papaya contains an abundance of vitamins and minerals. It also provides enzymes—the most important being papain, which greatly resembles pepsin in its digestive action. The natural papain enzyme is extracted from the papaya, made into tablets, and sold on the market—mainly as an aid for protein digestion.

Chinese Usage of Papaya

After the introduction of papaya into China, the Chinese quickly learned to appreciate the usefulness of the papaya in rendering meat tender, as well as its alimentary and medicinal qualities. With reference to irregularity, the Chinese maintain that ripe papaya fruit eaten daily is an effective natural means of abolishing constipation.

Many people have attested to the truth of this Oriental claim, stating that papaya worked for them when all other natural means had failed.

Modern Chinese herbalists sometimes recommend papain tablets for treating external hemorrhoids, which in some instances has proven successful. Generally, one tablet is taken every three or four hours until the ailment has cleared up, which, when the remedy is effective, usually occurs within a week.

Reported Uses of Papain for External Hemorrhoids

• Mr. R.G. was one of several people who claimed to have avoided surgery for painful external piles, the condition having been successfully treated by using papain tablets as directed by a Chinese herbalist.

• It is interesting to find that a modern Occidental physician also found that papain tablets were effective in treating a case of external piles. Phillip J. Pollack, M.D. reported the case of a woman 52 years of age who suffered painful external hemorrhoids. Standard therapy—rectal suppositories, sitz baths, and bed rest—produced no response. Dr. Pollack then instructed the woman to take one papain tablet every four hours. In 48 hours "marked improvement" was noted in the patient. Swelling and pain both subsided. After three more days of the papain treatment, the improvement was considered complete. Surgery was not necessary.[1]

Note: Because the fruit is highly perishable, importation of papaya into the United States from tropical regions has been a problem. But recently arrangements were made to ship the melons from Hawaii to the mainland by jet planes. However, if you still find that fresh papayas are not always available at your supermarket, other forms—such as papaya juice, frozen papaya, and dried papaya—are readily available from health food stores and are considered good substitutes for fresh papaya. Papain tablets may also be obtained from health food stores or from herb firms.

YANG-MEI

English Name: Bayberry
Botanical Name: *Myrica cerifera*

---

[1]*Current Therapeutic Research*, May 1962.

This small tree grows near swamps and marshes, and belongs to the family of myrtles. It reaches a height of from 3 to 8 feet, and bears globular fruit resembling berries.

Bayberry has a longstanding reputation as an effective remedy for diarrhea and dysentery. The tea is prepared by placing 1 ounce of the cut roots in one-and-a-half pints of boiling water. The container is covered with a lid, and the tea is simmered for five minutes, then allowed to stand until cold. One cold cupful of the strained tea is taken two or three times a day. If bayberry is used in the form of a tincture, one-half to one teaspoon is taken in a small glass of water two or three times a day.

SHUI-CH'ANG P'U

English Name: Calamus, Sweet Flag
Botanical Name: *Acorus calamus*

Calamus is a reed-like plant which flourishes along the edges of streams, lakes, and marshes. It is a native of Eastern countries but has gradually spread to most parts of the world. Because of its pleasant fragrance, it bears the equally popular common name of "Sweet Flag." In olden times, calamus was recommended by Taoists as having the power to bestow immortality.

Uses

Calamus is largely used in native Oriental medicine for treating dyspepsia, hyperacidity, and certain bowel complaints such as spasms of the bowel, and the discomfort caused by griping gas pains in the bowels. It has also been recorded from earliest times as one of the most popular remedies of the native practitioners of India. Ainslie, in his *Materia Medica of Hindostan, 1813*, states that in consequence of its great value in the bowel complaints of children, a severe penalty was placed on the refusal of any druggist to open his shop at night to sell calamus when demanded.

Calamus is prepared with 1 ounce of the cut roots to one pint of boiling water. This is simmered slowly for five minutes, then strained. One teacup is taken three times a day. Or the powdered root contained in capsules may be used, one capsule each time as needed. For children suffering from colic, a weak tea of calamus is prepared and small amounts given at regular intervals.

TZU-YUN-KAO (Lithospermum Ointment)

Lithospermum is one of the top-ranking botanicals recorded in *The Herbal* by Emperor Shen-Ung. It is the principal ingredient of a Chinese herbal ointment widely recognized as an effective rectal remedy for hemorrhoids, and various skin conditions.

Lithospermum ointment also contains sesame seed oil and tang kuei.

TRADITIONAL CHINESE HERB COMBINATIONS

These herb formulas are available in capsules, and used by the Chinese to treat the following conditions:

Cimicifuga Combination

Constituents: Cimicifuga, bupleurum, tang kuei, scute (scullcap), licorice, rhubarb root.

Uses: Hemorrhoids, symptomized by constipation, slight bleeding, pain, and itching of the anus. In addition, Lithospermum ointment is applied locally. Cimicifuga Combination is also used to treat the initial stages of rectal prolapse.

Pueraria Combination

Constituents: Pueraria (kudzu root), ma-huang, cinnamon, peony root, ginger, jujube fruit, licorice.

Uses: Diarrhea and acute colitis.

Pinellia Combination

Constituents: Pinellia, goldthread (coptis), scute, ginseng, jujube fruit, ginger, licorice.

Uses: Diarrhea alternating with constipation, symptomized by stomach distress, nausea, or gas.

Minor Bupleurum Combination

Constituents: Bupleurum, ginseng, scute, pinellia, ginger, jujube fruit, licorice.

Uses: Constipation accompanied by gastric distress, loss of appetite, fatigue, and occasional nausea.

Major Bupleurum Combination

Constituents: Bupleurum, scute, pinellia, peony root, ginger, jujube fruit, citrus peel, rhubarb root.

Uses: This combination is used for persons of a strong constitution and good appetite, who suffer frequent bouts of constipation with hard feces.

Bupleurum and Peony Combination

Constituents: Bupleurum, peony root, atractylodes, tang kuei, hoelen, mentha, ginger, licorice, moutan, gardenia.

Uses: Constipation, especially in women going through the menopause, and in persons of a weak constitution who are easily fatigued.

Coptis and Rhubarb Combination

Constituents: Coptis, scute, rhubarb root.

Uses: For persons of a strong constitution who suffer from constipation with hard stools and stomach distress.

Hoelen Five Herbs Formula

Constituents: Hoelen, cinnamon, alisma, atractylodes, polyporus.

Uses: Acute, watery diarrhea.

Ginseng and Atractylodes Formula

Constituents: Ginseng, atractylodes, hoelen, dolichos, lotus seed, dioscorea, platycodon, coix, cardamom, licorice.

Uses: Hemorrhoids in persons of a delicate constitution with weakness, poor appetite, and mild anemia.

Magnolia and Ginger Formula

Constituents: Magnolia bark, ginger, atractylodes, jujube fruit, citrus, licorice.

Uses: Stomach distress with diarrhea after meals.

Tang Kuei and Peony Formula

Constituents: Tang kuei, peony, atractylodes, cnidium, hoelen, alisma.

Uses: This formula treats constipation in persons of a weak constitution who tire easily. It is said to be especially effective for those who take an ordinary laxative which not only fails to move the bowels, but which also produces griping gas pains.

Pueraria, Coptis and Scute Combination

Constituents: Pueraria, coptis, scute, licorice.
      Uses: Colitis, diarrhea.

Summary

1. There are a variety of bowel complaints which have yielded to the use of herb remedies and certain health measures.
2. Piles are symptomized by rectal pain, burning, itching, and sometimes bleeding. They can be internal or external.
3. "Bathroom straining" (repeated straining to move hard, dry feces) may cause fissures and/or piles. It also puts an abnormal strain on the heart.
4. The plant kingdom provides certain herbs and natural foods which help prevent or overcome constipation. They are not regarded as laxatives, but rather as normalizers and regulators of bowel functions.
5. Although hard substances such as roots and barks are generally prepared as decoctions (boiled for a certain length of time), delicate yellow dock root is an exception to this rule and must never be allowed to boil continuously. To allow it to do so would destroy the root's active properties.
6. Diarrhea and dysentery have a weakening (Yin) effect on the body. If such conditions are prolonged and are not corrected, they can be very serious and dangerous.

11

CHINESE HERBS FOR COPING WITH HEADACHES, NERVOUSNESS, STRESS, AND INSOMNIA

For years Western civilizations have been drifting away from natural living and natural laws. Statistics show that an incredible number of people are taking tranquilizers, sleeping pills, and similar drugs for nervousness, insomnia, and stress. More often than not, the distressed patient is handed a medical prescription for some type of barbiturate drug, and many of these medicines produce side effects and are habit forming. Aspirin, the popular over-the-counter drug for relieving headaches, also causes side effects in many people.

According to a report by the U.S. Public Health Service, more accidental deaths result from an excess of barbiturates than from any other type of acute drug poisoning. Sometimes the continued use of sleep-inducing drugs brings about a trance-like state rather than genuine sleep. In such instances, the insomniac cannot remember exactly how many pills he had already swallowed so he takes more. This puts him to sleep permanently. In other cases, people make the dangerous and often fatal blunder of taking sleeping pills just before or shortly after drinking liquor. In analyzing 21 deaths caused by alcohol and barbiturate poisoning, two British pathologists concluded that the condition acts incredibly fast to produce a fatal drop in blood pressure.

Coping with Stress

Over a hundred years ago, Thoreau, the great naturalist and philosopher, said, "The mass of men lead lives of quiet desperation." What Thoreau observed so clearly is still very much with us, although the desperation is no longer silent. Today our life is far more complex and rife with conflicting demands. Records show that four out of every five adults are suffering from some form of tension or anxiety. Despite all our modern conveniences to make life "easy," we suffer more stress in one day than our forefathers did in a month or even a year.

Traffic jams, harsh glaring lights, overcrowding, and domestic tension contribute to stress as does boredom, exposure to extreme heat and cold, serious illness or injury, fear of unemployment, and competition in business or sports. Prolonged or sudden exposure to loud noises plagues us almost everywhere—sonic booms, roaring jets, frantically beeping horns, screeching brakes, wailing sirens, and so on.

The threat of noise to humans has led to scientific tests on animals to find out how loud some sounds affect them. Prolonged exposure to noise caused rats to become sterile, and if the noise was continued still further, it eventually killed the rats through heart failure.

Authorities have reported that stress is involved in almost half of all known diseases. It is a major cause of lifestyle illnesses such as ulcerative colitis, asthma, gastric ulcers, and impotence. Stress is a contributing factor to impaired vision, high blood pressure, stroke, allergies, and many other conditions.

Dr. Hans Selye, famed expert on tension and stress, tells us, "No one can live without experiencing some degree of stress all the time. You may think that only serious disease or intensive physical or mental injury can cause stress. This is false. Crossing a busy intersection, exposure to a draft, or even sheer joy are enough to activate the body's stress mechanisms to some extent."

Stressing challenges are as varied as life itself, and in today's modern world we have less and less opportunity to return to a relaxed state after one episode of stress has passed, before another stressor appears.

Chinese Healing Methods

Chinese herbalists treat persons troubled with stress, tension, nervousness, insomnia, and nagging headache pains with specific herb remedies which are harmless and non-habit forming. Certain select herbs reputedly relieve various types of headaches; others help promote natural sleep; while still others feed and repair the worn nervous system. However, due to the diversity of causes, a specific herb tea or formula may help one person but not another. Under the circumstances, it is best to select one herbal remedy and give it a sufficient trial. If after you have done so it does not help, you can switch to another. In this way you may be able to find the one most helpful for your own particular need. (It should also be noted that the limited space of one chapter necessarily prevents the listing of each and every Chinese herb remedy for the disorders cited.)

Along with the usage of herbs, the Chinese explain that Nature also requires sensible attention to the diet. Junk foods should be replaced by wholesome, well-balanced meals. And since food must have time to digest, you should never retire immediately after eating a meal. This practice has been known to cause nightmares or the stress and discomfort of prolonged restless twisting and turning in bed. Sufficient sleep is necessary so that energy used during the day can be restored to exhausted bodies.

The Chinese also advise that insomniacs cut down on salt in the diet.

CHINESE HERB REMEDIES

CHI-HSUEH-TS'AO

English Name: Catnip
Botanical Name: *Nepeta cataria*

Catnip herb belongs to the mint family and has a pleasant, aromatic odor. It is reputed to be a good natural remedy for nervous irritability, nervous insomnia, and nervous headache when combined with other herbs and prepared as a tea. Following are some examples.

1. One teaspoon each of catnip, celery seeds, oats, valerian *(Valeriana officinalis)*, and scullcap *(Scutellaria laterifolia)* are mixed together and placed in a container, and one and a half pints of boiling water are poured over them. The container is covered, and the tea is allowed to stand for 20 minutes. One warm cupful of the strained infusion is taken three times a day

between meals, and one cupful is taken in the evening before you retire. The beverage is sipped slowly.

2. Another formula for treating nervous insomnia and nervous headache consists of 1 ounce each of catnip, scullcap, and peppermint. The herbs are thoroughly mixed and stored in a capped jar. One or two heaping teaspoons of the mixture are placed in a cup and filled with boiling water. The cup is covered with a saucer, the tea is allowed to stand until it is lukewarm and then strained, and a teaspoonful of honey is added.

For insomnia, one cupful is taken at bedtime. For nervous headache, one hot teacupful is sipped slowly every hour or two until relief is felt.

3. As a nerve tonic or a remedy for insomnia, ½ ounce each of catnip, scullcap, valerian, and passiflora *(Passiflora incarnata)* is mixed and placed in a container, and one quart of boiling water is poured on. The container is covered, and the infusion is allowed to stand for 20 minutes and then strained. One teacupful is taken four times a day one hour after meals and about one-half hour before bedtime.

4. This combination may be used for nervous irritability or headache: One ounce each of catnip, sage, peppermint, and marjoram *(Origanum majorana)*, well mixed, is stored in a capped jar. One heaping teaspoonful of the mixture is placed in a cup filled with boiling water, the cup is covered with a saucer, and the tea is allowed to stand for five minutes and then strained. One cupful is slowly sipped every one or two hours until relief is felt.

LU-TS'AO

English Name: Hops
Botanical Name: *Humulus Lupulus*

This is the common wild hop which is native to China, Japan, and many other lands. In Chinese it is called *Lu-ts'ao* and *Lai-mei-ts'ao*. Another Chinese name for the hops is *Le-ts'ao* because the stem of the plant is prickly and chafes the skin when it comes into contact with it.

The word *hops* is taken from the Anglo-Saxon *hoppen* meaning "to climb" because the twining perennial plant attaches itself to neighboring objects and attains a great height. The botanical name *Humulus* is derived from *humus*, "moist earth," the type of soil in which the plant thrives best.

Constituents and Medicinal Action

The active principle in hops is a glandular powder called *lupulin*. The peculiar fragrant odor is due to a volatile oil. The medicinal action of hops is cited as nervine, stomachic, tonic, soporific (induces sleep), and anodyne (relieves pain). For these reasons, hops are employed for nervous irritability, nervous sick headache, insomnia, neuritis, indigestion, and poor appetite.

In Chinese medicine hops are used in many different forms, such as teas, hop pillows, poultices, and fomentations.

The Hop Pillow—Nature's Sleep Aid

Centuries ago, hop pickers claimed that the strong aroma of the plant imparted a soothing, calming influence on the nerves. Pillows stuffed with hops were soon used in place of ordinary pillows to assure a good night's sleep in conditions of insomnia. As the years passed, their popularity spread to many other nations throughout the world, and they were even used by royalty. For example, records show that the use of a hop pillow was prescribed for George III in 1787, with excellent effect. It is also recorded that it was employed with very good results during an illness suffered by the Prince of Wales in 1879.

The soporific value of the hop pillow was mentioned in the 17th edition of the *U.S Dispensatory*: "A pillow of hops has proven useful in allaying restlessness and producing sleep in nervous disorders. They should be moistened with water containing a trace of glycerin, previously to being placed under the head of the patient in order to prevent rustling."

Another method of preparing a hop pillow is to fill a muslin bag loosely with hops, tie the opening securely, and attach the bag to your regular pillow with a basting thread. Of course, the muslin bag (or pillow case) will need to be washed, and the hops should be renewed every month.

Note: Some people sprinkle the hops with a little alcohol claiming it helps to bring out the soporific properties of the hops more fully.

Hops in Tea Form

Hop tea is used to relieve nervous insomnia, nervous irritability, and nervous headache. It is prepared in a covered vessel—1 ounce of hops to one pint of boiling water. The tea is simmered for two or three minutes, removed from the burner, allowed to stand for five minutes, and strained.

For nervous irritability or insomnia, one hot teacupful is sipped three times a day and once before bedtime. In conditions of nervous sick headache, one hot teacupful is sipped slowly every two hours until relief is felt. The tea is also reputed to be an excellent tonic for the stomach, relieving indigestion and promoting the appetite. (Hop tea has an extremely bitter taste and may be sweetened with honey.)

Combination Tea Formula

Hops are often combined with other herbs for use in conditions of nervous insomnia. One-quarter ounce each of hops, passiflora, and valerian is mixed, and one pint of boiling water is poured over them. The container is covered, and the tea is allowed to stand for three hours and then strained. One cupful, reheated and sweetened with a teaspoonful of honey, is taken one-half hour before bedtime.

Hop Poultices and Fomentations

Hop poultices or fomentations are applied externally to relieve the pains of neuritis, which is an inflammatory condition of the nerves or nerve sheath. Doctors explain that although it can affect any part of the body, neuritis is generally situated in the main nerves of the face, leg or arm. It may be caused by any number of things such as a cold, rheumatism, inflammation of some part of the body that also affects the nerves, or debility due to illness. Sciatica, facial neuralgia, and neuritis in the arm are all types of this disorder. When the sciatic nerve and branches are affected, the pain extends from the buttocks downward along the thigh to the knee and foot. When the arm is affected, the pain is felt from the back of the neck and top of the shoulder down the arm to the wrist or fingers. Sometimes there is a tingling or numb sensation. Facial neuralgia is symptomized by severe pains, generally on one side of the face.

Treatment

If the pain is in the face, the hop poultice or fomentation is applied in front of the ear or to the lower part of the back of the head. For pain in the buttocks and leg, the poultice or fomentation is applied approximately 3 inches from the base of the spine. When the pain is felt in the shoulder, arm, or fingers, the poultice or fomentation is applied to the upper part of the spine in line with the collar bone. These external applications placed on the specific areas mentioned, soothe the inflamed nerve where it branches out from the spinal cord.

How to Prepare Hop Poultices

A hop poultice is prepared by placing a large handful (or more) of hops in a muslin bag, tying the ends of the bag together with a piece of string, and steeping the bag in a covered container of hot water for a few minutes. When ready for use, the hop bag is quickly wrung out and applied, as hot as can be borne without causing a burn, to the specific area. The poultice is then covered with a folded dry towel to retain the heat as long as possible. In the meantime, a second poultice should be steeping in the hot water. As soon as the first poultice begins to cool, it is immediately removed and placed back into the container, while the second hot poultice is quickly wrung out and applied according to previous directions. The poulticing is continued in this manner until relief is obtained.

How to Prepare Hop Fomentations

If one prefers, fomentations may be used instead of poultices. In this case, a batch of hop tea is prepared in a covered vessel, with 4 ounces of hops to two quarts of boiling water. This is simmered for five minutes and then strained. A folded towel is dipped into the tea, quickly wrung out, and applied, as hot as can be tolerated without causing a burn, to the specific area. The wet towel is immediately covered with a dry one to retain the heat as long as possible. In the meantime, a second towel should be soaking in the hot tea (the vessel kept covered). As soon as the first towel begins to noticeably lose its heat, it is immediately removed and dipped back into the container of hop tea, and the second towel is wrung out and applied to the specific area. Fomentations are continued until relief is obtained.

Note: In using fomentations or poultices, the water or tea in the container should be kept hot during the entire period.

Accessory Treatment

One-half ounce each of hops, burdock, scullcap, valerian, and vervain *(Verbena officinalis)* are mixed together and half of the total mixture is placed in two pints of cold water and brought to a boil. The container is covered, and the decoction is simmered for ten minutes and then strained. It is taken warm, one tablespoonful several times a day. It reputedly soothes the inflamed nerves and gradually builds up the entire nervous system.

MA-PIEN-TS'AO

English Name: Vervain
Botanical Name: *Verbena officinalis*

As mentioned previously in the chapter on women's health, this plant is not to be confused with the lemon-scented verbena of our gardens. Vervain grows wild in low grounds, has no odor, and bears small purple flowers. When cultivated, the flowers reach a larger size. In Chinese the plant is given two different names, *Ma-pien-ts'ao* and *Lung-ya-ts'ao*.

Nerve Tonic

Medicinally, the herb has an ancient reputation as a strengthener of the nerves and for this purpose is generally prepared as a combined formula. Here is one of many such combinations. One ounce each of vervain, scullcap, and valerian are mixed together and three pints of boiling water are poured over them. The container is covered, and the tea is allowed to stand for 20 minutes and then strained. One warm teacupful is taken three times daily.

Headache Remedy

Vervain also has a long-standing reputation as a remedy for relieving various types of headaches—such as mild, congestive, or nervous-sick headache or those caused by fatigue or tension. One or two heaping teaspoonfuls of the cut, dried herb are placed in a teacup filled with boiling water. The cup is covered with a saucer, and the infusion is allowed to stand until cool. It is then strained and reheated. One teacupful is taken three or four times daily (or more often in severe cases) until relief is obtained.

In a few instances, this simple vervain tea has also brought relief from the pains of migraine headache. For example, a young man who had endured considerable stress stated he had suffered periodic bouts of migraine for years and it could not be cured. One day his family received a copy of a health magazine in which vervain tea was mentioned for the relief of migraine. He said, "I insisted on trying it. After the first few cachets of dried vervain in my tea, the migraine pains left and have not been felt since."

Although the tea will not help in every case of migraine, the Chinese claim it is harmless and well worth trying.

Formula for "Liverish" Migraine

Some authorities maintain that liver trouble is one of the most common among the many different causes of migraine headache. Normally the bile that forms in the cells of the liver is thin and clear and flows freely through the gall bladder ducts. The bladder empties periodically. But if the bile thickens (generally due to consumption of fatty and indigestible foodstuffs or some temporary congestion of the bile ducts), the flow is slow, and the gall bladder does not empty. This back-up of bile into the bloodstream is believed to be the cause of severe migraine headaches.

Once the thickened bile starts to flow, the nauseated, "liverish" migraine sufferer begins to vomit the greenish-yellow bile, sometimes every several hours both day and night, often for two or three days. When at long last the excess bile is completely eliminated, the headache is finally relieved. But so long as the backed-up bile is retained in the system, the nausea and blinding headache persist. Therefore, to get the bile flowing as soon as possible during a migraine attack and to keep it flowing more often, Chinese herbalists advise the sufferer to drink one or two glasses of plain hot water. Drinking the water usually starts an amount of the bile flowing which can then be eliminated through vomiting. The glasses of water are continued every hour or two as needed, until the excess bile is completely eliminated. This means of washing out the bile from the system shortens the duration of the attack and more quickly relieves the blinding migraine headaches.

Although the hot water treatment may bring more prompt relief during a spell of "liverish" migraine, it will not cure the condition. That is, it will not prevent future attacks from occurring. Therefore, the real aim is to heal the ailment and produce lasting results. Following are examples of Chinese herb formulas which have reputedly proven helpful in a number of cases of "liverish" migraine.

One-half ounce each of vervain, dandelion root, ginger root, marshmallow root, motherwort, wild carrot *(Daucus carota)*, centaury *(Erythraea centaurium)*, and fringe tree *(Chionanthus virginicus)* are mixed together and simmered in one quart of boiling water for 15 minutes in a covered vessel. The decoction is strained, and one teacupful is taken three times a day before meals. This formula is taken for several weeks, or longer if necessary, because the effects are reputedly slow and gradual. It is said that the periods between the migraine attacks should lengthen, and the severity of the attacks should lessen.

A Notable Ingredient

Although, each herb listed in the above formula is considered very valuable, the botanical known as fringe tree deserves special attention since the Chinese have reported good effects on "liverish" migraine from the employment of this one herb alone. It is used in the form of a fluid extract, 12 drops in a little warm water, three times a day after meals. No milk should be taken. The Chinese claim that milk is *yin* and works against the medicinal action of fringe tree.

The fluid extract of fringe tree combined with the fluid extract of an herb known as Greater Celandine *(Chelidonium majus)* is another remedy which has reportedly brought relief to sufferers of "liverish" migraine. Equal amounts of the two fluid extracts are mixed together, and one teaspoonful in a little warm water is taken three times daily after meals. (In some instances, this combination has also been known to dissolve gallstones, when the treatment is continued long enough.)

Dietary Tips and Accessory Treatment for "Liverish" Migraine

In addition to the use of the herb remedies for "liverish" migraine, the Chinese advise sufferers to avoid eating or drinking anything cold. All foods or fluids should be warm or hot. It is also claimed that victims of this type of migraine headache are sensitive to external cold as well as internal cold. Therefore, the body should never be permitted to become chilled, especially in the upper abdomen and waist areas. In cold weather, extra warm clothing should be worn around the bodily areas mentioned, and any exposure to strong winds should be avoided at all times.

Fried foods and dairy products such as milk, cream, eggs, and cheese are to be omitted from the diet. If the person is troubled with irregularity, steps should be taken to keep the bowels open. This may be accomplished with the use of natural aids. (Refer to the chapter on bowel complaints.)

As a dietary supplement, one tablespoonful of lecithin granules obtained from soybeans (obtainable from health food stores) may be taken twice daily. (Lecithin reputedly has a beneficial effect on the liver and gall bladder.) The granules may be sprinkled over foods or added to fluids such as soups, coffee, or juices.

The amount of lecithin granules cited rarely if ever disagrees, but there are exceptions, and a few people find it too rich. In such cases, the amount is simply reduced or may be completely cut out.

WU-CHIA-P'I

English Name: Eleuthero
Botanical Name: *Eleutherococcus senticosus*

This tall shrub grows wild in various areas of the Far East and belongs to the same Araliaceae family as Panax ginseng. The flowers are violet or yellowish, and the leaves are similar in appearance to those of ginseng. Because its branches are spiked with thorns, people in olden times called the plant Touch-me-Not and Devil's Bush, and these synonyms are still in use today. More modern names for the Eleutherococcus bush are simply Eleuthero (pronounced El-oo-ther-oh) and "Siberian Ginseng."

In China, eleuthero is employed as a tonic and as a remedy for a great number of disorders, including nervousness and stress. It is generally used in the form of a tincture or extract.

Russian Scientific Studies on Eleuthero

Soviet scientists have taken a great interest in Chinese herbs and have discovered that eleuthero, a member of the ginseng family, is not only native to various areas of China, but also grows wild and abundantly in southern regions of the Soviet Union. It is for this reason, and the fact that the plant has undergone years of scientific study by a battery of Russian researchers at the Far Eastern Center of the Siberian Division of the USSR Academy of Sciences, that the herb is called "Siberian Ginseng." Results of these tests have established that eleutherococcus possesses an incredibly wide range of therapeutic activity, thereby substantiating many of the claims made for the herb by the Chinese. For example, prepared as a fluid extract and used as a tonic, it restores loss of vigor and vitality, increases endurance, gives more mental alertness, and so on. As a remedy, it reduces elevated sugar content in mild and moderate cases of diabetes, normalizes low blood pressure and mild forms of high blood pressure, protects against stress, has a beneficial effect in functional nervous disorders, and much more.

In this chapter we will briefly consider some of the Russian studies on eleuthero in relation to nerve conditions and stress.

Anti-Stress Action of Eleuthero on Animals

Russian scientists have established that a preparation of eleuthero has a marked protective action against most types of stress. For example, lengthy series of experiments on animals involved stress factors such as increased muscle loads, swimming for long durations, exposure to extreme heat and cold, chemical intoxication, surgery, and confinement in a closed vessel. In all of these experiments it was found that where eleuthero extract was administered, an anti-stress action was produced. For instance, one group of rats was injected with a preparation of eleuthero, and a second group was not. One hour later, both groups were made to swim in water until absolute exhaustion (death). The group not receiving the plant extract all developed bloating of the adrenals; decreased adrenal ascorbic acid; and shriveling of the thymus, spleen, and lymph nodes. Among the rats that received eleuthero, these destructive changes were hindered. It was also noted that the endurance of the treated rats increased remarkably. In comparison to the first group, they were able to swim 52 minutes longer until total fatigue (death).

Studies on Anti-Stress Action of Eleuthero on Humans

Under strict Soviet scientific guidelines, the anti-stress effect of eleuthero was studied on humans. After a long-term series of tests that took years, it was concluded that the plant extract increases human resistance to a wide variety of stress factors. The herb preparation helped people cope better under the ordinary stress and tension of modern everyday living; counteracted threats to typical stress-induced illnesses; produced a soothing and calming effect on people who had endured months of pressure and tension; eased the strain of worry and bottled up anxiety; relieved tensions of business and sports competitions; and delivered a protective effect against the stress of surgery, accidents, certain chemical toxins, radiation, and chronic illnesses.

In brief, Soviet scientists have firmly established that for people who find themselves in a trying situation or those who are engaged in any activity which taxes their endurance or stresses their body in other ways eleuthero extract can provide a protection that enables them to get through these periods with far less damage than they might otherwise incur.

Eleuthero Tested on Nervous Disorders

Probing further into the secrets of eleuthero, Soviet experts discovered that the plant extract had a pronounced therapeutic effect on functional nervous disorders, even in chronic patients who had been previously treated by a variety of different medications which had not helped.

Clinical studies with the plant extract were carried out on patients suffering from nervous exhaustion or nervous and emotional disturbances (not insanity). Their symptoms ranged from hair-trigger irritability to moodiness, lethargy, apprehension, menopausal "blues," insanity, persistent insomnia, depression, loss of vigor, and chronic fatigue.

In most patients, the administration of eleuthero extract brought about an improvement in sleep, restoration of energy and strength, a marked sense of well-being, and a renewed interest in life and work. The extract also displayed its normalizing effects in many areas. For example, while relieving symptoms of weakness, exhaustion, moodiness, and depression in patients suffering from these conditions, it produced a calm, restful, and well balanced effect on emotionally excited patients.

How Eleuthero Was Administered

The eleuthero treatment in these cases of nervous exhaustion and nervous and emotional disturbances lasted for four to five weeks. One dose of 20 to 40 drops of the extract was taken three times a day. To achieve a stable therapeutic effect, Dr. Brekhman, a prominent member of the Soviet scientific team, says: "It is recommended to give two or three courses at one or two week intervals." He adds that: "The preparations from eleuterococcus are non-toxic and harmless even when administered recurringly over a long period of time."

Note: A "course" means one month or five weeks of daily doses of eleuthero extract. At the end of that time, the doses are discontinued for one or two weeks, and then another course of eleuthero is taken.

Eleuthero—Widely Used

Eleutherococcus senticosus is manufactured for use and is widely available to the Russian public. In addition, a cold drink called "Bodrost" (cheerfulness) contains eleuthero and is very popular among the Russian people.

In one of the reports published by Soviet scientists in an International Congress, eleutherococcus was included in the list of therapeutic agents which can be of interest for space medicine (e.g. to help protect Russian cosmonauts against stress and to give them better endurance in space).

Eleutherococcus senticosus extract is currently available in the United States and can be obtained from health food stores or herb companies.

MI-TIEH-HSIANG

English Name: Rosemary
Botanical Name: *Rosmarinus officinalis*

There are several varieties of rosemary, such as the silver and gold leaves under cultivation in gardens, but the variety known as *Rosmarinus officinalis*, a small shrub with pale blue flowers and fragrant evergreen leaves, is the kind used medicinally. Its botanical name comes from the Latin *ros*, dew, and *marinus*, of the sea, since the wild plant grows abundantly near the seashore. This herb was introduced into China from Rome many centuries ago.

Medicinal Uses

Rosemary contains a special camphor, a volatile oil, a bitter principle, and a resin. Prepared as a tea, it reputedly soothes the nerves and relieves nervous insomnia, mental fatigue, and simple or congestive headaches. One heaping teaspoonful of the cut leaves is placed in a cup, and boiling water is added. The infusion is covered with a saucer, allowed to stand for five minutes, and then strained. One cupful of the hot tea is sipped slowly three or four times a day between meals.

Spirits of Rosemary

Here is another method of using rosemary for the relief of simple or congestive headache. As soon as the headache begins, a small bottle of spirits of rosemary is held to the nose, and the fumes are inhaled. In addition, a few drops of the preparation is rubbed gently but thoroughly on the temples, on the forehead, on the veins of the neck, and behind the ears. This treatment reputedly gives prompt relief.

Combined Rosemary Tea Formulas

As a remedy for nervous-sick headache, one-half teaspoonful each of rosemary, sage, and peppermint leaves is placed together in a cup which is filled with boiling water. The cup is covered with a saucer, and the tea is allowed to stand for five minutes and then strained. One cup of the hot tea is sipped slowly every hour or two until relief is obtained.

In a few instances migraine headache sufferers have reported relief with the use of a formula consisting of 1 ounce each of rosemary, scullcap, vervain, and wood betony *(Betonica officinalis)*. The herbs are thoroughly mixed together, and 1 ounce of the mixture is placed in one pint of cold water and brought to a boil. The container is covered, and the tea is simmered for two minutes and then allowed to stand until cold. The tea is then strained, reheated, and taken warm—one teacupful three times a day between meals and once before bedtime. The tea is used daily until relief is felt.

One woman who suffered periodic bouts of migraine for six years reported permanent relief after several weeks' use of the above herbal formula.

AI-HAO

English Name: Mugwort
Botanical Name: *Artemisia vulgaris*

In botanic medicine, mugwort tea is cited as nervine, tonic, stimulant, diaphoretic, and emmenagogue. As a nervine, the tea is prepared in a covered vessel. One pint of boiling water is poured over one heaping tablespoon of the dried leaves. The tea is allowed to stand for 15 minutes, then strained. It is best taken in small doses—one warm teacupful in the morning and one in the evening, or one tablespoonful three or four times a day (mugwort has a very bitter taste and may be sweetened with a little honey).

The Chinese maintain that mugwort tea is often helpful in relieving conditions of sleepwalking. This particular beneficial effect has also been commented upon by various Western herbalists. For example, C.F. Lyle writes: "The connection between the brain and the spinal cord is so intimate that herbs which affect the spine are likely to have some action on the brain. Mugwort, for instance, stimulates the spinal cord and relieves congestion in the brain. Sleepwalking is often combated by mugwort. It is a good brain tonic."

CHING-CHICH

English Name: Marjoram
Botanical Name: *Origanum marjorana*

The botanical name of this plant comes from *orios*, "a mountain" and *gamos*, "joy," in reference to the attractive appearance the plants give to the areas in which they grow. Marjoram has a fragrant odor, and warm aromatic taste, both of which properties are preserved when the herb is dried. It is popular as a seasoning in cookery, and has a very ancient reputation as a medicinal agent. A tea prepared with marjoram is said to relieve headache, and is also considered an effective remedy for insomnia.

Mrs. L.E.S. writes:

"I was looking for something that would help me sleep nights and this I found among the pages of old almanacs. Take one-half teaspoon powdered marjoram in one cup of hot milk at bedtime. It is very soothing. Here I have had marjoram in the house for some time and didn't know what it was for. Have been taking it for some time and find it so wonderful. I can now enjoy a good night's rest. Also, I have been telling some people who take sleeping pills to try it. What a simple good it is."

HUAI-HSIANG

English Name: Anise
Botanical Name: *Pimpinella anisum*

Among its remedial uses, aniseed in warm milk is considered by the Chinese to be a preventative of insomnia and nightmare. It is prepared by placing one-half teaspoon of the seeds in a cup and adding hot milk. The cup is covered with a saucer and the beverage allowed to stand for a few minutes, then strained. It is drunk warm at bedtime.

CHAI-HU-KUEI-CHIH-TANG
(Bupleurum and Cinnamon Combination)

This Chinese herbal formula is available in capsules, and is considered the remedy *par excellence* for treating stress and stress-related ailments. It contains bupleurum, cinnamon, ginseng, pinellia, licorice, scute, peony root, jujube fruit, and ginger.

Since ancient times, bupleurum has been regarded as a superior herb for its powerful harmonizing effect on the organism, relieving tension, nervousness, and hyperactivity. Ginseng, the tonic herb, is well known for its ability to increase strength and vitality, and to reduce reactions to a stressful lifestyle. The seven other herbs in this Chinese formula work synergistically so that the combination is much more effective than the use of any of the single herbs alone.

Basic Function of the Formula

Restoring balance to the body is the basic function of this herbal combination. It helps the adrenal glands to adapt to stress, and strengthens the liver, stomach, and intestines so that you feel more able to cope with tensions that might otherwise cause stress-related ailments. By relaxing the nervous system and tensed muscles, energy is being conserved. As the body begins to function more efficiently you will be able to handle stress much better, and also live and sleep more comfortably.

How Soon Will Benefits Be Obtained?

Two or three of the herb capsules are taken three times a day, about half an hour to an hour before meals. Generally within one or two weeks the level of tension and nervousness is reduced, along with an improvement in energy and mental outlook. Sleep patterns improve.

After three months of regular use, balance and well-being are restored, and in general all stress symptoms will have vanished. These results become stabilized after another three to six months use of the formula. If stress symptoms are light or infrequent to begin with, a much shorter period of use is generally sufficient.

Note. This Chinese formula is currently so popular among the people of Japan that it is medically approved by the Japanese government and covered there by health insurance.

Summary

1. Centuries of Chinese experience have shown that specific herbal aids for coping with jittery nerves, tension, insomnia, and nagging headache pains are effective, harmless, and non-habit-forming.
2. The pains of certain types of neuritis have often yielded to the use of herbs in various forms such as teas, fomentations, or poultices.
3. In addition to using herbs, faulty dietary habits should be changed. Junk foods are to be replaced with wholesome, well-balanced meals. The Chinese also advise insomniacs to cut down on salt in their diet.
4. Because food must have time to digest, you should never retire after eating a meal, as this practice has been known to cause nightmares and restlessness.
5. According to Chinese herbalists, liver trouble is one of the most common causes of migraine headache. Along with the use of herb remedies, sufferers of "liverish" migraine should avoid eating or

drinking anything cold. Dairy products as well as fried foods are also to be omitted from the diet. If the sufferer is troubled with constipation, steps should be taken to restore regularity.

6. Chai-Hu-Kuei-Chih-Tang (Bupleurum and Cinnamon Combination) is considered the remedy *par excellence* for treating stress and stress-related disorders.

12

PLANT REMEDIES
FOR CIRCULATORY DISORDERS

A Word About Hypertension

In medical terms, high blood pressure is known as *hypertension*. Blood pressure means the force of the blood against the walls of the arteries. When the pressure is abnormally high, it naturally causes abnormal wear and tear on the blood vessels. In severe cases, the pressure can cause the strained capillaries (tiny blood vessels) to rupture, which may result in a heart attack or stroke (cerebral hemorrhage). Stroke is the third leading cause of death in the United States. The brain is believed to be particularly susceptible to hemorrhage because it is enclosed in the skull and cannot expand when the blood pressure increases.

Kidney diseases, particularly inflammation, can cause hypertension, however only a very small percentage of the cases of high blood pressure are accounted for by kidney disease. More common is that type of blood pressure known as "essential hypertension." This type is presumed to exist without any well-defined cause being known.

The usual symptoms of high blood pressure are dizziness, headaches, and noises or ringing in the ears. Along with any remedy used for hypertension, the following regime is generally recommended: sufficient rest; regular exercise; abstinence from tobacco, coffee, and alcoholic beverages; a low-salt diet; minimization or, if possible, avoidance of stress-provoking situations; and control of the cholesterol count by correct diet or other means.

A Word About Hypotension

Low blood pressure is medically called *hypotension.* In this condition the push or force of blood against the vessel walls decreases, and the cells fail to receive an adequate supply of nutrients carried by the blood. Fatigue, sensitivity to cold and heat, rapid pulse beat on exertion, and lack of endurance are the usual symptoms of low blood pressure. A person with this condition requires more sleep than a healthy individual and generally finds himself more tired when he awakens in the morning than when he went to bed.

CHINESE HERB REMEDIES FOR CIRCULATORY DISORDERS

WU-CHIA-P'I

English Name: Eleuthero; "Siberian Ginseng"
Botanical Name: *Eleutherococcus senticosus*

Prepared as an extract, this member of the ginseng family is used as a natural remedy for normalizing the blood pressure, raising the pressure if it is too low and reducing it in mild or moderate conditions of high blood pressure. Yet this action does not interfere with normal blood pressure. Therefore, the extract may be used for other purposes—e.g., those cited in the chapter on nerve tension and stress—without concern that it will disturb normal blood pressure.

Although eleuthero extract has proven effective in many instances in relieving mild or moderate forms of hypertension, it is cited as especially effective (a specific) for conditions of low blood pressure.

Scientific Studies of Eleuthero on Blood Pressure

Results of carefully controlled studies of Soviet scientists have established that eleuthero extract does indeed have a normalizing effect on blood pressure. Dr. Brekhman writes: "It is known that eleutherococcus is one of the best remedies for curing hypotension [low blood pressure] but at the same time it reduces the elevated blood pressure in many hypertensive [high blood pressure] patients, or, in other words, displays its normalizing, adaptogenic action."[1] He points out that in conditions of high blood pressure the reduction is gradual and moderate, except in severe forms of high blood pressure, which do not respond to the eleuthero extract.

How Eleuthero Extract Is Used

Dr. Brekhman recommends from 20 to 40 drops of the extract in a little water to be taken before meals two or three times a day, to make the total daily dose of 80 drops. The course of treatment lasts for 25 to 30 days. If necessary the course may be repeated again at one- or two-week intervals. In other words, when one course has been completed the treatment is discontinued for one or two weeks, after which another course of 25 to 30 days treatment is taken.

Benefits of Eleuthero in Atherosclerosis

Clincial studies of the beneficial effect of eleuthero extract on atherosclerosis were undertaken by Dr. A. P. Golikov in Leningrad. In most patients, the condition involved mainly the coronary vessels and the aorta (large artery of the heart). In some cases the condition was complicated by hypertensive vascular diseases. Patients complained of weakness, exhaustion, pains in the heart, and pains beneath the breast bone. Most had increased cholesterol serum levels, and also showed signs of cardiac insufficiency.

Each patient was given a complete examination, and then placed on a course of eleuthero treatment, one dose of 25 to 30 drops of the extract three times daily. The course lasted for 25 to 30 days. Of other medication, only nitroglycerine and validol were given when necessary. These particular patients remained on the job while undergoing the eleuthero treatment.

After only one week from the start of the eleuthero treatment, and especially after one month, the patients improved significantly. Weakness and exhaustion vanished, cardiac pains and headaches became less severe or disappeared entirely, especially in patients with normal or low blood pressure. Along with these therapeutic results, the eleuthero treatment was accompanied by an improvement of circula-

---

[1]Lucas, R., *Eleuthero—Health Herb of Russia* (Spokane, Washington: R & M Books, 1972), pp. 29-30.

tion, normalization of blood pressure, reduction of cholesterol levels, and favorable shifts in protein and lipid metabolism.

The positive effects lasted for two to four months after the first course of eleuthero treatment. Three to four months later, subsequent courses of the plant extract produced an even more stable improvement of the patients' general state.

During four years, some patients received six to eight courses of eleuthero treatment, without any additional medicines. In all cases, results were reported to be good. Commenting on this, Dr. Brekhman says: "Thus if favorable shifts in the organism can be produced by eleutherococcus alone, without additional therapeutic measures, one may assume that the use of this preparation in combination with specific antisclerotic medicines may still be more effective."

HU-TS'UNG

English Name: Onion
Botanical Name: *Allium cepa*

There are several varieties of onions native to China, but the common onion which is largely cultivated in the Southern regions of the land is believed to be of foreign origin. It is called *Hu-ts'ung* and *Hui-hui-ts'ung*—the latter term meaning "Mohammedan onion," indicating its derivation from the West.

In China the onion is a favorite article of the diet. It is eaten with rice, millet, or bread, together with green vegetables.

Medicinal Uses

The onion belongs to the same botanical family as garlic and leeks and has been used for centuries for treating a host of different ailments ranging from circulatory disorders to the common cold. Because of its incredibly wide range of usage, onions are employed in a variety of forms—for example, freshly extracted onion juice; onions eaten raw, boiled, roasted, fried, or baked; chopped or grated onions applied as compresses or prepared as hot poultices; teas made with onions; finely grated onions mixed with honey or prepared as syrups; and so on.

In this chapter we will restrict our attention to the Chinese usage of onions in relation to circulatory disorders. The Chinese maintain that onions relieve high blood pressure; help eliminate fluid in the cardiac and pleural sacs; and, when eaten boiled or fried, will help prevent or dissolve dangerous blood clots.

Modern Medical Report on Onions

The Western medical profession is taking considerable interest in the therapeutic possibilities of onions for treating high blood pressure and other problems of the circulatory system. For example, a team of British doctors has demonstrated with tests on humans that boiled or fried onions can help reduce the possibility of heart attacks by raising the blood's ability to prevent or dissolve deadly clots. This information was reported in the following article which appeared in the *West London Observer*:

ONIONS AND THROMBOSIS

In France, horses who develop clots in the legs are treated with garlic and onions. A chance statement to this effect by a human patient led four Newcastle doctors to investigate the possible effect of onions on blood clotting.

The essential element in the formation of a clot is the change of substance called fibrinogen in the blood to insoluble fibrin, which forms a fine mesh; the "scaffolding" of the clot.

The blood of a healthy person has a measurable ability to "dissolve" this fibrin—a fibrinolytic activity, as doctors call it—and it has been known for some time that a fatty meal reduces this activity.

Would onions stop this reduction or even reverse it, and so make the formation of a clot unlikely? This is the question the four doctors tried to answer.

They gave a fatty breakfast to each of 22 patients, and confirmed that two or three hours later the fibrinolytic activity of their blood certainly was reduced.

On a separate occasion they gave the same patients the same fatty breakfast, accompanied by 2 ounces of onions, fried for some of the patients, boiled for others.

Two or three hours later the fibrinolytic activity of their blood was found to be markedly increased; and the odds against the change being a chance finding were found to be less than 1 in 1,000. Research is now proceeding to discover which substance in onions could be responsible for this dramatic effect.

Is it of any importance?—Well, everyone knows that man, and particularly modern man, is plagued by clotting disease—thrombosis of leg veins, for instance, and more important, of coronary arteries.

Anything that will increase the blood's fibrinolytic activity might be very important in the treatment or prevention of these conditions; and all the known drugs that have fibrinolytic activity have some undesirable characteristic. Onions might provide the answer.

In the meantime, one might speculate on why onions, fried or in a stuffing, are the traditional accompaniment to such fatty foodstuffs as steak and pork and goose, and why they are almost invariably cooked in fat. Has man's instinct been a few centuries ahead of his reason?

Whatever the truth may turn out to be, onion and garlic addicts need apologize much less in the future, while at medical banquets the leek, that close relative of the onion, will doubtless be de rigueur, acceptable at once to both the social and the professional conscience of the diners.

Note: Pharmaceutical firms are now busy searching for the basic ingredient in onions that may lead to the development of a cheap, non-harmful medication.

SANG

English Name: Mulberry Tree
Botanical Name: *Morus alba*

The cultivation of the mulberry tree in China dates from antiquity. According to ancient tradition, Si-ling, the empress of Huangti (B.C. 2967), taught the people how to use mulberry leaves for rearing silk worms. (Silk worms feed upon mulberry leaves.)

Several varieties of the tree are found in all parts of China. The *fruits* of the common mulberry *(Morus alba)* are known as *Shen*. When fully ripened they are called *Hsun* or *T'an*. In commerce they are sold under the name *Sang-shen-tzu* and made into a jam called *Sang-shen-kao*, in which form the fruits are preserved for medicinal purposes.

Therapeutic Uses

The juice of the ripe berries, diluted with water and used in considerable quantities, is reputed to improve the circulation and to have a tonic effect on the heart. It is also said to produce diuresis and therefore to be helpful in some instances for relieving conditions of cardiac dropsy.

WU-CHIA-P'I
(Eleutherococcus)

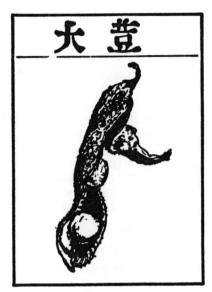

TA-TOU
(Soy Bean)

HU-TS'UNG
(Onion)

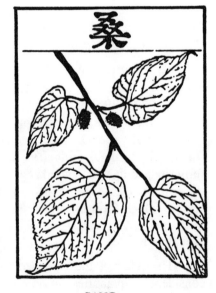

SANG
(Mulberry)

A Scientific Study

According to a medical report, 18 heart patients were treated by mulberry therapy, and all but two showed marked improvement. Pain and shortness of breath were reduced, and in some cases swelling of the ankles vanished.

SHAN-CHA

English Name: Hawthorn
Botanical Name: *Crataegus oxycantha*

This small thorny shrub or tree is native to Asia, Africa, and Europe but is naturalized in many other parts of the world. It produces a red fruit (hawthorn berries) with yellow pulp, which remains on the tree after the leaves drop off in autumn.

In Chinese medicine the hawthorn is used as a heart tonic and to normalize high blood pressure. It is also said to be a good remedy for various forms of heart trouble, and for producing a healthy circulation of the blood.

Chinese Claims for Hawthorn Shared by Other Practitioners

Dr. T. H. Bartram of England refers to the value of hawthorn as follows:

"A well-known herbal sheet-anchor for general heart trouble is of course, hawthorn. Berries can be used with success in most cardiac disorders, especially hypertrophy. It is appropriate where the psychological pattern is one of melancholy and irritability. It works best where the pulse is weak and rapid, with concurrent dropsy and dyspnea (labored and difficult breathing). It is doubtful whether digitalis, the most widely used heart remedy in the world today, can accomplish more than this common tree. One thing is certain—the menacing effects of digitalis are avoided in treatment by hawthorn."

Faschauer of Germany reported that 100 heart patients requiring continuous therapy were given liquid extract of hawthorn and the results were generally beneficial. Marked subjective improvement was noted in patients with mitral stenosis, and patients with heart disease of old age.

In reference to hawthorn berry, Dr. Eric Powell writes:

"This (hawthorn) is prepared in tincture of fluid extract form and the dose varies from 15 to 60 drops in water before meals three times daily, young people requiring smaller doses than adults. Crataegus (hawthorn) is probably the best rejuvenator of the heart ever discovered, and it is absolutely harmless. The herbal schools have employed it with great success since the discovery was made known. Although it may be given in homeopathic potency, it is usually administered in the form of the tincture or fluid extract. Valvular deficiency, enlargement, and some forms of inflammation yield to the gentle influence of Crataegus.

"This writer is quite satisfied that it is without equal as a remedy for most heart cases, and he speaks with some authority as he, himself, was cured with Crataegus when given up to die of heart disease when a child. He has been using Crataegus professionally for some 35 years with the most pleasing results."

Dr. Powell adds:

"All sufferers from heart trouble should give the feet—only the feet—a hot bath every night before retiring. Have the water well up over the ankles and as hot as possible, adding more hot water every minute or so. Bathe the feet for about ten minutes; dry well, then pull the toes and loosen up the feet with the hands. This will help to equalize circulation, soothe the nerves, remove congestion around the heart, and induce restful sleep."

Reported Use of Hawthorn for High Blood Pressure

Mr. R.B.A. of Leicester writes:

"We have found that hawthorn has had a dramatic effect on my wife's high blood pressure. Together with a salt-free diet, we feel that we have achieved results that ten years of drugs have failed to do.

"I feel the use of hawthorn has saved my wife from a slow, lingering death. Side effects of the prescription drugs have been too frightening to put into words."

YÜEH-KUEI

English Name: Cinnamon
Botanical Name: *Cinnamonum cassia*

Chinese herbalists explain that many older people suffer from cold hands and feet, especially at night, which is a Yin (weak) condition. For temporary relief, they suggest eating a very small pinch of powdered cinnamon before going to bed. They also point out that the cinnamon should be of the highest quality, the kind sold in Chinese herb shops. The best quality can be determined by a bitter-sweet taste. If the taste is too bitter, and not oily, the quality is poor.

YUNNAN PAIYAO

This Chinese name means "Yunnan White Herb." Yunnan is the name of the border province in Southwest China; Pai means white; and Yao, herb or medicine. It consists of a powder substance manufactured by a scientific process from a special type of tree known as the "white tree," which is found only in Yunnan province. It became famous for its effectiveness in treating wounds during the Japanese invasion of China.

For decades Yunnan Paiyao has been employed both in the Orient and Europe as a valuable remedy for cuts, bruises, hemorrhoids, traumatic wounds, and for activating blood circulation and dispersing blood clots. When the powder is applied to a bleeding wound and bandaged, the bleeding reportedly stops very quickly.

Strokes

According to Chinese herbalists, one particular function of Yunnan Paiyao which is not yet widely known, is its value as a remedy for strokes. Consider the following impressive accounts:

• A prominent Chinese man, 77 years of age, credits Yunnan Paiyao with saving his life. He writes:

"Early one morning I suffered a stroke and fell to the floor. A friend who was visiting me became alarmed and rushed to help. I remembered that I had Yunnan Paiyao in the house, so I pointed to the other room and murmured, 'Yunnan Paiyao—Yunnan Paiyao.' My friend understood, and immediately gave me two of the capsules with a small glass of water. Shortly after swallowing the capsules I was able to get up on my feet, and was taken to the hospital.

"The doctor confirmed that I did have a stroke, and said he was amazed that I was able to walk into the hospital, and had recovered so quickly."

• In another case, an 80-year-old Chinese man was hospitalized after suffering a severe stroke. The next day, a close friend who was an herbalist, heard what had happened and went to see him. He writes:

"Mr. C's family was standing by his bed, with such sad faces that I was fearful my friend had died. He was in very serious condition, unable to speak, and could only stare at us. I was told the doctor was doing everything he could but did not hold out much hope. In desperation I spoke with the doctor and explained all about a remedy we use for such conditions and asked if I could give it to my friend. The doctor said he did not object because although he thought it would do no good, at least it would do no harm.

"I gave my friend Yunnan Paiyao four times that day, and the next day he was able to speak. I gave him the remedy again, and on the third day he was able to go home.

"Later my friend told me he wished he had known about Yunnan Paiyao long ago, as his brother had died years before of a stroke. He felt that the remedy could have saved his brother's life."

How Yunnan Paiyao Is Used

Yunnan Paiyao is available in small bottles, packed ten to a carton. Each bottle contains 4 grammes of the herb powder. For internal use, the contents of one bottle are divided into eight dosages, and one-eighth is taken at a time, stirred in water or tea. It is used four times a day, and each small bottle lasts two days. The powder is also available in capsules on blister sheets, 16 to a sheet. One to two capsules are taken four times a day.

Included with the bottles and capsules are what the Chinese call, "Safety Pills." The pill is used only as an emergency first-aid measure in cases of accidents resulting in severe injury, until the person can be rushed to a hospital. The pill is given first, by breaking it up in a little water or tea, then the herb powder is given. The emergency first-aid "Safety Pills" are not necessary for strokes or other conditions.

Further Instructions

• Broad beans, fish, sour or cold food, should not be eaten within one day after using Yunnan Paiyao.

• Yunnan Paiyao should not be used during pregnancy.

CHIANG

English Name: Ginger
Botanical Name: *Zingiber officinalis*

According to news reports, it is the opinion of researchers at Cornell University Medical College that ginger may help prevent strokes and hardening of the arteries. During tests on agents to slow down blood clotting, a lab technician who was checking blood cells or platelets that he had donated for the study, noticed they were not clotting as they should. He recalled that the evening before, he had eaten a considerable amount of ginger marmalade, and further, that studies at the University of Minnesota had linked similar antiplatelet activity to Chinese food. The technician then dropped an extract of ginger on normal platelets and found that they, too, failed to clot.

A hematology researcher says it is believed that a substance in ginger called *gingerol* inhibits an enzyme that causes cells to clot. The same enzyme is blocked by aspirin, proven effective in preventing recurrence of so-called "little strokes." These attackes are triggered by microscopic artery clots which flow through the bloodstream until they block arteries in the brain.

TIENCHI GINSENG

English Name: No equivalent
Botanical Name: *Panax notoginseng*

One of the several varieties of ginseng is called *tienchi* or *sanchi*. The root, which is valued for its medicinal properties, contains saponins, flavonoids, and sterols which reportedly produce a beneficial action on the circulatory system, especially for problems of the veins and arteries.

Tests at the Peking Institute of Physical Culture showed that the use of tienchi strengthened the constitution, improved the functioning of the cardiovascular system, and helped the body return to normal after exercising. Climbers at 15,000 feet on the Tibetan plateau, who had taken tienchi, had no trouble with irregular heart beat; whereas, others who did not take tienchi had irregular changes in the electrocardiograms.

A clinical preparation of tienchi was given for two months to 680 hospital patients suffering from coronary disease and angina pectoris. The therapeutic rate effect was 60 - 95% and electrocardiograph improvements were 40 - 50%. It was found that processed powdered tienchi can reduce the number of attacks of angina pectoris, and quickly eliminate or alleviate the symptoms. Patients who depended on nitroglycerine in tablets were able to reduce the dosage.

It was also found that when tienchi is taken regularly, cholesterol and lipid metabolism seem to improve, which lessens hardening of the arteries and several other problems of older people.

How Tienchi Is Used

Tienchi is used only in processed form, never raw. It is available on the market in the form of processed slices of the root called Tian Qi Pian. The contents of one box of Tian Qi Pian is about 2⅔ ounces. It is prepared for use by cooking one-half of the contents with chicken soup, simmering it slowly for two or three hours.

TA-TOU

English Name: Soybeans
Botanical Name: *Glycine hispidia*

The soybean has an ancient history. It was cultivated in China more than 4,000 years ago and was considered one of the five sacred grains along with rice, barley, wheat, and millet. The renowned Taoist doctor Szu-miao, who lived at the beginning of the Tang period and who was given the honored title of "King of Medicaments," was the first to note the various types of soybeans, such as Ta-tou and Wu-tou.

In China, the soybean has been nicknamed "China Cow" because it produces so much protein that for generations it has been used in many parts of the land as a substitute for milk. The soybean is also employed in many Chinese food preparations such as soy flour and soy relish, but the three that are of almost universal use in Oriental cookery are soybean oil, soy sauce, and soybean curd.

Soybeans in the United States

The first soybeans were brought to the United States in 1804 by a Yankee clipper ship returning from China. A few people sowed the seeds and perpetuated the plant, but there wasn't much interest in the plant. It was not until well over a century later, during World War II, that the American people began to realize the full potential of the valuable plant, and farmers throughout the country began to grow the bean in increasing numbers.

Today, many hundreds of millions of bushels of soybeans are grown yearly in the U.S. This remarkable legume is the only member of the plant kingdom which gives complete protein comparable to all forms of animal meats. Soybeans contain 11 times as much protein as milk, twice as much protein as meat or fish, and one and one-half times as much protein as cheese.

Other Valuable Nutrients

Along with an abundance of protein, soybeans also contain vitamins A, E. K, and some of the B factors. Other nutrients found in the beans include potassium, iron, phosphorus, calcium, and amino acids. In addition, soybeans are rich in unsaturated fatty acids of which the most important is *lecithin*.

Lecithin for Coping with Cholesterol

Lecithin is composed of bland, water-soluble granules refined from soybeans and is available from health food stores and various herb firms. Many Chinese-American herbalists recommend soybean lecithin as a dietary supplement, claiming that it helps regulate the metabolism, reduces cholesterol, and supplies nutriment to the brain, nerves, and glandular and sexual system.

Cholesterol is a major ingredient of plaque, a build-up of fatty particles that frequently become deposited within the arteries. When the arteries become clogged, blood circulation to all parts of the body, especially to the brain, is reduced. This shortage of blood to the brain can cause mental confusion, forgetfulness, and high blood pressure. Deposits of fatty particles also cause the heart to work harder in order to pump the blood through the clogged passageways. Here is where many heart and coronary troubles begin, if the heart is forced to undertake more work than it is able to do.

Cholesterol build-up can also bring about complications such as nervousness, gallstones, eczema, psoriasis, a certain type of arthritis, and atherosclerosis (hardening of the arteries).

How Lecithin Is Used

As dietary supplements, generally one tablespoonful of granular soybean lecithin is taken twice daily and one or two tablespoonfuls of soybean oil are taken daily. The granules may be used in any number of ways; e.g., stirred in juices, sprinkled over cereals, and added to meat or vegetable dishes. The oil may be used over salads and as cooking oil.

Proper diet is also stressed. Animal fats should be avoided because they have a high prevalence of cholesterol. Foods fried in deep fat or prepared with saturated fats should be greatly reduced or competely cut out. The same applies to pies, cakes, and other pastries that are prepared with hydrogenated shortening or synthetic fats. The more hydrogenated or saturated fats you consume, the more lecithin you need to handle them.

The time required for relieving or preventing cholesterol deposits by taking soybean lecithin varies with each person.

Note: Lecithin is also available in capsules and in liquid form.

Scientific Evaluation and Reported Uses

Many of the Chinese claims for the therapeutic value of lecithin is supported by modern medical findings:

• In an article published some years ago in the *Journal of the Mt. Sinai Hospital,* David Adlersberg, M.D. and Harry Sobotka, Ph.D. reported on five cases of high cholesterol in which a "striking decrease in serum cholesterol level was achieved by addition of comemrcial lecithin to the diet." One woman, age 41, had a cholesterol count of 620. She began taking 12 grams (two tablespoonfuls) of soybean lecithin daily, and in two months her count was down to 420. After another month, her count was down to 300. Another woman, 38 years of age, was troubled with multiple health problems, including high cholesterol in her blood and fatty deposits in her sk'n. Her extremely high cholesterol count of 1370 was sharply reduced to 445 when she took 15 grams of lecithin a day for a period of three months. The cholesterol count of a 35-year-old man dropped from 440 to 260 while he was taking two tablespoonfuls of lecithin daily for two months.

Another case was that of a 55-year-old woman who was diabetic and very obese. Her cholesterol count was 360. Six weeks later, after she took a little more than two tablespoons of lecithin every day, her count had dropped to 235. To see what would happen, the doctors took her off the lecithin and found that her cholesterol count rapidly rose again.

• The staff of the *British Medical Journal* recommends soybean oil for treating an excess of cholesterol in the blood, adding that the oil may also help in preventing blood clots and heart attacks.

• After many years of careful analyses and evaluation, Dr. Lester M. Morrison says that he is "certain that lecithin is one of our most powerful weapons against disease." He adds that it "is an especially valuable bulwark against development of 'hardening of the arteries' and all the complications of heart, brain, and kidney that follow." He also feels that soya oil is "the most healthful of all food oils."

Dr. Morrison cited many cases in which the cholesterol count was reduced with the use of lecithin. To mention one example, he reported that 12 out of 15 patients experienced an average reduction of serum cholesterol of 156 milligrams after three months of taking soybean lecithin supplements daily. He points out that a low-fat diet alone had failed to lower the cholesterol level in these patients.

Dr. Morrison also mentions that two of these patients had a history of angina pains, but after they took lecithin for three months "the symptoms of angina disappeared..."

The initial amount of 36 grams (6 tablespoons) of lecithin administered by Dr. Morrison is relatively high. However, he reported that follow-up work indicated that a maintenance dose of one or two tablespoons of lecithin daily was effective in sustaining normal cholesterol levels. (Normal cholesterol levels are said to range from 200 to 250 milligrams.)[2]

• A 60-year-old man with dangerously high blood pressure and severe nosebleeds spent a month in the hospital. When he returned home, his doctors were not very optimistic about his condition. He began taking a tablespoon of lecithin daily for three months, and his blood pressure dropped over 100 points

• In an article published in the *American Laboratory* (July, 1973), Jacobus Rinse, Ph.D., a chemist, wrote that back in 1951 he suffered severe angina attacks. His physician told him he had ten years to live, providing he carefully avoided all types of strenuous exercise.

---

[2]*The Low Fat Way to Health and Longer Life* (Englewood Cliffs, N.J.: Prentice-Hall, Inc., 1958).

Drawing on his knowledge of chemistry, Dr. Rinse theorized that taking soybean lecithin would help keep the cholesterol liquefied in his system. He began a dietary program of using supplements, which included one tablespoon of soybean lecithin granules, and a tablespoon each of raw wheat germ, bone meal, brewer's yeast, and soybean or safflower oil. He used this mixture in cereals and occasionally in yogurt.

He reported that for years, since he began taking these dietary supplements, he has never been troubled with angina. He also cited the experiences of many friends and acquaintances with circulatory problems who said they were benefited by a nutritional program featuring lecithin.

Multiple Benefits

Numerous reports also back up the Chinese claim that there are many other benefits that can be traced to the addition of soybean lecithin in the diet. Following are some examples.

• A nurse said that external applications of liquid lecithin successfully cleared up her infant's persistent diaper rash. Another nurse who heard about it thought that liquid lecithin might possibly heal bedsores in hospital patients. To try out the therapy, she selected a gentleman patient (at the hospital where she worked) who was weak and frail and had two bedsores on the lower spine.

The nurse obtained permission of the patient's doctor to apply external applications of liquid lecithin to the bedsores. Several other nurses cooperated, and on each shift the bedsores were first cleansed with hydrogen peroxide, then coated with liquid lecithin and bandaged with a non-stick dressing. The dressing was changed at least three times during a 24-hour period. Care was also taken to keep the patient off the bedsore area by correct positioning of his body.

The nurse reports that they were all greatly surprised to find that definite improvement was noticeable within two to three days. She adds that the patient is still in the hospital and very ill, but the bedsores seem to be healing nicely. Since hospital pharmacies do not stock lecithin, she explains, she purchased it at a local health food store.

• Dr. Dietrick of El Paso, Texas reported that he has treated many diabetic patients successfully with lecithin. He found that after a few weeks of lecithin the insulin requirement gradually decreased, and eventually the patients were able to return to a normal diet. Dr. Dietrick says that the cure was accomplished with six tablespoonfuls of lecithin and 100 milligrams of vitamin E daily. He adds: "It would seem quite possible that the cells of the pancreas which secrete insulin may have become starved for lecithin due to an insufficiency in the diet, and that for this reason they had reduced their manufacture of insulin. When sufficient lecithin is again supplied, it is quite conceivable that those cells might resume their normal secretion of insulin..."

• Mr. A.M.C. wrote:

"From October to December, 1958, my vision was so bad that I could not read newsprint. I saw my eye doctor, who said he could not do anything for it. I asked what caused it, and he said it was caused by bad circulation.

"Remembering an article I had read about lecithin, I began to take raw liquid lecithin, one teaspoon three times daily. Three weeks later my vision was restored to normal. I told my doctor about it and he said, 'Oh, yes, you have gotten your bloodstream cleared out.'"

• One man reported that hearing in his right ear had been impaired for many years and that he also frequently experienced a ringing sound. He said he was aware of the value of lecithin in cleaning the bloodstream of cholesterol plaques and fatty particles, so he decided to try it and took a large amount of lecithin daily with his meals. He says: "Much to my surprise the ringing in my ears has stopped and there has been an improvement in my hearing. I don't know which of the elements of the lecithin has caused the improvement; I don't know how far the improvement may go. But I'm going to continue my lecithin program since its quite pleasant to not have that ringing in the ears."

• Success in treating psoriasis with soybean lecithin was reported by Drs. Paul Gross and Beatrice Kesten of the Department of Dermatology at the Columbia-Presbyterian Medical Center. The doctors placed 235 patients on lecithin and a low-fat diet. Because of the restricted diet, the medics considered it important to administer vitamin supplements such as A, D, and the B vitamins, but were certain that lecithin was the agent responsible for the therapeutic effects on the condition of psoriasis.

Of the 235 patients, 155 were considered adequately treated, and the rest either refused to cooperate or abandoned the program before definite conclusions could be reached. Of those who followed the regime, only 37 experienced no improvement. Twenty-three became well and remained well after one year of treatment and three years of observation. Twenty-nine were highly pleased that their psoriasis was being controlled. The remaining 66 subjects showed some improvement, but required special ointments in addition to the lecithin.

• Other medical experimentations have credited lecithin for controlling psoriasis. In an article written by Dr. Herman Goodman, a leading dermatologist, he described a new medicine, "one of a group of lipids—fatlike chemicals—which include lecithin and vitamin A," which proved successful on a small number of psoriasis patients.

• In her book, *Let's Eat Right to Keep Fit*, Adele Davis wrote: "Even the stubborn eczema-like condition known as psoriasis usually disappears rapidly when salad oils and lecithin are added to the diet."[3]

• Dr. Edward Hewitt reported that he has observed great improvement and complete cures in several cases of mental illness when sufficient lecithin was added to the diet. He also maintains that many cases of arthritis are due to cholesterol deposits, and if arthritis is of this type lecithin added to the diet will effect a cure.

• According to Dr. R.K. Tompkins and his colleagues, all of Ohio State University College of Medicine, gallstones can be prevented when adequate lecithin is included in the diet. At an annual meeting of the Federation of American Societies for Experimental Biology, these investigators reported that "Over 90% of human gallstones are composed chiefly of cholesterol. The maintenance of cholesterol in solution in bile is the key to prevention of gallstone formation. Several investigations in recent years have suggested that a class of compounds called phospholipids are necessary for preventing cholesterol precipitation from bile. Our study indicates that human bile can be made richer in these phospholipids by feeding a commercial preparation of lecithin (obtained from soybeans), the principal phospholipid of bile. This increase in phospholipid content of human bile appears to enhance the ability of the bile to hold cholesterol in solution."

• In addition to lowering the cholesterol content of the blood and being a potent agent against development of hardening of the arteries and all the complications that follow, according to Dr. Lester Morrison, "Lecithin has other remarkable therapeutic qualities as well. One that we are just beginning to explore is its ability to increase the gamma globulin content of the blood proteins. These gamma globulins are

---

[3]*Let's Eat Right to Keep Fit* (New York: Harcourt, Brace & World, Inc., 1954), p. 38.

known to be associated with nature's protective force against the attacks of various infections in the body.

"In the bloodstream of patients who used lecithin as recommended, we found evidence of increased immunity against virus infections. This is of special interest, since scientists have reported finding this lecithin-induced immunity against pneumonia."

Summary

1. When prepared as an extract, the plant known as Eleutherococcus reportedly normalizes the blood pressure, raising the pressure if it is too low and reducing it in mild or moderate cases of high blood pressure. Yet this action does not interfere in any way with normal blood pressure.
2. In conditions of hypertension the following regime is generally recommended: Adequate rest; regular exercise; abstinence from tobacco, coffee, and alcoholic beverages; a low-salt diet; minimization or avoidance of stress-provoking situations; and keeping the cholesterol count normal by correct diet or other means.
3. The Chinese maintain that the humble onion is helpful for relieving various types of circulatory disorders. It is reputed to be of special value as an aid for preventing or dissolving dangerous blood clots.
4. The diluted juice of ripe mulberries is said to improve the circulation and to produce a tonic effect upon the heart.
5. Cholesterol consists of fatty particles that frequently lump together and become deposited within the walls of the arteries.
6. Cholesterol buildup can cause complications such as nervousness, gallstones, eczema, psoriasis, high blood pressure, strokes, a certain type of arthritis, and various heart and coronary ailments such as hardening of the arteries.
7. Soybean lecithin, when added to the diet, acts as an emulsifying agent for cholesterol. When cholesterol tends to lump together, lecithin breaks it up into tiny particles, enabling it to circulate through the body and preventing it from solidifying or congealing into large lumps and clinging to the sides of the arteries.
8. In addition to lowering excessive cholesterol, soybean lecithin supplements provide many other remarkable health benefits.

13

SUAN—NATURE'S MEDICINE

Suan is the Chinese name for garlic. This little bulb has been known in China from earliest times and was mentioned in the *Calendar of Hsia*, a book written 2,000 years before Christ. According to Chinese tradition, when Emperor Huang-Ti was climbing a mountain some of his followers ate the leaves of a poisonous plant and became deathly ill. By eating wild garlic which was found growing in the area, their lives were saved. From that time, the bulb was introduced into cultivation.

A Timeless Remedy

The use of garlic as a folk remedy is age-old. The Chinese, Romans, Greeks, Hindus, Egyptians, and Babylonians all claimed that garlic cured intestinal disorders, infections of the respiratory system, skin diseases, flatulence, wounds, worms, and delayed the symptoms of aging.

Many years ago, Professor Tallarico wrote:

> Lakovsky related the marvels of garlic and the onion because of their content of elements and specific essences. He says that in certain forests of Siberia a variety of wild garlic grows, called locally 'ceremissa.' Every autumn there is a pilgrimage to those forests when the aged, the paralyzed, the sick, and those afflicted with all kinds of diseases repair there to eat of the wild garlic for days, or even weeks. Afterward they return to their homes relieved of their ills, rejuvenated, and healed. It is further said that in Russia and Poland there are groups of very pious and very poor Israelites, who from time to time,

interrupt their religious exercises to break their fast upon bread
and raw garlic. Cancer is unknown among those people, whose
lifespan averages better than a century.

Medical Research on Garlic

Through laboratory experiments, an enormous amount of scientific interest in garlic has resulted. Reports from all over the world are
slowly confirming many of the empirical beliefs in the healing power
of this humble herb. G. Piotrowski of Switzerland, Kristine Nolfi,
M.D., of Denmark, and French scientists Poullard, Noether, and
Uquilia all demonstrated that garlic reduces high blood pressure. In
Brazil, a group of physicians reported the successful use of a garlic
extract among more than 400 patients with intestinal infections. Dr.
Hans Reuter of West Germany and two cardiologists in England found
that garlic is effective in lowering blood cholesterol, thereby reducing
the risk of heart attacks. Russian clinics and hospitals use garlic in the
form of volatile extracts which are vaporized and inhaled for respiratory ailments. Dr. Yee of China also treats respiratory ailments with a
specially prepared garlic inhalant. Kazuhiko Asi, Ph.D., of Japan cites
the low incidence of cancer among people who consume ample
amounts of garlic daily. In the U.S., Drs. Kotin and Stein reported
using garlic for treating cases ranging from respiratory disorders to
diarrhea, nervousness, cramps, and other ailments. Every case obtained relief within one month, some within one week.

Allicin—Potent Germ Killing Element in Garlic

Biological chemists have discovered that when garlic is cut or
crushed, much sophisticated biochemistry takes place, resulting in a
germ-killing element called *allicin*, which combats germs that can be
destroyed by penicillin. As reported by Dr. John H. Bailey, the allicin
in garlic attacks *staphylococci*, one of the germs that are found in
boils.

It was also demonstrated that allicin can destroy germs which so
far have proved to be immune to penicillin. One example is the germ,
Bacillus paratyphoid A, which creates a disease closely resembling
typhoid fever.

There are several types of paratyphoid bacteria, and this family of
germs creates a complicated variety of ailments which often makes it
extremely difficult for physicians to diagnose. On some occasions,

these germs cause symptoms similar to summer complaints; e.g., diarrhea or dysentery. In other cases, they produce kidney complications, rheumatism, or other ailments.

One drawback, however, is that allicin is a harsh irritant which many people cannot tolerate, as the consumption of this substance in large quantities found in garlic when the raw bulb is crushed or cut, may irritate the mouth or esophagus, or may cause anemia, or further irritate such conditions as stomach ulcers. However, a major breakthrough in this area has been made, resulting in a highly specialized garlic preparation.

KYOLIC—ORIENTAL GARLIC SUPREME

Wakunaga's multimillion-dollar research center in Japan is one of the most advanced facilities in the world in the field of herbs and biotechnology, and a substantial portion of the resources of this center is allotted to the scientific study of garlic.

Some years ago, Manji Wakunaga, a strong advocate of Chinese herb remedies, joined forces with Dr. Eugene Schnell, a German chemist who realized that if the amount of allicin in cut or crushed garlic could be reduced to a level low enough not to irritate the body, yet high enough to be effective in combination with garlic's other components, the result would be the perfect garlic for mankind. Dr. Schnell's exclusive 20-month "Cold Aging" process of garlic produced the desired effect.

In the U.S. this special garlic preparation is called Kyolic; in Canada, Leopin; and in Japan, Kyoleopin.

Organically Grown

As with most organic herbs and plants, the quality of garlic depends upon the soil and climate in which it is grown. If the soil is depleted of vital nutritive elements, so is the garlic. Kyolic garlic is organically grown in rich composted soil, without the use of pesticides, insecticides, or herbicides. It is grown and harvested at its nutritional peak in the farmlands of Hokkaido, Japan's northernmost island. After the harvest, the best cloves are selected and shipped in large bundles to the processing plant of the Wakunaga Pharmaceutical Company headquartered in Osaka, Japan. Here, garlic juice is extracted from the cloves and undergoes a curing process without heat, in large steel tanks for 20 months. Through this unique process, the quantity of allicin with garlic's other ingredients results in a balanced level that can easily be tolerated by the body. In addition, the odor components of garlic are modified so that the odor is neither detectable on the breath nor through the pores.

Kyolic contains all the essential nutrients of the whole, live garlic bulb; e.g., minerals, vitamins, enzymes, amino acids, sulphur compounds, allinin and allicin. It is especially rich in the important mineral selenium. According to medical research studies, selenium may suppress or prevent cancerous growths, in certain circumstances.

Various Forms of Kyolic

Kyolic garlic is available in various forms. For example—in tablets—in powder contained in gelatine capsules—in bottled liquid extract with a container of empty gelatine capsules—and in liquid only. The empty gelatine capsules are easily filled with the use of the handy spouted bottle, and taken immediately. If left to stand, the capsules quickly dissolve.

Kyolic garlic is also available in combination with other nutritive substances such as garlic/lecithin—garlic/parsley/alfalfa—garlic/calcium lactate—garlic/vitamin C, and so on.

REMEDIAL USES OF KYOLIC GARLIC

A Physician's Experiences with Kyolic

In an issue of his publication[1], Dr. William H. Khoe, M.D., Ph.D., D.H.T., D.Ac., cited some of his medical experiences with the use of Kyolic garlic. He writes:

---

[1] *The Khoe Newsletter*; Feb., 1982.

In my studies I have found Kyolic to be a superior product because it has rarely produced side effects. Last summer when we went to Japan and were invited to see the factory and Wakunaga Farm, I saw that the garlic was grown in an area free of pollution. No chemical fertilizers were used and those who were with me on the trip agreed that this was the cleanest factory we had ever seen.

The special process that the garlic goes through makes it practically free of any side effects. In many countries garlic is grown in areas which are polluted. In this era in which we are living, our environmental pollution is getting worse every year. Our air is polluted. Our food is polluted. Our soil is polluted. We are living in a polluted era. For an individual to clean this up is impossible. So the next best thing we can do for our patients is to detoxify them with this product [Kyolic].

Dr. Khoe then goes on to mention how he uses Kyolic in his practice. For example, he says he has found it relieves pain in the treatment of arthritis. He also writes that itching of the vaginal region (pruritis vulvae) and itching of the anus (pruritis ani), "have been treated with this product using a cotton swab."

For vaginal moniliasis (fungus infection), Dr. Khoe suggests inserting two liquid Kyolic capsules in the vagina at night before retiring, and covering with a pad so as not to stain the bedsheets.

He adds that he has used Kyolic garlic for patients with diarrhea and colitis. "The dose is 16 capsules a day, four times a day, for a week, and then four twice daily."

In reference to the benefits of Kyolic for the hair; Dr. Khoe says: "We have patients who have been taking capsules of liquid Kyolic and to their great surprise their hair is turning back to its normal color. This does not happen with everyone, but with many who have told me this spontaneously, although I had not asked them to comment on it."

For the condition of pinworms in children, Dr. Khoe states that he has found liquid Kyolic garlic to be one of the better biological remedies. He writes:

"I shared this knowledge with some of our doctor friends when I gave a lecture to the Philippine Congress in Manila. You fill a gelatine capsule with Kyolic, then lubricate it with vegetable oil or Vaseline, and insert it into the rectum. We have seen, and they have reported, that pinworms disappear in less than a week."

Dr. Khoe concludes by saying:

"Research work has been done, not only in Japan, regarding Kyolic but also in this country in some of the universities. In my opinion, Kyolic is a God-sent product to help the human race survive in a toxic environment."

Additional Uses

In a later issue of his publication[2], Dr. Khoe presents a list of further indications for the use of Kyolic liquid garlic. Following are several excerpts from his writing:

Eyes	Place a few drops into an eye-glass containing distilled water. Use as an eye-wash a few times a day for infections. Has relieved eye infections.
Ears	Use a few drops in the ear canal for the treatment of ear infections, including fungus infections of the ear canal.
Nose	For the treatment of nasal congestion and watery discharge of nasal passages. This is done by inhaling garlic vapor [by removing the cap from the liquid Kyolic garlic].
Throat	One teaspoon of Kyolic diluted in water can be used for throat soreness and infection. Used for tonsillitis and pharyngitis.
Skin	A few drops of Kyolic on a Q-Tip may be used for isolated skin lesions, such as bites and stings of insects. It can also be applied on abrasions.
Hypertension	12 capsules a day (four—three times a day) before meals, have controlled hypertension.
Arthritis	Here again, one must find the etiology of arthritis. However, with a diet free of simple sugars, the use of ten to 12 capsules a day has relieved many patients from their arthritis pain.
Diabetes	By using ten to 12 capsules a day, one can decrease the insulin intake. A number of patients, after having completely changed their diet for a number of months, no longer require insulin.
Gastritis	Here, too, one must first find the etiology. If there is no serious cause, even ulcers and gastritis can be helped.
Cancer Treatment	I have not used this for cancer treatment per se. However, Kyolic has been used as an

---

[2]*Khoe Newsletter*, 1984.

Constipation

adjunct to the treatment of cancer. It has been successfully used together with radiation therapy, and it has cut down the side effects of radiation burn. Kyolic can give the patient a feeling of well-being when it is used in conjunction with radiation or chemotherapy. Kyolic has been very successful in the treatment of constipation. The dosage is four capsules before retiring.

Besides the use of Kyolic in the abovementioned diseases, it is also used in our practice for heavy metal poisoning. I have been using Kyolic in the treatment of Alzheimer's disease. Of course, it is combined with other modalities.

The use of garlic, and especially Kyolic, has been a great improvement in the care of what I call the diseases of modern civilization, including the many chemicals that are used in our daily life.

Note: When Dr. Khoe speaks of using ten, 12, or 16 capsules a day, he is referring to the daily total, which is to be taken in divided doses, such as four capsules three times a day, making a total of 12.

CASE HISTORIES USING KYOLIC GARLIC

Many people in the U.S. and other parts of the world have reported good results with various forms of Kyolic garlic. Consider the following examples:

• "I am on my third bottle of liquid Kyolic. I had a cardiogram this week by my doctor and again it showed an improvement. But what is most remarkable is the fact that my feet are not as cold as they used to be other winters. The garlic must have helped my circulation very much. Other winters, or even in summer when the weather was cool, my feet would be so icy-cold it would take hours under the electric blanket to get them to warm up. I haven't had cold feet like that all winter. I am taking four capsules of the liquid Kyolic garlic a day."— Mr. O.V.

• "Just recently I returned from a trip back east. While there I was under great stress due to an ailing mother. I got very little rest, but for some reason I did not experience the stress headaches as before.

"I can only say that I am sure the six or more capsules of Kyolic that I took each day played a big part in helping me to maintain the mental and physical stamina needed under the circumstances. I mentioned to my husband after I returned from my trip that I couldn't believe how I was able to cope, having had continual stress headaches previously. I have been on the dry Kyolic for over five months."—E. McN.

• "I have found Kyolic garlic to be much superior and versatile in uses than any product of its kind. Those of my patients whom I have prescribed it for have found it to be of value in their ailments. In my own case it has made it possible for me to discontinue the use of antihypertensive medication for the first time in ten years. Not only that, but my blood pressure is about 12 points lower diastolically than I was ever able to achieve with medication."—Mr. A.F.—D.C.

• "Rubbing my feet nightly at bedtime with Kyolic liquid garlic, and covering them with a pair of clean white cotton socks, cleared up a bad case of athlete's foot."—G.C.

• "A former employee of ours, Mr. C.L., told me about his father who was suffering from heart disease for several years. Mr. L., Sr. had experienced numerous heart attacks over the past 15 years, so many in fact that his physician suggested that he might hold the Guinness record for the most heart attacks and still survive. C's father was under constant medical supervision, but his condition continued to deteriorate, to the point where he was virtually bedridden, being unable to work, drive, or perform any normal activity.

"I advised C to send his father some Kyolic 101 Garlic Capsules as a possible benefit for his condition. The Senior Mr. L., reluctantly took four capsules of the Kyolic 101 formula each day. Within a few weeks, the older Mr. L's condition improved to the point where he was able to do normal activities including driving a car for the first time in many years. After six months of taking the Kyolic every day, Mr. L was able to play golf and had virtually a normal life. Both father and son give Kyolic full credit for this remarkable improvement."—B.C.

• "I heard a lot about garlic being a good remedy for colds, but I was hesitant to try it because I also heard it lowers high blood pressure. Since my blood pressure is normal, I thought the garlic might cause it to drop. Fortunately, I read where a medical doctor said that garlic normalizes high or low blood pressure, but does not disturb normal blood pressure. With this assurance, I tried Kyolic garlic tablets the next time I felt I was starting to come down with a cold. Within a few days, I felt fine."—F.T.

- "I have been taking Kyolic garlic for my high blood pressure. I did not suddenly stop taking my doctor's prescription even though after several months the effect was unsatisfactory. Within a week after adding Kyolic, my blood pressure is happily at a level that is 'normal' for my 75 years. I may gradually try to reduce the prescription if the Kyolic will hold the blood pressure within acceptable limits."—N.D.

- "I am a singer entertainer who was introduced to Kyolic at a Thanksgiving party in 1984, where I performed. After the festive banquet, I was given a sample of Kyolic and took one to see if it would help my stomach, and it did. I have been taking it ever since, two to three daily, and I want to report the astounding results.

"I have had skipped heartbeats for many years. I was sent to a heart specialist as my blood pressure would be high at times due to professional stress. I was put on various medicines without result and to a point where my whole system was affected. I stopped all pills and decided to do it on my own. I reduced my weight from 196 to 185 lbs., exercised, and retired. My blood pressure would vary from 139 over 88, with the skipped heartbeats remaining on the cardiogram.

"In March 1985, after six months on Kyolic, I had a full physical and the result was unbelievable. Cholesterol 220, blood pressure 135 over 85 with all other organs working normally (liver, kidneys, pancreas, etc.), and *no* skipped heartbeats!

"In September, I had to see my doctor to have some papers signed. The attending nurse took my blood pressure and reported it was 130 over 70, and no skipped heartbeats. I did not diet nor refrain from any type of food. I eat as before but find I can easily eat anything in moderation and keep my weight around 175 lbs."—Mr. A. de M.

- "Kyolic with vitamin C was used as a supplement in a nutritional program designed by me to enhance performance for a specific group of world-class track and field athletes."—R.K., M.D.

- "A friend spent several thousand dollars on medical treatments for a stubborn skin rash, without results. At the suggestion of a neighbor, she tried a special diet and Kyolic liquid garlic. In a few weeks, the skin rash had completely cleared up and she was back at work."—R.R.

- "Customers kept telling me about the remarkable therapeutic properties of the odorless garlic, Kyolic. Having a medical background, I was rather skeptical. Then, during a recent trip to Japan, I visited the research laboratories of Wakunaga Pharmaceutical Co., the makers of Kyolic. What I saw and learned confirmed the stories I had heard about Kyolic, and made me a permanent user."—Mr. M.D., Registered Pharmacist.

• Mrs. V.G. suffered from a severe case of *Candida Albicans*, a fungus infection which can produce up to 79 foreign toxins in the body. She complained of headaches, numbness, tingling, pounding in the head, fluid in the ears, poor memory, incoordination, extreme fatigue, depression, clicking noises in the head, dark spots under the eyes, and vaginal discharge.

Mrs. V.G. was also allergic to certain foods, and troubled by chemical sensitivity. She explains:

"I stopped going into certain stores because of the smell of almost all new materials in fabric and clothing shops. Even super-markets bothered me in certain areas such as the aisle where the laundry detergent and soaps are. A person's cologne and perfume also bothered me. In fact, I thought I was going to die one time on an airplane as someone had perfume on and I thought I'd have to ask for oxygen. I couldn't even drive in traffic without becoming sick to my stomach and experiencing asthma symptoms.

"I also could not tolerate certain things in my home, such as the smell of vinyl shades, the polyester in the bedspread, cigarette smoke, household cleaners, etc. I was also allergic to dust, mold, and mildew, and most of the time I walked around with a mask on. I was unable to work, and after my husband and I had spent our life savings on orthodox medical treatments which failed to eliminate my problems, I consulted a natural healing practitioner."

Mrs. V.G. was placed on a special diet and advised to take Kyolic garlic. The first week she took eight teaspoons of *liquid* Kyolic every day, and one week later included six *capsules* daily of the Kyolic 103 formula. These amounts were continued for another three weeks, after which time she was able to return to work. Two weeks later, she reduced the amount of Kyolic liquid to six teaspoons per day, but continued with the same number of capsules she had been taking. This was followed for one month, then the liquid garlic was reduced to four teaspoons per day, while the number of capsules remained the same.

Six weeks later she wrote: "I am still on four teaspoons and six capsules a day, and will continue this a while longer, reducing the liquid a teaspoon at a time, but will remain on the capsules."

Mrs. V. G. reports the results she has obtained:

"The symptoms that have *disappeared* since I've been on the new diet and Kyolic are: Vaginal discharge, numbness, tingling, clicking in the head, headaches, depression, confusion, and dark spots under my eyes. My chemical sensitivities are also completely gone, and now I can go out anywhere.

"The symptoms that have *improved* are: Fluid in my ears, pounding in my head, memory, alertness, reasoning, and my hair has a shinier appearance.

"Lab tests have shown that my unusually high yeast count has been reduced to a 'normal' level, and my immune system has recovered. I feel absolutely terrific and have more energy than I ever remember having in my life."

Summary

1. The use of garlic as a folk remedy in China and other lands is age-old.
2. Medical reports from all over the world are gradually confirming many of the empirical beliefs in the healing power of garlic.
3. Biological chemists have discovered that when garlic is crushed or cut, it produces an element known as allicin, which combats germs that can be destroyed by penicillin. However, allicin is a harsh irritant which many people cannot tolerate.
4. A highly specialized Oriental garlic preparation known as Kyolic has been developed, whereby the amount of allicin is reduced to a level low enough not to irritate the body yet high enough to be effective with garlic's other valuable components.
5. Kyolic garlic is grown in rich, composted soil, without the use of insecticides, herbicides, or pesticides.
6. Kyolic garlic is available in various forms—e.g., liquid, capsules, etc.—and also in combination with other nutritive substances.
7. Many people have reportedly found Kyolic to be a power-house of disease fighting agents that makes it an effective healer of various ailments.

LIST OF MAIL ORDER HERB DEALERS

The list of herb dealers below is given solely for the convenience of the reader for purchasing the herbs and herbal products described in this book. You may write for their catalogs or price lists.

Kwan Yin Chinese Herb Co.,
 Inc.
P.O. Box 18617
Spokane, WA 99208

Nature's Herb Co.
281 Ellis St.
San Francisco, CA 94102
(catalog 50¢)

Haussmann's Pharmacy
534-536 W. Girard Ave.
Philadelphia, PA 19123

Golden Gate Herbs, Inc.
P.O. Box 810
Occidental, CA 95465

Indiana Botanic Gardens, Inc.
P.O. Box 5
Hammond, IN 46325

In Canada
Nu-Life Nutrition, Ltd.
871 Beatty St.
Vancouver, B.C., Canada

INDEX

231